LONGFORD: ESSAYS IN COUNTY HISTORY

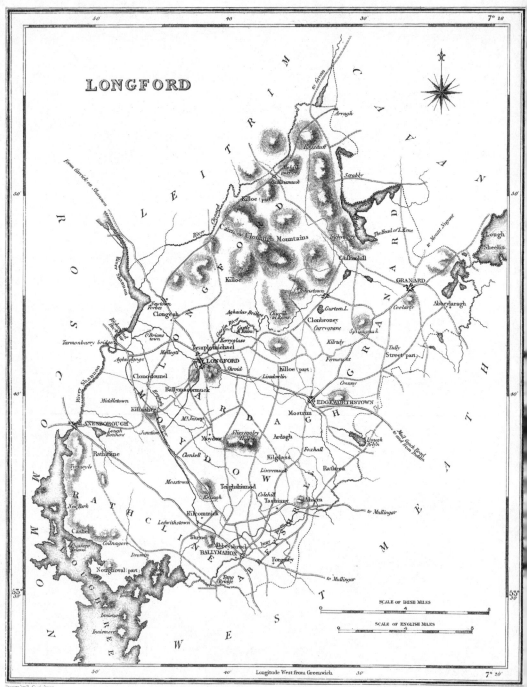

LONGFORD

SCALE OF IRISH MILES

SCALE OF ENGLISH MILES

Longitude West from Greenwich

Longford:
Essays in County History

edited by

RAYMOND GILLESPIE

and

GERARD MORAN

THE
LILLIPUT PRESS
DUBLIN

First published in 1991 by
THE LILLIPUT PRESS LTD
4 Rosemount Terrace, Arbour Hill,
Dublin 7, Ireland

A CIP record for this
book is available from
The British Library

ISBN 0 946640 51 3

Jacket design by Jole Bortoli
Set in 10½ on 12 Bembo by
Koinonia Ltd of Manchester
and printed in England by
Billings & Sons Ltd of Worcester

Contents

Notes on Contributors

Tom Dunne teaches history at University College, Cork. He has written *Maria Edgeworth and the Colonial Mind* (NUI, O'Donnell Lecture, 1984) and *Theobald Wolfe Tone: A Colonial Outsider*. He has also edited *The Writer as Witness: Historical Studies*, xvi.

Raymond Gillespie has written a number of books and articles on seventeenth-century Ireland including *Colonial Ulster: The Settlement of East Ulster, 1600-41* and *Conspiracy: Ulster Plots and Plotters in 1615*. He has also edited collections of essays on local history including *'A Various Country': Essays in Mayo History, 1500-1900* and *The Borderlands: Essays on the History of the Ulster Leinster Border*.

James Kelly teaches history at St Patrick's College, Drumcondra. He has written widely on the political history of eighteenth-century Ireland.

Liam Kennedy lectures in economic and social history at Queen's University, Belfast. He has edited and contributed to *An Economic History of Ulster, 1820-1939* and is author of *Two Ulsters*.

Desmond McCabe is completing a doctoral thesis on law and order in early-nineteenth-century Mayo at University College, Dublin.

Kerby Miller is Associate Professor of History at the University of Missouri, Columbia. He is author of *Emigrants and Exiles: Ireland and the Irish Exodus to North America*.

Gerard Moran has written on the political history of late-nineteenth-century Ireland including *The Mayo Evictions of 1860* and articles in local and national journals. He is joint editor of *'A Various Country': Essays in Mayo History, 1500-1900*.

Fergus O'Ferrall is author of a biography of Daniel O'Connell in the Gill's Irish Lives series and of *Catholic Emancipation: Daniel O'Connell and the Birth of Irish Democracy*.

Preface

On 8 May 1837 John O'Donovan, topographer and Gaelic scholar, arrived in Granard to begin collecting material for the Ordnance Survey memoir on Longford. He was not optimistic about what he might find. 'I fear that the Annalie will not turn out an interesting territory,' he wrote. Few have tried to establish whether, from the historian's point of view, O'Donovan's fears were justified and there has been no full-scale study of the county since the work of James P. Farrell in the late nineteenth century. That there is, nevertheless, an awareness of the importance of the county's heritage is clear from the activities of the Ardagh and Clonmacnoise Antiquarian Society which functioned from 1926 to 1951 and the present Longford Historical Society founded in 1967. The Goldsmith Society, which now runs the annual Goldsmith Summer School, has also made a significant contribution to an understanding of the county's past.

This appreciation of the value of the study of Longford's history has been expressed in practical terms in the support which the editors have received in the preparation of this volume. Longford County Council, Longford Urban District Council, the Vocational Educational Committee, the Library Committee and Bord na Móna have all given generous financial support to make this publication possible.

Abbreviations

A.F.P.	*Archivium Fratrum Praedicatorum*
Arch. Hib.	*Archivium Hibernicum*
Cal.S.P. Ire.	*Calendar of State Papers relating to Ireland* (24 vols, London 1860-1911)
Coll. Hib.	*Collectanea Hibernica*
C.S.O.	Chief Secretary's Office
C.S.O.R.P.	Chief Secretary's Office Registered Papers
D.D.A.	Dublin Diocesan Archives, Archbishop's House, Dublin
D.E.P.	*Dublin Evening Post*
G.O.	Genealogical Office, Dublin
H.C.	Parliamentary Papers, House of Commons series
J.A.C.A.S.	*Journal of the Ardagh and Clonmacnoise Antiquarian Society*
N.L.I.	National Library of Ireland, Dublin
P.R.O.	Public Record Office, London
P.R.O.I.	Public Record Office of Ireland, Dublin
P.R.O.N.I.	Public Record Office of Northern Ireland, Belfast
S.P.O.	State Paper Office, Dublin
T.A.B.	Tithe Applotment Books in P.R.O.I.
T.C.D.	Trinity College, Dublin
U.C.D.	University College, Dublin
U.C.G.	University College, Galway

I
INTRODUCTION

Land, Politics and Religion
in Longford since 1600

RAYMOND GILLESPIE AND GERARD MORAN

> Geographers generally admit that Longford is the most central county in
> Ireland; historians and general writers scarcely admit that such a place exists
> at all; whilst the general public ... know as little [of the history of the county] as
> they know or care about the history of Hong Kong or Timbuctoo.[1]

The accuracy of these observations, written in 1886 by James P. Farrell, the first
editor of the *Longford Leader*, as the introduction to his *Historical Notes and Stories
of County Longford*, is demonstrated by the scarcity of historical writing about the
county. With some notable exceptions it has not received the attention which
many other counties have, either from nineteenth-century antiquarians or
twentieth-century local historians.

It is not that Longford lacks any intrinsic interest for the historian, and while
on a practical level the estate archives of Longford are neither abundant nor easily
accessible, this is also true of other counties. One reason for its neglect may be
that the history of Longford lacks any central organizing event around which a
narrative can be constructed. The county never experienced a plantation on the
scale of those in Ulster or Munster; nor was it usually a scene of land agitation,
as the Connacht counties were, in the late nineteenth century. What is interesting
about the development of County Longford is that it was rarely a focus of national
attention, and the fact that it was almost forgotten by the government poses the
question of what influences were at work in shaping the county's society from
the seventeenth century to the present.

This problem is of more than normal interest for the historian because of the
geographical position of the county. Its central location defies attempts to classify
it as part of a wider region such as Ulster, Connacht or Leinster, and the complex
interaction within Longford of forces characteristic of not one region but several
adds to the confusion. In the nineteenth century the Meath/Cavan border
delineated 'the northern edge of a market-orientated economy in Leinster as
opposed to the peasant world of south Ulster'.[2] Yet this boundary, if continued
southwards, runs through the middle of County Longford so that, for example,
before the Famine the population density in Longford increased towards the west
and north of the county: 'from the moderate densities of Leinster there was a rise
to the high densities generally characteristic of Connaught and Ulster'.[3] The
religious composition of the county's population, its voting practices in the
nineteenth century and the ability of the O'Farrells to manipulate differing power

blocks to survive the political difficulties of the seventeenth century all point to the divergent influences which shaped Longford society.

The county is the counterpart of the medieval O'Farrell lordship of Annaly, which was divided into a northern and a southern half occupied by O'Farrell Bane and O'Farrell Boy respectively. This north-south divide was a reflection of Longford's topography. The northern part of the county, as described in Samuel Lewis's *Topographical Dictionary of Ireland* (1837), was in 'a state of nature' with little prospect of draining or improving. In the sixteenth century this area had been covered in woodland, mainly scrub, but it was cleared in the early seventeenth century to provide fuel for the ironworks located there. Farther south, between Edgeworthstown and Longford, lay a belt of good well-drained land, along which the main road through the county ran. West of Longford town the land was poorly drained while in the south of the county, around Ballymahon, the land was fertile and well cultivated. This pattern was discernible even in the seventeenth century. According to the Civil Survey description of 1654, the southern baronies of Shrule, Rathcline and Moydow were good land fit for tillage and grazing, and Moydow was improved mainly using manure. In Longford barony the southern part between Edgeworthstown and Longford was fit for grain as well as grazing but farther north only the hardy oats or rye would survive. This division between north and south was reflected in the adjoining barony of Granard.

While the road network of the nineteenth century was poorly developed the Royal Canal which ran through Longford town was an important link with the outside world. To the west of the county the river Shannon, which had been used by ships since the seventeenth century, also had steamships which used Lanesborough on the Longford-Roscommon border as a port in the 1840s.

I

Longford's history reflects the interaction of forces at work in the shaping of modern Ireland. Some changes brought about by these forces were very gradual and the underlying trends were, at times, scarcely perceptible to contemporaries and clearly discernible only in later generations. Others, such as the day-to-day workings of politics, had more immediate impact. The problem for the historian is one of balance; the essays by Gillespie, Kelly, and Kennedy and Miller examine various long-term changes in county society while those by Dunne, O'Ferrall, McCabe and Moran explore short-term developments. The framework used is a traditional one with each writer examining one or more of the key variables regularly used by national historians in explaining the evolution of modern Ireland: land, politics and religion. Historical problems in which these several strands interacted have attracted most attention from both local and national historians, and the essays here are no exception.

The seventeenth-century redistribution of land on a religious basis has prompted much analysis at both national and regional levels. The eighteenth-century Penal legislation attracted the attention of later nationalist historians and is only now beginning to be reassessed in a less partisan light. The amalgamation of the land question, the rise of the new political idea of nationalism and the revitalization of the Catholic Church in the nineteenth century has prompted historians to draw together the themes of land, politics and religion. It was in this context that Farrell's work on the history of Longford was written in the late nineteenth century and it is significant that it carried the imprimatur of the local nationalist MP Justin McCarthy and encouragement 'from all the clergy to whom I have written'.[4]

While the framework for these essays is traditional the writers' approach to it is less so. The danger of using a well-tried structure for national history when exploring local problems, especially an area with problems as complex as those of Longford, is that the detail of local society will be lost under the weight of a list of national or regional events. These essays keep both the local and national contexts in mind. Desmond McCabe's essay, for example, suggests the importance of the law as a unifying influence extending over the whole country but also demonstrates that the manner of its application varied with local circumstances. This process of adaptation is also clear in Fergus O'Ferrall's contribution, which reveals the importance of the rising middle class as 'brokers' who moulded national political ideas to their own needs. Of course the relative importance of different groups of 'brokers' changed over time. The Catholic clergy, for example, played a comparatively minor role in the events of Catholic Emancipation but by the 1860s had established their control over the political life of the county, as Gerard Moran's study of the 1868 election in Longford shows.

These three essays demonstrate the interaction between the political ideas as formulated in Dublin and the requirements of county society. However, they also indicate that Longford contributed to the political thinking of the day. While in the late eighteenth century Richard Lovell Edgeworth of Edgeworthstown may have taken little part in formal political activity, as described by McCabe, O'Ferrall and Moran, he had, as Tom Dunne's essay makes clear, strong views on the power relationships within the county. Dunne describes his attempts to reshape the relations between the various elements in Longford society; native and newcomer, landlord and tenant. Such moulding of political relationships at local level is no less important than the local manifestations of national political issues, yet it is a subject with which local historians have not yet fully come to terms. Understanding the political life of a region is not as simple as studying the history of national institutions based in the region; it extends to understanding the power relationships between all the various groups within the county. Thus O'Ferrall's description of the Catholic Emancipation in Longford is set in a much wider context of religious polarization, economic difficulty and social flux.

In religion as well as politics these essays bring new insights. The role of local ecclesiastical history as traditionally understood was set out by Bishop James MacNamee in the introduction to his *History of the Diocese of Ardagh* published in 1954: 'In a work of local history like this one can scarcely expect to come upon

any original views or revolutionary theories on the subject itself or its cognates.'[5]
MacNamee limited himself to the traditional preoccupation of identifying the
early ecclesiastical sites of the county, establishing the succession of the bishops
and compiling parish histories based on a succession of parish priests. Undoubtedly this is important groundwork for the study of the Church in Longford, but
it is the beginning of the process rather than the end. The list of MacNamee's
subjects is as important for what it leaves out as for what it contains. There was
no examination of popular religious belief, for example, nor did MacNamee try
to trace the changes in the relative importance of the Church over time or the
effectiveness of the communication of its message to the laity. Some of these
questions are broached in James Kelly's essay on the history of the Catholic
Church in Ardagh. Unlike MacNamee's analysis, in which the Church is
portrayed as having changed little from the time of St Patrick, Kelly shows the
impact of the 1650s in retarding the growth of the Church in the diocese, with
repercussions into the eighteenth century. Its slow development in the nineteenth century as a more efficient pastoral and administrative institution is the key
to understanding the modern Catholic Church in the diocese. Kelly's interpretation thus modifies Emmet Larkin's revolutionary view of the 'devotional'
revolution of the late nineteenth century, suggesting a more gradual institutional
change.[6]

No regional study of religious change can be content with an examination
of Church structures, which are nationally determined; it is also necessary to look
at the relative strength of and relations between the various religious groupings
in the region. Longford provides a good case-study because of its substantial
Protestant population. Liam Kennedy and Kerby Miller examine their history
over almost three centuries, providing an important counterweight to the
description of the Catholic community in James Kelly's essay.

The question of landownership also runs through the essays in this volume.
This is hardly surprising given that it was the main source of wealth and, at least
until the late nineteenth century, as Gerard Moran demonstrates, of political
power. It is the most prevalent theme in the nineteenth-century historical
writings of James Farrell, as witnessed by space given over in his *History of the
County Longford* to printing the patents of the early-seventeenth-century plantation of the county and the confiscations of the Cromwellian settlement.[7]

In his treatment of the subject Raymond Gillespie describes not the pattern
of landownership but rather the means by which a landed estate was acquired,
maintained or lost. This reveals the inadequacy of plantation or confiscation, the
processes most clearly visible in the records of central government, in explaining
the experience of the landowners in seventeenth-century Longford. However,
it is only when land is tenanted and developed that it becomes a valuable asset.
In this context Liam Kennedy and Kerby Miller's essay has an importance beyond
the area of religion for they also examine the changing pattern of the overall
county population over time and how this was affected by wider economic and
social changes. Tom Dunne discusses some of the ways in which change could

be effected by considering how one landlord, Richard Lovell Edgeworth, went about developing his estate.

These essays highlight the interrelationship between local and national history and they must call into question MacNamee's contention that the examination at local level of themes traditionally written about in a national context does not give rise to 'original views or revolutionary theories'. Admittedly the types of questions which the local historian asks of his sources and the answers he discovers are often rather different to those presented in national studies. This is the result not of a difference in the quality or importance of the study but rather a difference in perspective. Much historical writing on the issues of land, politics and religion has been from the perspective of the Dublin administration and based on its records. Viewed from Dublin the sort of variations in the application of the law described by Desmond McCabe, for example, appear as problems for the administrative system, while from the perspective of the region they are best interpreted as necessary adaptations to local needs. Similarly, as Fergus O'Ferrall points out, Catholic Emancipation may have been understood in one way by the Dublin politicians but it was perceived in very different ways by inhabitants of the diverse regions within Ireland.

All of this is not to argue that there is in some way a dichotomy in the understanding of the past, a national and local response to events, only one of which is 'correct'. Men did not live in two worlds. Even the most isolated region in the country was subject to outside influences and the people of Longford did not inhabit an independent provincial society. After 1603 one law governed the whole country and men frequently met the representatives of central government in the form of the justice of the peace, county sheriff, the officials of various local courts and tax collectors. It would also have been difficult to avoid the parish clergy and, at least occasionally, the bishop, all of whom were part of the nation-wide organization of the various Churches. While regional economic considerations may have been paramount, national economic trends affected most areas to some extent. Men lived not in one social network but in several: the nation, the county, their market area, the parish and their immediate neighbourhood, all of which overlapped. The difference between national and local was one not of substance but of perspective, although frequently the perspective of the locality best represents the contemporary reality.[8]

Local historians in Ireland, and indeed elsewhere, have been slow in appreciating the complexity of their subject, failing to recognize that local history is a specialized technique of historical study rather than the poor relation of the discipline.[9] They are often content to chart the points at which national history touched their own county or to retreat into the minutiae of topography, family history or the succession of parish priests or bishops for their own area. The reality is that history written at national level provides only partial answers to the problems presented and other perspectives are badly needed to correct and deepen our understanding of the evolution of Irish society. Local history is the groundwork fundamental to our understanding of the country as a whole. As one of the first of the modern Irish local historians, the Waterford apothecary Charles Smith, wrote in 1746, 'If gentlemen would make proper searches in their respective neighbourhoods into every thing ... the ... history of the kingdom might soon be put into a proper light.'[10]

II

These essays cannot claim to be a comprehensive history of the region in the way that James P. Farrell's or Bishop MacNamee's were. Many themes which local historians should properly investigate are not examined here. How, for example, did Longford, a region so poor that it could not support a parochial structure in the late seventeenth century, become in the later eighteenth century an apparently prosperous area, exporting linen, grain and cattle. One source of this prosperity was the rural linen industry which by the middle of the eighteenth century had become one of the pivots of the Longford economy, with about 2000 looms operating in the county. In the 1760s the production of coarse linen was being overtaken by fine linen weaving, mainly for non-Irish markets. Large quantities of linen yarn were also supplied to surrounding counties. However, the early part of the nineteenth century saw a dramatic decline in this trade,[11] with the result that the county could no longer support the high levels of population reached in the late eighteenth century. By the 1820s and 1830s emigration from the county was running at almost 1.1 per cent of the population a year, the highest in the entire country.[12] This rise in emigration, coupled with the decline of the linen industry, is central to the history of the county after 1800, affecting the agricultural economy, landlord-tenant relations and the extent of commercialization.[13] The decline in such an important source of income inevitably led to tensions within the community. The rise of the Threshers in 1806-7, although ostensibly a result of the level of clerical dues, may well be linked with changes in the handicraft earnings of poorer families. Similarly, the decline of the linen economy, which supported many people on small holdings, gave rise to increased competition for resources and it is no coincidence that the most common causes of agrarian violence in 1845-6 were competition for land and conacre rents.[14]

An awareness of these changes in the rural economy is vital to an understanding of other aspects of Longford history. One must analyse the structure of the pre-Famine rural economy in order to appreciate how the Famine of 1845-9 affected the county. In the years before the Famine Longford was not as dependent on the potato as many of the areas of the southern and western seaboards. However, the death rate in the county during the Famine, while certainly lower than the adjoining counties of Roscommon and Leitrim, was higher than nearly all other Leinster counties.[15] It should be possible to investigate the disruption of these years in Longford by examining the workings of the Poor Law; the effects of the Famine locally were certainly out of proportion to the event itself.[16]

The Famine set in motion a train of events which had a profound effect on the history of the county in the late nineteenth century. Population falls as a result of emigration led to farm consolidation. The role of the potato in popular diet and in farming changed quickly: there was a fall of 40 per cent in the acreage of land growing potatoes between 1845 and 1859 and the agricultural economy was reshaped. The importance of drystock farming steadily increased, with the number of cattle in the county almost doubling between 1854 and 1904. The skills of the Longford people also changed as schooling expanded and the level of illiteracy fell: between 1851 and 1861 the numbers of illiterate fifteen- to nineteen-year-olds fell from 34 per cent to 25 per cent.[17] The impact of the Famine can be understood only in the context of the weakness of the pre-Famine economy and both topics require the attention of local historians in Longford.

These essays provide only a starting-point in the opening up of new perspectives. Rather than being a forgotten county Longford should be seen as a region of particular importance in the complex social, cultural and religious evolution of modern Ireland. In reality it is a frontier county straddling not a political border but one which has been firmly fixed in men's minds in the course of Irish history.

NOTES

1. J. P. Farrell, *Historical Notes and Stories of County Longford* (Dublin 1886), p. 1.
2. T. Jones Hughes, 'Landholding and settlement in the counties of Meath and Cavan in the nineteenth century' in Patrick O'Flanagan, Paul Ferguson, Kevin Whelan (eds), *Rural Ireland, 1600-1900* (Cork 1987), p. 104.
3. T. W. Freeman, *Pre-Famine Ireland* (Manchester 1957), p. 181.
4. Farrell, op. cit., pp. viii-ix.
5. James J. MacNamee, *History of the Diocese of Ardagh* (Dublin 1954), p. xii.
6. Emmet Larkin, 'The Devotional Revolution in Ireland, 1850-75' in *American Historical Review*, lxxvii (1972), pp. 625-52.
7. J. P. Farrell, *History of the County Longford* (Dublin 1891), pp. 42-131.
8. For more detail on this see Raymond Gillespie, Gerard Moran, 'Writing local history' in Raymond Gillespie, Gerard Moran (eds), *'A Various Country': Essays in Mayo History, 1500-1900* (Westport 1987), pp. 11-23.
9. For an account of this attitude see H. P. R. Finberg, 'How not to write local history' in H. P. R. Finberg, V. H. T. Skipp (eds), *Local History: Objective and Pursuit* (Newton Abbot 1967), pp. 71-86.
10. Charles Smith, *The Antient and Present State of the County and City of Waterford* (Dublin 1746), p. xv.
11. The percentage of the labour force reportedly engaged in industry and handicrafts in the county fell from 42.5 per cent in 1821 to about 30 per cent by 1841 (tabulated in Cormac Ó Gráda, *Ireland Before and After the Famine* [Manchester 1988], p. 36).
12. J. H. Johnson, 'The distribution of Irish emigration in the decade before the Great Famine' in *Irish Geography*, xxi (1987-8), p. 82.
13. For a useful idea of the extent of the effects of the introduction of linen see W. H.

Crawford, 'Economy and society in south Ulster in the eighteenth century' in *Clogher Record*, viii (1975), pp. 241-58.

14. M. R. Beames, *Peasants and Power* (Sussex 1983), p. 295.

15. P. M. A. Bourke, 'The extent of the potato crop in Ireland at the time of the Famine' in *Journal of the Statistical and Social Enquiry Society of Ireland*, xx, part 3 (1959-60), p. 7; J. Mokyr, *Why Ireland Starved* (London 1983), p. 267.

16. For a useful beginning see Owen Devany, 'Minutes of Longford poor law guardians during the Great Famine' in *Teathbha*, i, no. 4 (1978), pp. 329-36.

17. Ó Gráda, op. cit., p. 146.

II
OVERVIEWS 1600–1926

A Question of Survival: the O'Farrells and Longford in the Seventeenth Century

The themes of land, politics and religion have probably never been so closely intertwined in Irish history as in the seventeenth century. According to one recent survey of the years from 1534 to 1690,

> though an age of economic advance and intellectual activity [it was] above all an age of disruption. Prolonged and fundamental conflict over sovereignty, land, religion and culture produced changes more catastrophic and far reaching than anything Ireland had experienced since the Anglo-Norman invasion ... or was to experience again till the great Famine, the land war and the struggle for national independence.[1]

As a useful index of how far this social revolution had progressed at various points in the seventeenth century historians have used estimates of the extent of landownership by Catholics, which can be calculated from the land surveys made in the course of the century. Using these sources Catholic landownership fell from 61 per cent in 1641 to 22 per cent in 1688 and in 1703, after the Williamite settlement, to 15 per cent. The percentage declined further in the eighteenth century.[2] Useful as these estimates are in demonstrating the scale of the social revolution in the country as a whole they do not give the local historian a sense of either the magnitude or the mechanisms of change in his own area. It is possible to calculate the changes on a county basis but these can often be distorted by the activities of one or two large landowners. County Antrim, for example, remained apparently strongly Catholic throughout the seventeenth century. This trend is explained by the fact that the main landowner, the Catholic Earl of Antrim, owned almost 46 per cent of the county. Similarly Galway's apparent Catholicism was due to the vast estates of the Earl of Clanricard.

The general figures do not provide an explanation of the processes whereby land passed from the hands of the sixteenth-century Catholic owners to new seventeenth-century Protestant landlords. The temptation is to see the plantations of the early seventeenth century, the Restoration land settlement and the Williamite confiscations as themselves constituting the mechanism for the changes in landownership. According to this approach land was confiscated from men simply because they were Catholic. Hence the local historian's story of the seventeenth century is often one in which Protestant newcomers appropriated Catholic land through a policy of confiscation and settlement. Undoubtedly this happened in some areas of the country, especially Ulster where a thoroughgoing plantation policy was applied. Yet Ulster was atypical of the general trend; even after the most sustained period of plantation, the first forty years of the seventeenth century, it was almost the only area in which landownership by Catholics had fallen below 50 per cent. Even into the eighteenth century there are many examples of families who survived from the old order: the O'Haras of Annaghmore in Sligo, the Maguires in Fermanagh, the O'Neills in Antrim.[3] Frequently the plantation process removed traditional constraints from collateral septs of a native Irish family, allowing them to rise to prominence with the decline of the senior lineage. There was also a dramatic rise in the number of Old English landowners from the Pale who acquired lands in newly opened up areas of the midlands and Connacht either as estates for younger sons or as an expansion of their own estates.[4] Besides these, new Catholic groups also entered the land market for the first time in the seventeenth century. Most notable among these were the merchants from the older towns who began to acquire substantial lands outside the towns.[5] A few Catholics from the professions, such as the Quinns, later earls of Dunraven, in Limerick invested their profits in land. To confound further any straightforward link between religion and land-holding there were also many Catholics among the Scots and English settlers of the seventeenth century in both Munster and Ulster. At a slightly lower social level many Catholic native Irish became substantial tenants on Protestant-owned estates by exploiting the tenurial confusion of the seventeenth century; a phenomenon much criticized by the bardic poets who were the upholders of the traditional values of the social order.[6]

All of these examples should serve to warn us of the dangers of any easy identification of religious affiliation with the significant redistribution of land which occurred in seventeenth-century Ireland. The ability to evolve and implement survival strategies in the face of religious and political change depended on more than simply religious belief. Rather it was determined by a whole set of attitudes to land, including knowledge of law, access to capital, economic ideas, and political manoeuvring. For instance a landowner who regarded land as a way of providing for followers, who were a symbol of status in Gaelic polity, stood little chance of retaining his lands for long in the increasingly commercial world of the seventeenth century. Low rents coupled with increasing outgoings would rapidly drive him into bankruptcy. Similarly a landowner who was not prepared to use the political and legal structures of the Dublin administration to confirm and enlarge his holding could expect only to be taken advantage of by those who were. Of course even if a single landowner devised a suitable strategy for survival unforeseen circumstances could disrupt the best-laid plans. Failure to produce a male heir, for example, often resulted in the collapse of family fortunes.

Studying these survival strategies, which are in turn a reflection of a cultural outlook, is a matter which is best tackled at a local level. Longford is a particularly good region for such a study since there the native medieval family of O'Farrell survived the changes of the seventeenth century to emerge in the eighteenth century with a substantial part of their landholding intact. An understanding of the reasons for this survival depends on tracing the O'Farrells' knowledge of, and reaction to, the innovations in law, politics and economic outlook resulting from the spread of the power of the Dublin administration throughout the country from the middle of the sixteenth century.

It is clear that by the beginning of the seventeenth century the O'Farrells of Longford were conversant with the practice of English law and the mechanisms of court politics. A commentator of 1608 noted that they were well informed as to the law and they were certainly using the Dublin assize courts in the sixteenth century to resolve land disputes.[7] Moreover they had demonstrated on a number of occasions in the late sixteenth and early seventeenth centuries their ability to use the Dublin administration to further their own ends. In 1570 the lordship of Annaly had been transformed into the county of Longford and at the same time both principal septs of the O'Farrells had surrendered their lands to the Dublin administration and received a regrant of them. They also assumed the local government of the county with Faghany O'Farrell, who had been granted English liberty in 1552, being appointed captain of the territory for life.[8] In 1588 Faghany attempted to increase his hold over the office by asking for a new grant of his lands, including the right of his son Iriell to hold the office of seneschal.[9] The other O'Farrell family, the O'Farrell Boy, took exception to this move since they assumed that the office would be granted to them on Faghany's death. Faghany's family began by appealing the case directly to the principal Secretary of State in London, Lord Burleigh, and maintained an agent at the English court, Edward Nangle, to advance their case. The other contender for the office, Fergus, was also in correspondence with Burleigh and with Sir Francis Walshingham, the other Secretary of State. Fergus, too, kept an agent at the court in London to protect his interests and enlisted the aid of Baron Delvin of Westmeath to press his case before Burleigh. The case was fought before not only the Irish Privy Council but also the English Council in the 1590s. The result was inconclusive but the conduct of the case highlights the O'Farrells' detailed knowledge of the political process at its various levels both in England and in Ireland.

The ability of the O'Farrells to use their knowledge of the system to protect themselves from potential colonization was well demonstrated by their campaign against the Nugent family from Westmeath, who wished to acquire lands in the county. This was part of a more general expansion of Pale families into adjoining counties in the late sixteenth century. In 1593, for example, Theobald Dillon, a Palesman who already had lands in Connacht, purchased land in Longford. Sir Francis Shaen, another Palesman, also claimed to have extensive lands in Longford which had been laid waste as a result of the Nine Years' War.[10] Most of these acquisitions were small but it was the family of Nugent, the barons Delvin and later earls of Westmeath, which posed the greatest threat to O'Farrell hegemony in Longford. They had been receiving grants of Church land in Longford from the middle of the sixteenth century but their most concerted attempt to build up their estate in the county came in 1603. At the end of the Nine Years' War Delvin claimed that because some O'Farrells had been in rebellion large amounts of their land should have been forfeit to the King. In fact at the end of the war the O'Farrells involved had been given a pardon. Delvin's actions were, however, motivated not by a concern for the crown's rights in Ireland but rather by the fact that he had been awarded an open-ended grant for land and wished to use it to acquire land in Longford. The land had to be confiscated by the crown before the grant could be made. The matter dragged on for several years before Delvin's case was finally dismissed.

As part of the settlement of the dispute, however, a survey of the county was made and royal title to the county was conceded by the O'Farrells. This had important repercussions since the establishment of royal title to an area was a necessary precursor of a plantation scheme, such as that then being devised for Ulster.

The most successful attempt of the O'Farrells to prevent serious erosion of their position was in the delaying tactics which they used to ensure that the plantation of the county operated to their advantage. A plantation scheme for Longford was mooted as early as 1611, shortly after the implementation of the Ulster scheme, by the Lord Deputy Sir Arthur Chichester.[11] This was a relatively modest plan, along the lines of those followed in Monaghan and Cavan in the late sixteenth century comprising the establishment of freeholders and compounding by native Irish overlords for the exactions traditionally taken from their followers. Government, however, was concerned with problems elsewhere and the proposal was never implemented. A second scheme for plantation in 1615 was effectively vetoed by the O'Farrells who compiled a long memorandum for submission to the King demonstrating that 'it is more for your Majesty's honour, profit and service to confer the lands of the county Longford upon the natives than to dispose it by way of plantation'. The two chief O'Farrells, one of whom, Connell, was the MP for the county, appeared before the Privy Council in London and accepted the King's title to the county but managed to have the project deferred.[12]

Given the momentum of the movement for plantation in the early seventeenth century and the strategic importance of the county, deferral was the best that could be hoped for. A scheme was devised by the then Lord Deputy, Oliver St John, by late 1618. As finalized for implementation in September 1619 this scheme bore little resemblance to that applied in Ulster ten years earlier.[13] All freeholders who had held over 100 acres were to be restored to three-quarters of their lands. This guaranteed the position of the main lines of the O'Farrells. Of the 142 native Irish and Old English who received land in the plantation the five main O'Farrell families obtained about 10,000 plantation acres or nearly 7 per cent of the area of the county. Twelve other lesser O'Farrells were granted 4854 plantation acres or about 3.7 per cent of the county. Eighteen Old English families also received grants of land since they were landowners before 1619. These included the Earl of Kildare and various familes of the Nugents. However, the largest beneficiary in this group was the Earl of Westmeath who was granted 2917 plantation acres or 2 per cent of the county. The lands not granted to the native Irish or Old English were set aside for New English settlers from a wide range of backgrounds. Some, such as Francis Edgeworth or Patrick Hanna, were government officials who received their land as a reward for loyal service. (Edgeworth was something of a land speculator in his own right.) Others, such as the Forbeses, later earls of Granard, came from Scotland attracted by the prospect of quick profit and it was not until the 1670s that they finally sold their Scottish lands.

The land for these grants was made available by declaring that all freeholders who held under 100 acres before 1619 were to become tenants to the new grantees. The terms of their tenancy were set down in the conditions of the plantation scheme. They were to hold their lands by lease of three lives or twenty-one years, receive their lands in English acres rather than the native land measure of cartrons, or townlands, and make improvements to the land by sowing hemp and enclosing 10 acres for every 60 they held. O'Farrell reaction to the plantation was delayed until October because of the harvest. Then they began negotiating on the provisions for taxation in the scheme and succeeded in gaining some concessions.[14]

This scheme rationalized the landholding pattern of the county. Although 43 freeholders are recorded in the surrenders of 1570 only 17 received grants in the plantation. It reduced many of the smaller landowners to tenants and established a network of large estates which were more economically viable than the small freeholdings created by the custom of partible inheritance in the county. One of the main forms of inheritance used in sixteenth-century Longford was the custom of gavelkind whereby a man's holding was divided equally among all his sons on his death. As one chancery bill of 1588 put it, 'the lands descending from the ancestor to be divided between the next heirs male excluding all daughters and females'.[15] Not surprisingly this led to considerable fragmentation of holdings which became smaller with each generation unless one individual was powerful enough to consolidate several. It may be that some individuals in the south of the county were more successful in doing this than their northern counterparts since the 1570 indentures recorded 36 freeholders in the territory of O'Farrell Boy as opposed to only 7 in the territory of O'Farrell Bane.[16] The network of estates created in 1619 was further rationalized in the course of the early seventeenth century as many of the first grantees, such as Daniel Gookin, sold their lands to other settlers.[17]

In the confusion which inevitably accompanied the implementation of any major scheme, many of the larger O'Farrell families used the techniques of English law to defraud the smaller families of land. Mistakes were also made by the administrators in allocating land to smaller families whose claims were often difficult to prove. The smaller families replied in like manner with not only a number of cases in the court of chancery but also a petition to the Dublin government.[18] Such actions raise the question of how the O'Farrell families had learned the techniques of political and legal manipulation. The main explanation lies in the proximity of Longford to the Pale. As early as the 1520s O'Farrells had links with Gerald, ninth Earl of Kildare, who was then Lord Deputy, and such contacts with Pale families as landowners continued into the late sixteenth century.[19] There were also important marriage connections between the Gaelic O'Farrells and the main Old English families of the adjoining counties. Fergus O'Farrell of Mornin in south Longford, for example, who died in 1599, married first a daughter of the Earl of Westmeath and later Eleanor Plunkett, a daughter of the Baron Dunsany. Similarly, James Mac Iriell O'Farrell who died between 1610 and 1612 married Mary Plunkett, daughter of the eighteenth Earl of Fingal, and their son, Roger, married Alison Dillon, daughter of the third Earl of Roscommon.[20]

Contact with the Old English community of the Pale was not limited to marriage and landownership: there were also strong economic links with the commercialized east coast. From the fifteenth century towns had developed at Longford and Granard, both centred on O'Farrell castles, which were attracting merchants from the Pale. In 1480, for instance, it was complained in parliament that these towns were attracting business from the Pale 'which if they [the towns] are long continued will bring great riches to the king's enemies and great poverty to the king's subjects'.[21] This growth of towns in Longford was part of a wider development in the Irish midlands and extending north to Cavan, where O'Reilly went as far as to mint his own money. Southwards into County Westmeath, Mullingar developed from the fifteenth century as a result of its trading links with the Dublin merchants. Since freedom of the town was necessary to trade it was claimed in the early seventeenth century that the freemen of Dublin had always been freemen of Mullingar and vice versa.[22] This sort of urban development was not the norm in Gaelic Ireland. Usually, the surpluses generated in the economy were redistributed not through the market but rather as token payments to an overlord in return for protection and other services. Redistributed in turn through feasting, they became mutual bonds of obligation between lord and follower.[23]

The scale of this innovative contact with the market should not be overstated. Custom still played an important part in the life of the inhabitants of Longford. About 1629, for example, the clergy of Ardagh claimed that tithes could not be collected because the inhabitants of the area were not used to paying according to the legal scales recently introduced but preferred the custom of the country.[24] Nevertheless the early encounter with the market type of economy, meant that the inhabitants of Longford were well placed to take advantage of the rapid economic developments of the early seventeenth century. As with many other areas of the country, a significant number of patents for markets and fairs was granted in the years after 1603. Unlike many of the fairs established in other parts of the country, these Longford fairs proved to be lasting features. Of the nine grants of patents to hold fairs made before 1640 only one, that of Taghshinny, near Ballymahon, established by James Mc Connell O'Farrell in 1620, was not operating in 1685. Indeed by 1685 two fairs each at Cullyvore and Mostrim, or Edgeworthstown, were operating without a patent.[25] By contrast over 75 per cent of the fairs established in Ulster by 1641 had failed by 1685.[26]

The Pale to the east of Longford was not the only area which had an important influence on the shaping of the county in the early seventeenth century. With the rapid development of Ulster as a result of both formal plantation and informal colonization opportunities there became considerably scarcer and settlers began to look elsewhere, often southwards to Longford. Many of the new settlers who were part of the Longford plantation had earlier been involved in the Ulster scheme. Robert Gordon, for instance, son of Sir Robert Gordon of Lochinvar in Scotland, who eventually acquired the lands of five other Scots planters in Longford, had previously held land in Donegal as part of the Ulster plantation.[27]

This was a settlement not only by landowners: many brought with them tenants from their Ulster lands and there was also a more generalized drift south of those whose opportunities seemed limited in Ulster. Younger sons, for example, who would not inherit their fathers' lands in Ulster saw new areas of settlement such as Longford as a way to establish themselves with land. In this way, as Liam Kennedy and Kerby Miller demonstrate below, a substantial Protestant community grew up in north Longford and by 1641 an area of Sir John Seaton's land in north Longford was called 'Scots quarter'.[28]

This was not an entirely new trend. The O'Farrells of north Longford had contacts with Ulster families in the late sixteenth century and disturbances which began in Ulster often spilled over into Longford. In 1595, for example, the Annals of the Four Masters noted that O'Donnell 'arrived with his troops at the dawn of day in the two Annalys (these were the countries of the two O'Farrells, though the English had some time before obtained sway over them) ... and set every place to which they came in these districts in a blaze of fire ... They took [the castle of] Longford, for they had set fire to every side and corner of it.'

Thus the society which emerged in County Longford during the seventeenth century was the product of the interaction of two contrasting influences from Ulster and the Pale. The balance between them, however, varied. Communication between Ulster and parts of Longford was sometimes difficult. Archbishop Plunkett, for example, complained in 1672 that the diocese of Ardagh was a long way off from Armagh and difficult to reach in winter, views echoed by George Rawdon from Lisburn in County Antrim in 1681. However, the view from Dublin could be equally despondent. In 1681, Lord Conway complained of the inaccessibility of Longford from Dublin and asked rhetorically of the Earl of Granard, 'How can a man that lives in the county of Longford do any business but his own private affairs.'[29]

This combination of influences gave Longford a distinct identity in the seventeenth century. One indication of this is the problem which most contemporaries had in trying to classify it. Fr David Wolfe, the Jesuit missioner, was convinced in 1574 that the O'Farrells were Ulster lords while a description of the country in 1598 firmly assigned them to Leinster.[30] Longford's separate character was demonstrated in a number of ways in the early seventeenth century but perhaps most dramatically in 1623. When choosing agents to represent Irish interests at the London court during a debate on the development of the wool trade, Longford, Meath and Westmeath declared that they wished to set themselves up as a separate province 'and a body apart' from Leinster. After some debate the matter was referred in January 1624 to the English Privy Council, which refused to allow such a move.[31]

The familiarity of the Longford O'Farrells with the legal and economic ideas of the Pale and with the rapidly changing world of seventeenth-century Ulster meant that the county was in a position to take advantage of the economic upturn which characterized the late seventeenth century. One measure of the development of the county is the valuations made of its ecclesiastical benefices. In 1585, for example, the deanery of Ardagh was valued at £14 but by 1633 this had risen to £66. In other parishes the increases were even more spectacular. Granard's valuation increased from £14 in 1585 to £120 in 1633 and Templemichael rose from £4 to £20 over the same period.[32]

There is little doubt that a significant proportion of this increase was made possible by the considerable investment in the county by the settlers who came as part of the plantation. The depositions taken after the outbreak of rebellion in 1641 which asked settlers to list their losses provide a picture of sustained growth over the previous twenty years. John Edgeworth of Edgeworthstown deposed that his father had spent £600 on buildings on his lands which by 1641 he reckoned were worth £260 a year.[33] This certainly compares favourably with the expenditure of an Ulster planter on a similarly sized property. Some substantial tenants also invested in improvements; Matthew Foules, for example, claimed to have spent £350 on his substantial holding at Ballylough near Granard.[34] On the Dutton estate leases stipulated such improvements and one lease made in 1632 for forty-one years required £200 to be spent on building and fencing instead of being paid as an entry fine.[35] Even some of the absentee landowners took care to see that their lands were developed and their rents increased. James Young, for example, sublet his entire estate to another Scot, Thomas Mortimer, for seven years. He required Mortimer to settle tenants, to build a dwelling house and corn mill, to keep a manor court in which to settle tenants' disputes and, most importantly, to ensure that rents were increased after the first year of any tenancy.[36]

Another sign of growth in the economy was the rapid development of towns in the county, many of which had been there in embryo since the fifteenth century. There was a saddler, butcher, vintner and a number of merchants in Longford town by 1641. New towns, such as St Johnston, also grew, with a shoemaker, tanner, blacksmith and joiner in the town in 1641.[37] At least part of this growth was due to the rapid development of Dublin in the early seventeenth century and the expansion of its hinterland. In 1641 at least one man, John Steele, a weaver from the barony of Moydow in the south of the county, included in his losses commodities he was bringing to Dublin.[38] Not surprisingly the native Irish also benefited from this upturn and at least one factor contributing to the spread of the rising in Longford in 1641 was the frustration felt by some native Irish who had become wealthy enough to expand their landholding but were prevented from doing so by the conditions of the plantation even though there were settlers happy to sell land to them. Indeed a group of O'Farrells who petitioned Viscount Dillon in November 1641 recorded this as a source of discontent.[39]

If the contact with Ulster had benefits for the O'Farrells in the early seventeenth century it also created difficulties. On 22 October 1641 a number of the major native Irish lords of Ulster went into rebellion to express their dissatisfaction with economic and political developments in Ireland. Given Longford's geographical location it was only a matter of time before the trouble spread into the county from Cavan; by 27 October 1641 there were disturbances in the north of the county and by 29 October rebels from Leitrim were also active in that area. This situation created considerable problems for the people of Longford. To the east, the Old English of the Pale remained loyal to the King and refused to join the rising until early December. By mid 1642, pushed into rebellion by force of circumstance, they had established the Confederation of Kilkenny. According to one Longford deponent the reaction of the Sheriff of the county, Iriell O'Farrell, was to declare that he supported the King. The problem was the meaning of such a declaration, since the Ulster rebels also claimed to be loyal to the King and to be rebelling only against the 'evil counsellors' who were advising him. They produced proof of their claim in the form of a commission from the King authorizing them to act in his name. This was, in fact, a forgery but it was certainly believed to be genuine at the time by most of those in Longford and was frequently referred to in the depositions taken shortly after the rising as a justification for the rebels' actions.[40]

The confusion created by this conflict between different claims of loyalty was well displayed in a petition of 10 November 1641 signed by twenty-six O'Farrells, but not the two major families, and addressed to the Governor of the county, Viscount Dillon. In this they set out their grievances: their inability to purchase lands in the escheated counties, the Act of Uniformity, the quirks in the law which made land titles unstable, the failure of the native Irish to receive grants of Irish land in plantations and the disturbances in neighbouring counties. The tenor of their complaints was, significantly, not how badly they had been treated by the new order but rather their inability to gain acceptance in the political life and patronage system of the Dublin administration. They asked for guidance from Dillon but received none. Their confusion was reflected in the fate of three of the signatories. One, Cormac O'Farrell, was serving under one of the northern conspirators, Philip O'Reilly of Cavan, by December 1641; another, Brian, was serving with the royalist forces at the same date; and a third, Lisagh, was fighting in the Confederate army by 1648.[41] According to one deponent another group of O'Farrells went to Dublin to seek guidance as the rebellion spread but received no help and left after a fortnight.[42] Other O'Farrells took more drastic action and at least one, Captain Charles O'Farrell, went to England to serve the King when the civil war broke out there.[43]

The longer the war went on the more extreme the situation became. Rumours, such as that related by Margaret Conygrave of St Johnston that the King had been captured by the Scots, the Queen banished to France and her confessor mutilated and executed, added to the confusion.[44] Issues of loyalty to the king became less clear-cut and, according to one Longford deposition, by January 1642 proclamations were still being made by the rebels in the name of the king but named no king and his identity was 'a dangerous question'. Another deponent reported in the same month that the Longford rebels were proposing to make Owen Roe O'Neill, recently arrived from the Continent, king of Ireland and to drive out the English and Scots.[45] Some of the O'Farrells did try to maintain order within the county. Faghany O'Farrell, one of the justices of the peace for the county, deposed that he had tried to control the 'Irish rabble' but it proved impossible; others stated that various O'Farrells had tried to protect them from the rebels.[46] By February 1642 two of the main O'Farrell families of the county, represented by Francis O'Farrell of Moate in Longford and James Farrell of Tenelick, were in rebellion.[47]

One of the most important elements in rallying the O'Farrell families in the cause of the Confederation in the 1640s was the arrival of Richard O'Farrell in Ireland with Owen Roe O'Neill in early 1642. Richard was a younger son of Connell O'Farrell of Tenelick, who had been MP for Longford in the parliament of 1613-15, and belonged to one of the two most important branches of the southern O'Farrells. He spent most of the war outside Longford and as it drew to a close in 1652 he, together with the commanders of his regiments (many of whom were O'Farrells and included Lewis, his brother, and Connell, his cousin), were allowed under the terms of the peace to go to continental Europe. There they served first under Spain and later, under the exiled Charles II, in France. At the Restoration in 1660 these men were well placed to receive favours from the newly restored King, including substantial grants of land in the Restoration land settlement.[48]

In Longford itself the 1650s were a difficult time. The effects of war had been severe and in 1652 the county was described as waste. Many of the older market centres collapsed and the Civil Survey description of the barony of Ardagh recorded that there was neither fair nor market in the barony although some had been operating there before 1641. The fair of Longford town itself survived and the rest were evidently refounded soon after as they were operating in 1685. The problems of the war probably account for Longford's fall in the share of the Irish subsidy between 1634 and 1662.[49] It is difficult to know how much impact the Cromwellian policy of transplantation had on the county. Certainly all the main O'Farrell families who survived the war were declared transplantable (one transplantation certificate survives) although in one case, that of Francis O'Farrell of Mornin, it is clear from later evidence that he never left the county.[50]

The restoration of Charles II in 1660 brought a new set of problems for the O'Farrells. The death of Francis O'Farrell without an heir in the late 1640s had meant that the lands of the northern O'Farrell Banes passed out of that family.[51] However, at least some of the land passed into the hands of other O'Farrells. Roger O'Farrell of Barry, for example, who held 1000 acres according to his widow, died in 1653 leaving two daughters but no son to inherit the land. This land was passed to another O'Farrell, James. Other smaller branches had also been affected either by warfare or demographic accident during the 1650s. Most important for the survival of the family was the new set of political contacts forged by the various O'Farrells who had been in the royal court in exile in the 1650s. The Act of Settlement included specific provisions for the restoration of land to Lewis O'Farrell and Connell O'Farrell of Tenelick, who was still holding the land in 1706.[52] Thus this branch of the family landholding can be traced from the late sixteenth century into the early eighteenth century.

Equal in importance to political contacts was access to money in order to defend any newly established position against legal and other threats. A number of O'Farrells were given grants of land in the Restoration land settlement, yet many of these do not feature in the land surveys made shortly afterwards, presumably because they could not finance the protracted legal battles which often went on over such grants. One significant exception to this was Francis O'Farrell of Mornin, the representative of the main line of O'Farrell Boy, the southern branch of the family. He had fought with the Duke of Ormond on the royalist side during the 1640s, was declared transportable to Connacht by the Cromwellians, but was restored to his lands. His restoration had to be defended against other claimants and this required large sums of money, both for legal fees and more dubious reasons. Francis had used one of his Old English friends, Edward Dillon of Streamstown in County Westmeath, to make contact with Sir James Shaen, later Surveyor General, who he hoped would procure a provision for his restoration in the Act of Explanation, which modified the earlier Act of Settlement. He offered Shaen £2000 to speak to the Earl of Anglesea about the matter. The money was found by assigning to Anglesea Francis's allocation of land in Connacht under the Cromwellian land settlement, which he had never visited, and by selling the timber on the land to Captain Adam Molyneux. The bribe, neatly concealed as a mortgage on land, had the desired effect and the lands were restored. This branch of the family thereby became the largest O'Farrell landholders in Longford, with over 1860 acres in 1706 scattered throughout the baronies of Longford, Abbeyshrule and Moydow, and maintained their land-holding in the county from the sixteenth into the early eighteenth centuries. The land passed from Francis, who died in 1692, to his grandson James. The family's political and religious outlook can be gauged by the fact that Francis's son Roger was the member for Longford in the Patriot Parliament and was killed fighting for King James at the siege of Derry. He was attainted in 1691.[53]

The lands of the O'Farrells of Mornin remained in the family until the early eighteenth century when they were sold to Robert Jessop of Derry because the family was deeply in debt. Such developments highlight the importance of factors other than formal confiscation in the changing pattern of landholding during the seventeenth century. A number of O'Farrell families sold out at the beginning of the eighteenth century. James O'Farrell of Barry, for example, sold his lands to Wentworth Harman of Dublin in 1708 at the relatively good price of over fifteen times the rental value. Harman had already acquired land in the county in 1695 by his marriage to Frances Shepard, daughter of Anthony Shepard of Newcastle, and his purchase from O'Farrell laid the foundations of the large King-Harman estate of the nineteenth century.[54] At the same time John O'Farrell, the second largest O'Farrell landowner in the county according to the 1706 crown rental, also mortgaged a substantial portion of his lands.

As the early seventeenth century had created a network of consolidated estates which had been reorganized and enlarged in the Restoration land settlement, so the problem arose as to how this was to be maintained. One important element was to ensure that the land was not fragmented by splitting the inheritance up among a number of sons as had been the case in the sixteenth century. The O'Farrells seem to have adopted the practice of primogeniture by the early seventeenth century. The will of Roger O'Farrell of Mornin, who died in 1637, specified that the lands were to go to his eldest son, Francis, and he provided £500 each for his second son and his three daughters, the money to come from his wife's or his mother's lands.[55]

The problem of the provision for younger sons was a difficult one and careers had to be found for them. One example of their fate is provided by the family of Iriell O'Farrell of Mornin who had at least four sons. The eldest, James, acquired the family lands and the second eldest, John, lands at Ardenragh. Fergus, the third, entered the Church and died on the Continent as a bishop, while the youngest, Morrogh, died in the Spanish army.[56] Both Church and army played a vital part in absorbing potentially disruptive younger sons. Here the role of continental Europe was crucial, especially after the 1650s when at least some of the O'Farrells had experience there. However, connections with the Continent were not a new departure for the inhabitants of Longford. Indirect contacts through the Pale in the late sixteenth century, when increasing resort was being made to the colleges in Europe for education, probably familiarized the O'Farrells with the opportunities there. According to a chancery bill of 1592 Edward Farrell claimed that he was serving with the Queen's forces in the Low Countries when his two brothers dispossessed him of land. In 1618 it was also noted that James O'Farrell of Tenelick, 'one of the chiefest men in the country', had served the Queen in France and Flanders.[57] This flow of recruits into continental service continued throughout the early seventeenth century and a number of O'Farrells served in the Spanish army in Flanders. After the outbreak of war in 1641 many returned, such as Phelim O'Farrell who was noted by one deponent in 1642 as 'lately come out of Holland'.[58] The drift continued both into continental and English armies in the late seventeenth century. In 1675, for example, Fergus Farrell of Longford, aged twenty-five, was recorded as being in the King's guard of horse in London. Some later returned to Longford, such as Captain Gerald O'Farrell who served in Flanders under the French king until September 1685. Then in response to a proclamation that all Irish subjects were to return to Ireland he petitioned for a commission in the forces of a Longford settler, Sir Thomas Newcomen, and was supported by another Longford settler, the Earl of Granard.[59]

A second major outlet for younger sons was the Church. As James Kelly's essay below demonstrates, the Counter-Reformation was already beginning to affect Longford by the early years of the seventeenth century. The native Irish were travelling to Europe for training as clergy, some later returning to the county. The Dominican Lawrence O'Farrell, who was martyred in the 1650s, had been educated in Lisbon and was later prior of the Dominican college there before returning to Ireland. Perhaps the most famous example of this group was the Capuchin Richard O'Farrell, who wrote a history of the 1640s in Ireland.[60] Richard appears to have been a younger son of one of the families who had become tenants in the Longford plantation. In 1630 he went to the Low Countries where he studied at the Irish colleges at Lille and Douai before being ordained in 1634.

Such resorts to productive outlets for younger sons are further examples of the survival strategies which the various families of O'Farrells adopted in the seventeenth century. Such strategies made it possible for those who remained to take advantage of the economic upturn of the late seventeenth century to consolidate their position after the Restoration land settlement. The lack of estate papers for the county makes it difficult to describe the impact of this upturn in detail but there is some evidence of it in contemporary descriptions of the county. Nicholas Dowdall's account of Longford in 1683 recorded considerable exports of wool and noted that there was also sufficient corn grown to serve local needs.[61] Timber was another important export, especially in the region close to the Shannon in the west of the county, the river being used for transport. The town of Longford was recorded as being like 'a large country village having but a few good houses in it', though a slightly later description noted many good English-style houses being built in the town.

All of this activity was reflected in the improvements being made by the local landlords to their estates. By the 1680s the Earl of Longford had rebuilt his house, remodelled his gardens and added fish-ponds. At Granard Sir Arthur Forbes had reclaimed lands, planted orchards and hop-yards and built a fine walled garden containing Scots fir, pine, juniper, cedar and lime trees. The O'Farrells were also prominent in this movement and Dowdall recorded Sir Connell as having wrought much improvement on his land through enclosures and bridge-building.

There is little doubt that the position of the O'Farrells declined relative to that of the newcomers in the course of the seventeenth century. This decline was not due exclusively to confiscation and colonization, even though the main families remained Catholic throughout the century. (As Nicholas Dowdall commented of the O'Farrells in 1682, 'yet they never dispersed as other septs of Ireland did but continue still in this county and I suppose are the most entire and numerous of all the Irish septs this day'.[62]) The extent of the changes between the settlement of 1619 and the crown rental of 1706 is clear from the fact that by the early eighteenth century the title of only four acres of O'Farrell land could be traced back to the plantation. One major factor in the decline of the family's fortunes was the death without heirs of Francis O'Farrell in the late 1640s, as a result of which about 2 per cent of the county which had belonged to the O'Farrells passed out of their hands. Secondly while the contacts of the O'Farrells with the Pale and Ulster ensured that they were well placed to survive the economic and social changes of the seventeenth century, the pressures of warfare and economic change were too great for the smaller landowners. The 43 O'Farrell freeholders of the 1570 surrenders had been reduced to 17 landholders by 1619. The number fell further to about six by 1706. Their share of the profitable land in the county had fallen from about 10 per cent in 1619 to about 3 per cent by 1706.[63] The same fate befell the Old English landowners whose share had fallen from about 22 per cent in 1619 to slightly over 18 per cent by 1641 and had almost vanished by 1706. The general trend of the seventeenth century was towards larger estates. As smaller landholdings came up for sale many of the other O'Farrells were not in a position to purchase them because of either lack of cash or, as they had complained in 1641, political restrictions on their land dealing.

There is no doubt that Ireland experienced a social revolution in the seventeenth century as large quantities of land passed between different social and ethnic groups. While Longford was clearly involved in that social revolution the mechanisms by which it was generally achieved were clearly more complex than simple confiscation and colonization. The less dramatic impact of changing social, economic and political structures was of central importance but can often be detected only at a local level. Seventeenth-century Ireland will not be properly understood until the local dimension has been more fully explored.

NOTES

1. T. W. Moody, F. X. Martin, F. J. Byrne (eds), *A New History of Ireland*, iii (Oxford 1976), p. lxiii.
2. J. G. Simms, 'Land owned by Catholics in Ireland in 1688' in *Irish Historical Studies*, vii (1950-1), pp. 180-90; Moody, Martin, Byrne, op. cit., iii, p. 428.
3. For example see Thomas Bartlett, 'The O'Haras of Annaghmore *c.* 1600 - *c.* 1800: survival and revival' in *Irish Economic and Social History*, ix (1982), pp. 34-52; W.A. Maguire, 'The lands of the Maguires of Tempo in the seventeenth century' in *Clogher Record*, xii, no. 3 (1987), pp. 305-19.
4. For example see Mary O'Dowd, 'Landownership in the Sligo area, 1585-1641', Ph.D. thesis, U.C.D., 1980; Brian Mac Cuarta, 'Newcomers in the Irish Midlands', M.A. thesis, U.C.G., 1980, chapter 1.

5. Breandán Ó Bric, 'Galway townsmen as owners of land in Connacht, 1569-1641', M.A. thesis, U.C.G., 1974.
6. Bernadette Cunningham, 'Native culture and political change in Ireland, 1580-1640' in Ciaran Brady, Raymond Gillespie (eds), *Natives and Newcomers: The Making of Irish Colonial Society, 1534-1641* (Dublin 1986), ff. 158-9.
7. Historical Manuscripts Commission, *Report on the Buccleuch Mss*, i (London 1899), p. 77; Historical Manuscripts Commission, *Report on the Salisbury Manuscripts*, xix (London 1965), p. 165; P.R.O.I., Chancery Bills, G 323.
8. The relevant documents are abstracted in J. P. Farrell, *History of the County Longford* (Dublin 1891), pp. 21-6; James Morrin (ed.), *Calendar of the patent … rolls of Ireland, Henry VIII-Elizabeth* (Dublin 1861), p. 238.
9. The documents are given in Farrell, op. cit., pp. 26-34.
10. Farrell, op. cit., pp. 35-41; *Cal. patent rolls Ire., Hen. VIII-Eliz.*, p. 268; on Shaen see Bernadette Cunningham, 'Political and social change in the lordships of Clanricard and Thomond, 1569-1641', M.A. thesis, U.C.G., 1979, ff. 196-8.
11. *Cal. S.P. Ire., 1611-14*, pp. 49, 50, 51-2, 148, 312-13, 415; *Cal. Carew Mss., 1603-24*, pp. 66-8, 208-11.
12. *Cal. S.P. Ire., 1615-25*, pp. 108-11; *Acts of the Privy Council 1615-16*, p. 558.
13. The text of the scheme is printed in Mary Hickson, *Ireland in the Seventeenth Century*, ii (London 1883), pp. 284-7; *Cal. S.P. Ire., 1615-25*, pp. 231-2, 263-4.
14. *Cal. S.P. Ire., 1615-25*, p. 266.
15. P.R.O.I., R.C. 9/7, f. 268; P.R.O.I., Chancery Bills, T 87.
16. Farrell, op. cit., pp. 21-6.
17. For details see Mac Cuarta, op. cit., ff. 141-3.
18. T.C.D., Ms 672, ff. 149-52, 155-160.
19. P.R.O.N.I., D 3078/1/15/45,51; D3078/1/26/1-7; P.R.O.I., R.C. 6/1, f. 222.
20. Royal Irish Academy, Upton Mss 25/93, 94.
21. J. F. Morrissey (ed.), *Statute rolls of the parliament of Ireland, 12th and 13th to the 21st and 22nd year of the reign of King Edward IV* (Dublin 1939), pp. 818-21.
22. J. T. Gilbert (ed.), *Calendar of the Ancient Records of Dublin*, iii (Dublin 1892), p. 202.
23. For example, Raymond Gillespie, 'Lords and commons in seventeenth century Mayo' in Raymond Gillespie, Gerard Moran (eds), *'A Various Country': Essays in Mayo History, 1500-1900* (Westport 1987), pp. 45-7.
24 *Cal. S.P. Ire., 1647-60*, pp. 45-7.
25. The patents are listed in *Report of the Commissioners appointed to enquire into the state of the fairs and markets in Ireland*, H.C. 1852-3 (1674) xli, appendix; John Burke, *Hiberniae merlinus* (Dublin 1685).
26. The failures in Ulster are examined in Raymond Gillespie, 'The small towns of Ulster, 1600-1700' in *Ulster Folklife*, xxxvi (1990), pp. 18-26.
27. For a detailed analysis of the undertakers' backgrounds, see Mac Cuarta, op. cit., ff. 95-118.
28. T.C.D., Ms 817, ff. 196, 291; a Presbyterian congregation supplied from the presbytery of Laggan in Ulster had been established in Longford by 1676, P.R.O.N.I., D 1759/1E/2.
29. John Hanly (ed.), *The Letters of Saint Oliver Plunkett* (Dublin 1979), p. 300; Edward Bewick (ed.), *The Rawdon Papers* (London 1819), pp. 266-7; *Cal.S.P. Domestic, 1683*, p. 248.
30. *Cal. S.P. Rome, 1572-8*, p. 152; Edmund Hogan (ed.), *A Description of Ireland in 1598* (Dublin 1878), pp. 113-16.
31. *Acts of the Privy Council, January 1623 - March 1625*, pp. 168-9.

32. P.R.O.I., R.C. 9/7, f. 242; T.C.D., Ms. 1066; Ms. 1067.

33. T.C.D., Ms 817, f. 144.

34. T.C.D., Ms 817, f. 146.

35. P.R.O.I., Lodge's records of the rolls, vi, f. 103.

36. P.R.O.I., R.C. 5/6, ff. 325-7.

37. T.C.D., Ms 817, ff. 134, 135, 142, 162v; the former sovereign of St Johnston claimed losses of over £1000 in the 1641 rising including £150 worth of goods in his shop in the town, (f. 150).

38. T.C.D., Ms 817, f. 161.

39. The text of the petition is in J. T. Gilbert (ed.), *A Contemporary History of Affairs in Ireland, 1641-52*, i (Dublin 1879), pp. 367-8; for an example of the difficulty of a settler wishing to sell land to a native Irishman in Longford, see *Cal. S.P. Ire., 1647-60*, p. 143.

40. T.C.D., Ms 817, ff. 148, 156; Raymond Gillespie, 'The end of an era: Ulster and the outbreak of the 1641 rising' in Ciaran Brady, Raymond Gillespie (eds), *Natives and Newcomers*, pp. 191-213.

41. Gilbert, *Contemporary History*, i, pp. 56-7, 265, 271, 367-8, 373.

42. T.C.D., Ms 817, f. 231v.

43. *Cal. S.P. Ire., 1660-3*, p. 363.

44. T.C.D., Ms 817, f. 140v.

45. T.C.D., Ms 817, ff. 194v, 201.

46. T.C.D., Ms 817, f. 231.

47. Gilbert, *Contemporary History*, i, p. 389.

48. Stanislaus Kavanagh (ed.), *Commentarius Rinuccinianus*, v (Dublin 1944), pp. 314-15; C. H. Firth, 'Royalist and Cromwellian armies in Flanders' in *Transactions of the Royal Historical Society*, new series, xvii (1903), pp. 71-2, 105; on the later history of O'Farrell's regiment in Tangier, John Childs, *The Army of Charles II* (London 1976), pp. 115-51.

49. Robert Dunlop, *Ireland under the Commonwealth*, i (Manchester 1913), p.140; R. C. Simmington (ed.), *Civil survey*, x (Dublin 1961), p. 41; *House of Commons Journal, Ireland* (1753), pp. 179-82; Julian Walton, 'The subsidy roll of county Waterford' in *Analecta Hibernica*, xxx (1982), pp. 51-2.

50. Historical Manuscripts Commission, *Ormonde Mss* (old series), ii (London 1899), pp. 134, 137, 163-4; the transplantation certificate is in N.L.I., Ms 8831/2307.

51. *Cal. S.P. Ire., 1663-5*, pp. 512-13.

52. *Cal. S.P. Ire., 1660-3*, pp. 253,366; *Cal. S P. Ire., 1663-5*, p. 60; P.R.O.I., Quit Rent Office papers, crown rental 1706.

53. Royal Irish Academy, Upton Mss 25/95; P.R.O.I., Lodge's records of the rolls, viii, p. 53; Bodleian Library, Oxford, Carte Ms 44, f. 656.

54. P.R.O.I., D 12970, D 12954.

55. P.R.O.I., R.C. 5/6, ff. 355-64.

56. Royal Irish Academy, Upton Ms 25/93,94.

57. P.R.O.I., Chancery Bills, C 229; *Cal. S.P. Ire., 1615-25*, p. 109.

58. T.C.D., Ms 817, f. 217.

59. Historical Manuscripts Commission, *Ormonde Mss* (old series), ii, p. 238; *Cal. S. P. Domestic, Feb.-Dec. 1685*, pp. 326, 379.

60. P. J. Corish, 'Two contemporary historians of the Confederation of Kilkenny' in *Irish Historical Studies*, viii (1952-3), pp. 220-1. In O'Farrell's account his family is recorded as having lost all their possessions in the Longford plantation, but since they were nonetheless able to receive him as a visitor in the same county in 1644 it is more

likely that they were freeholders with less than 100 acres in the plantation who were reduced to the status of tenants.

61. T.C.D., Ms 883/2, ff. 258-67.
62. T.C.D., Ms 883/2, f. 264.
63. The acreages are calculated from the return in Hickson, op. cit., ii, pp. 288-91, and P.R.O.I, Quit Rent Office papers, crown rental 1706.

The Long Retreat: Protestants, Economy and Society, 1660–1926

LIAM KENNEDY, KERBY A. MILLER, WITH MARK GRAHAM

The introduction of Protestantism and Protestant settlers to Ireland in the early modern period exercised a profoundly complicating effect on the political evolution of the island and its peoples. Social cleavages based on ethnicity and religion, while varying in intensity during the succeeding centuries, were to prove enduring. In many parts of Ireland differences and divisions coloured - not always darkly - communal, neighbourhood and even personal relationships. Ultimately the break-up of the United Kingdom in 1921, the accompanying partition of Ireland and the modern conflict in Northern Ireland, cannot be understood in isolation from these historical processes. Yet relatively little is known about the economic, social and demographic structures of Protestant communities over long periods of time, particularly outside Ulster. It is true that a large number of literary works, and a small number of historical accounts, explore the demise of southern Protestantism in this century. The tone is frequently elegiac, with the focus on 'Big House' society. Class bias apart, these celebrations of crumbling piles and eccentric inhabitants are largely confined to a terminal phase in the history of Irish Protestant life.[1]

The objective of this essay is to pioneer the long-range study of southern Protestant communities, tracing periods of vitality as well as decline, and relating their fluctuating fortunes to wider currents of historical change. Given the underdeveloped state of Irish political and religious demography this cannot be attempted on a large scale as yet, but a beginning can be made at a regional level. For County Longford and some neighbouring parishes in Westmeath it has proved possible to assemble population estimates and related materials on a consistent basis through time, though admittedly at disconcertingly large intervals before the early nineteenth century.

Many elements in community life remain obscure of course, but the demographic evidence provides at least a framework for an outline account of Protestant economy and society in the Longford region between the restoration of the Stuart monarchy in 1660 and the formation of an independent Irish state.

I

The origins of the Protestant settlements in Longford lie in the reign of James I and are described in greater detail by Raymond Gillespie above. In 1620 the crown resolved to confer a quarter of the lands of the county 'upon such British

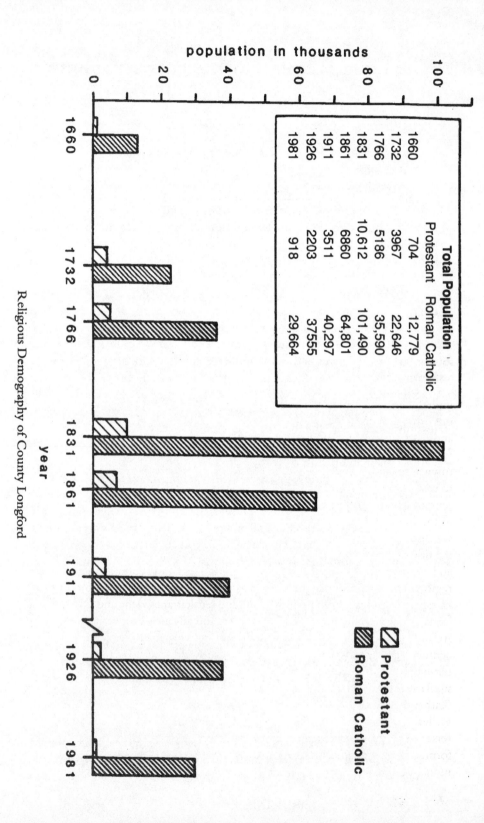

population in thousands

year

Religious Demography of County Longford

	Total Population	
	Protestant	Roman Catholic
1660	704	12,779
1732	3967	22,646
1766	5186	35,590
1831	10,612	101,490
1861	6860	64,801
1911	3511	40,297
1926	2203	37555
1981	918	29,664

Protestant

Roman Catholic

Table 1. Numbers of Irish and English in (a) Longford and (b) Westmeath baronies in 1660

	BARONY	IRISH	ENGLISH	% ENGLISH
(a)	Longford	990	168	15
	Granard	3540	165	4
	Ardagh	2428	48	2
	Moydow	1963	10	1
	Rathcline	2123	208	9
	Abbeyshrule	1735	105	6
		12 779	704	5
(b)	Kilkenny West	3180	188	6
	Clonlonan	2293	308	12
	Rathconrath	4378	188	4
	Moygoish	2715	120	4
	Brawny	–	–	–
		12 566	804	6

SOURCE: based on data contained in S. Pender, *A Census of Ireland c.1659* (Dublin 1939). See text for multiplier used.

undertakers as shall be conformable to the religion established in the churches of our other kingdoms'.[2] Land grants were made at the expense of the Old English and native Irish landholders of the sixteenth century. Grantees received these royal favours under strict conditions: 'grantees' tenants to build their houses in town reeds and not dispersedly, on penalty of £5 English for each transgression, to sow hemp at the rate of 1 [acre] for every 100 [acres]; not to levy uncertain rents or Irish exactions; not to demise lands for more than a term of life or 40 years to the mere Irish, or to persons not of English descent or surname …'.[3] There was also a prohibition, on pain of forfeiture, on practising gavelkind or assuming the title of the Great O'Farrell. Essentially this was the beginning of a systematic and imposed attempt to remodel the economic, social and cultural systems of the region. The intrusion may be viewed as part of a larger colonial project in the Elizabethan and Jacobean periods to subdue recalcitrant Gaelic and Old English lords, strengthen the position of the crown and advance Protestant interests in Ireland. These policies were pursued most actively in the early seventeenth century, the plantation of six Ulster counties being the most comprehensive and ultimately most successful of these ventures. While there are fundamental similarities between the Longford and Ulster plantations,[4] the legal basis differed. Rather than resorting to outright confiscation as in the case of Ulster a decade earlier, ancient royal claims to lands in Longford (and elsewhere) were resurrected. This was despite assurances given to the outraged O'Farrells, whose chiefs formed the indigenous ruling élite in the territory, in the reign of the previous monarch, Queen Elizabeth.[5]

Table 2. Numbers of Catholics and Protestants in (a) Longford and (b) Westmeath baronies in 1732

	BARONY	ROMAN CATHOLIC	PROTESTANT	% PROTESTANT
(a)	Longford	4414	905	17
	Granard	4600	987	18
	Ardagh	4755	1047	18
	Moydow	2584	291	10
	Rathcline	3945	355	8
	Shrule	2348	382	14
		22,646	3967	15
(b)	Kilkenny West	3758	410	10
	Clonlonan	3981	796	17
	Rathconrath	6179	400	6
	Moygoish	3704	232	6
	Brawny	1852	814	31
		19,474	2652	12

SOURCE: based on *Abstract of the Number of Protestants and Popish Families as Returned to the Hearth Money Office in 1732 Pursuant to the Order of the Commissioner of Revenue* (P.R.O.N.I. - MIC 310/1). See also note 10.

The scale of Protestant immigration is not known, but it cannot have been large. In any case the 1641 rising followed quickly, finding fertile ground in the economic and religious grievances of the Irish and Catholic gentry. The Forbes family, of Scottish origin, who had received extensive grants in the 1620s, suffered the siege and capture of their seat at Castle-Forbes, near the Shannon.[6] The castle of Longford, held by 'a renegade O'Farrell, who bartered his faith and fatherland for English gold and confiscated acres, was mercilessly sacked and the garrison slaughtered'.[7] Richard Edgeworth, father of the novelist Maria, claimed that the rebels attacked the Edgeworth residence at Cranallagh, 'set fire to it at night, and dragged the lady out, literally naked'.[8] More happily, according to family tradition, an attempt to dash out the brains of the infant heir, by swinging him against the corner of the castle wall, was foiled by a servant's ruse. Whatever about the nature and extent of atrocities, on which there is room for substantial dispute, there is no doubt that Protestant settlers and their dependants were driven out of many parts of Ulster and north Leinster during the 1640s. However, the Cromwellian settlement, with its own terror and confiscations, imposed a more complete pattern of Protestant estate-holding and ascendancy. The restoration of the monarchy in England in 1660 led to the readmission of some dispossessed Catholic gentry to parts of their estates, but the new landed élite was largely confirmed in its position.

Some rough impression of the numbers of Catholics and Protestants and of the balance between them in 1660 can be formed from the poll money returns for that year.[9] The numbers of people in each barony, as indicated by the returns, are clearly underestimates, referring at best to the adult population only. We have adopted W.J. Smyth's working hypothesis of a multiplier of 2.5 for use in converting the original data into population estimates (Table 1).[10]

Very probably, more confidence can be placed in the ratios between English and Irish (assumed to be synonymous with Protestant and Roman Catholic respectively) than in the absolute numbers of each.[11] It is apparent from Table 1, which also includes information on a number of baronies in south Westmeath, that the Protestant presence was weak in all parts of the region. Only in the barony of Longford did the Protestant-Catholic ratio rise to 1 in 6. In the region as a whole, Protestants were outnumbered 15 to 1, this thin scattering of households consisting largely of substantial landholders rather than a Protestant yeomanry or artisans. It is important to note also that the density of population in the baronies was low, which presumably helped to blunt economic conflicts between natives and newcomers, at the humbler levels of society at least.

By the early eighteenth century the Protestant position had strengthened considerably, both in terms of absolute and relative population (Table 2). In 1732 Protestants accounted for 15 per cent of the population of Longford county. If the population estimates can be trusted, then in Brawny Barony (in County Westmeath and containing the garrison town of Athlone) the Protestant share of the population had expanded to virtually one-third. It is true there had been set-backs during the Williamite wars when Longford and Westmeath were occupied by Jacobite forces, and Newtownforbes, Killashee and other county seats were burned to the ground.[12] Yet the events of 1689–91 and their aftermath succeeded in extending the economic power of the new landlord class through further confiscations, confirmed its political authority after an interlude of crisis, and restored Protestant confidence in the stability of the colonial social order. These circumstances laid the basis for a significant expansion of Protestant numbers. Natural increase no doubt played a role, but the scale of the increase suggests that the primary demographic mechanism must have been immigration. Landlords, particularly those with underpopulated estates, were anxious to attract Protestant tenants, as these were perceived to be more agriculturally progressive and more fully committed to the market economy than poor Catholic tenants.

This assumption that persons of recent English (or, less emphatically, Scottish) origin, or simply Protestants, would be more inclined to divide and enclose land, plant orchards and gardens, and build solid farm-houses lingered long after 1700, and even in the newspapers of the third quarter of the eighteenth century advertisements of farms to let quite often expressed an explicit preference for Protestant applicants ...[13]

In Longford some of these immigrant tenants were Presbyterians, possibly an overspill from the Scottish Presbyterian influx into Ulster in the 1690s and early 1700s.[14] As early as 1697, the county of Longford had a Presbyterian minister,

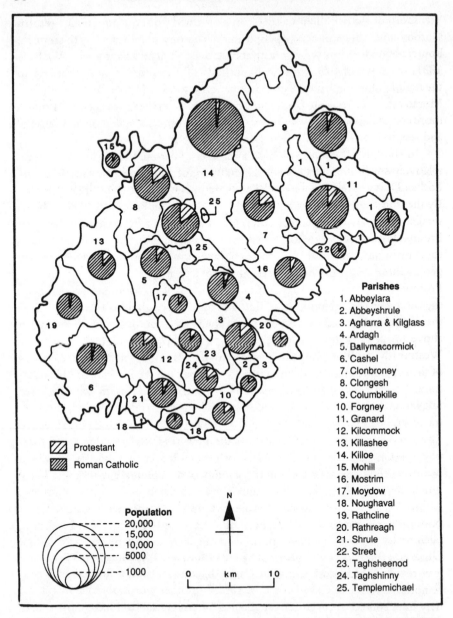

Parishes
1. Abbeylara
2. Abbeyshrule
3. Agharra & Kilglass
4. Ardagh
5. Ballymacormick
6. Cashel
7. Clonbroney
8. Clongesh
9. Columbkille
10. Forgney
11. Granard
12. Kilcommock
13. Killashee
14. Killoe
15. Mohill
16. Mostrim
17. Moydow
18. Noughaval
19. Rathcline
20. Rathreagh
21. Shrule
22. Street
23. Taghsheenod
24. Taghshinny
25. Templemichael

Protestant
Roman Catholic

Population
20,000
15,000
10,000
5000
1000

N

0   km   10

Spacial Distribution of Longford Catholics and Protestants by Parish in 1831 'transported' from Loughbrickland in County Down, who ministered in the Corboy and Clongesh areas.[15] However, most Protestant farmers, artisans, labourers and servants probably belonged to the Church of Ireland. Certainly in 1831, when we have fairly reliable information on the religious composition of the region, the vast majority of Protestants belonged to the Established Church.[16] Moreover, the Anglican Ascendancy is likely to have found its co-religionists more congenial than the sometimes truculent Presbyterians, protesting their civil and religious disabilities.

In the middle of the seventeenth century County Longford contained a relatively small number of leading families. The 1660 poll money returns list Forbes, Dillon, Archbald, Babington, Edgeworth and Pilsworth and a few others. By the mid eighteenth century, however, there had been a substantial influx of smaller Protestant gentry, as the county became subdivided into smaller estates.[17] Presumably these brought their own retainers and followers.[18] This would help to explain not only the increasing Protestant population but its changing geographical distribution. There is little relationship between the distribution of Protestants in 1660 and in 1732 (compare Tables 1 and 2; see also Table 4). By the latter date the baronies of Ardagh, Granard and Longford, in that order, held the largest numbers of Protestants in the county. In 1660 Ardagh ranked only just above Moydow, which, of all the baronies, held the fewest Protestants. In the Westmeath baronies, by contrast, there was much more continuity, the ranking of the baronies in terms of settlement size being little disturbed by the passage of time. Perhaps this indicated more mature settlements. In Longford county, uneven growth meant that gains in Protestant population were heavily concentrated in the north and east of the county, while the Shannonside and southern districts lagged behind. It seems, therefore, that during this formative period north Longford reflected, in attenuated form, religious demographic shifts occurring more generally in the northern half of Ireland. Indeed north Longford might be viewed as part of a frontier zone of Protestant settlement which embraced south Ulster, north-east Connacht and north Leinster. This raises the possibility that the districts centring on Granard and Longford town may have been recipients of migrants from core regions of immigration and settlement in Ulster. By the 1720s and 1730s economic distress and the falling in of leases with low rents in the northern province may have stimulated a further push into remoter regions like Cavan and Longford.[19] In other words, internal migration may have sometimes acted as a substitute for emigration to North America.

The religious census of 1766, conducted mainly by Church of Ireland ministers at the instigation of the Irish House of Lords, affords us our next detailed glimpse of the religious demography of the county (Table 3). The returns are compiled on a parish basis, hence no direct comparisons are possible with the baronial estimates for 1732 and 1660. We can, however, trace changes at county level. The Catholic population increased by 1.3 per cent per annum between 1732 and 1766, the Protestant total by 0.8 per cent. These represent vigorous rates of expansion for both denominations, but the discrepancy between the two

Table 3. *Numbers of Catholics and Protestants in County Longford arranged by Parish for 1766; also showing Russagh and St Mary's (Athlone) from Westmeath West*

PARISH	ROMAN CATHOLIC	PROTESTANT	% PROTESTANT
Abbeylara	1317	92	6.5
Ardagh	1908	201	9.5
Clonbroney	1882	434	18.7
Granard★	7893	840	9.6
Kilcommock	1129	190	14.4
Kilglass★	1620	211	11.5
Killashee	941	141	13.0
Mostrim	1793	439	19.7
Rathcline★	2802	125	4.3
Shrule	1312	146	10.0
Taghshinny★	1432	92	6.0
Templemichael★	9367	1902	16.9
'Other'†	2194	373	14.53
	35,590	5186	12.7
Russagh	329	11	3.2
St Mary's	1746	629	26.5

★ Group of parishes. These are: Granard and Columbkille; Kilglass, Agharra and Rathreagh; Rathcline and Cashel; Taghshinny, Moydow and Taghsheenod; and, finally, Templemichael, Clongesh, Killoe and Ballymacormick. (The original sources do not, unfortunately, disaggregate these unions or groupings.)
† 'Other' refers to the parishes of Abbeyshrule and Forgney, and to those parts of Mohill, Noughaval and Street contained in County Longford.
SOURCE: calculated from Rev. T. P. Cunningham, 'The 1766 Religious Census of Kilmore and Ardagh', in *Breifne*, ii, no. 4 (1961), pp.352-62 and Tennison Groves Mss, P.R.O.N.I., T.808/15264.

is, nonetheless, interesting. Differential migration and emigration seem the most likely explanations, though some of the forces discussed later in relation to the pre-Famine period may also have operated. Colonel Charles Clinton helped to organize a group exodus of Presbyterians from Corboy to North America in 1729.[20] The characteristic complaints of the period made by nonconformists – low incomes, high rents and tithes, penal measures against Presbyterians – probably constituted the 'push' factors behind the emigration.[21] On the 'pull' side, the lure of prosperity and independence in the New World must have exercised its own complementary effect. Members of the more numerous Church of Ireland denomination who were possessed of some capital are also likely to have emigrated to America during the middle decades of the century. At the higher levels of Protestant society, among the greater and lesser gentry, opportunities in the army, the Church and government represented outlets that, in many instances, would have involved absence or migration from the county.

Only very crude comparisons can be made between the spatial distribution of Protestants in 1732 and 1766 because parishes are not neat subunits of baronies. It would appear, on the basis of rough impressions, that settlement patterns were fairly stable, suggesting that the geographical framework of subsequent Protestant development had taken shape as early as the first quarter of the eighteenth century. Certainly for periods later than 1766 the ranking of parishes (or clusters of parishes) by size of Protestant population shows a high degree of continuity (Table 4).

II

The period from the 1770s to the Great Famine encompasses the most critical years for economic and political change in the region since the plantation. Demographic developments intertwined with other strands of social change. Total population expanded rapidly in all districts of the region, as a comparison of Tables 3 and 5 reveals.

But, while this vigorous increase was enjoyed by both Catholics and Protestants, it is clear that the former were multiplying at a faster rate. The result was that in Longford as a whole the ratio of Protestants to Catholics dropped from 1 in 7 to 1 in 10. This downward trend finds its extreme expression in the case of Mostrim where, exceptionally, the Protestant community shrank in absolute as well as relative size.

This weakening of the Protestant demographic and, by implication, political position is all the more striking given the apparent economic strength underpinning it. The landed élite of big landlords, middlemen, squireens and 'half-gentlemen' was composed mainly of adherents of the Established Church. Beneath these was a substantial middle class of strong farmers and townsmen engaged in trade, industry and the professions. While there was also a proletariat or semi-proletariat of small-holders, tradesmen and labourers, its weight within the Protestant social structure was far less than in the case of its Catholic counterpart.[22] Salient differences between Catholic and Protestant communities can be explored further by combining a variety of sources and using correlation analysis. The end product, a set of statistical relationships as presented in Table 6, helps to illuminate some important historical patterns.[23]

According to this summary account, there was some clustering of Protestants in relation to the 'Big Houses' of the gentry, they tended to be concentrated in the more fertile districts of the region, were likely to be found in areas characterized by village or town settlements, and were well represented where the local economy had (or once had) a significant industrial base. The converse of these relationships appears to hold in the case of Catholics. The demesnes of the gentry, it is worth noting, were also associated with areas of good farming land; hence, for example, the high density of imposing residences, which were

40   LONGFORD: ESSAYS IN COUNTY HISTORY

Table 4. *Comparing the ranking of subunits of the Longford region (baronies or parishes) according to size of Protestant population at different points in time*

Comparison	Rank correlation coefficient
1660 and 1732	0.10
1766 and 1831	0.76
1831 and 1861	0.97
1861 and 1911	0.98
1766 and 1911	0.80

SOURCE: calculated from information in the authors' Longford–Westmeath data file.

Table 5. *Numbers of Catholics and Protestants in County Longford, arranged by Parish for 1831; also showing Russagh, St Mary's (Athlone) and the total for Westmeath West*

PARISH	ROMAN CATHOLIC	PROTESTANT	% PROTESTANT
Abbeylara	2929	183	5.9
Abbeyshrule	1043	190	15.4
Ardagh	4735	245	4.9
Clonbroney	3809	1010	21.0
Forgney	1900	341	15.2
Granard★	17,677	1181	6.3
Kilcommock	3216	590	15.5
Kilglass★	4896	712	12.7
Killashee	3637	503	12.1
Mostrim	4424	320	6.7
Rathcline★	7953	170	2.1
Shrule	3601	247	6.4
Taghshinny★	5958	846	12.4
Templemichael★	31,988	3781	10.6
'Other'†	3724	293	7.3
	101,490	10,612	9.5
Russagh	705	73	9.4
St Mary's	6304	1088	14.7
	39,500	3115	7.3

★ Group of parishes.
† 'Other' refers to those parts of Mohill, Noughaval and Street contained in County Longford.
SOURCE: calculated from the *First Report of the Commission of Public Instruction, Ireland*, H.C. 1835 xxxiii.

virtually all Protestant, around Ballymahon in south Longford. The 'Big Houses' commanded the most valuable factor of production in the regional economy, land resources, and were of course important sources of patronage of all kinds. As Protestants of lower rank shared a common religious affiliation with members of the local Ascendancy class they might be expected to (and probably did) benefit disproportionately from the existing structures of economic and political power.

How then might we explain the shrinking proportion of Protestants? We can, for a start, exclude the role of migration within Ireland in the decades before the Famine. The 1841 census indicates little movement into or out of the county. Slightly more significant may be an inflow of Catholics into poorer, thinly populated townlands in north Longford in the later eighteenth century. Some refugees from Ulster, driven out by the Protestant Peep O'Day Boys, are said to have found their way into the county.[24] As against this must be set a small addition to the Protestant population of south Longford where the Countess of Rosse had introduced some Ulster tenants 'specially planted there to render yeoman service to the course of law and order when required'.[25] The more substantial forces altering the religious balance, however, must have been differential emigration, conversions from Protestantism, and possibly also differences in the propensity to marry. Exploring these in reverse order, our expectation is that by at least the early nineteenth century, Protestants on average practised later and/or less frequent marriage. This is predicated on the basis of a link between class structure, inheritance practices (particularly resistance to subdivision of holdings) and marriage behaviour.[26] In view of the economically privileged status of many of its members, it is likely that Protestant society tended to manage its marriage, inheritance and family dispersion strategies in a more careful fashion than was the case among Longford Catholics.

Conversions from Protestantism are a further possibility. This was a major source of concern among some churchmen, and might occur under a variety of circumstances. The archdeacon of Elphin lamented in 1814 that many had lapsed due to the 'past neglectful conduct and ignorance in spiritual things of too many of the Established Clergy'.[27] In similar vein Revd Robert Shaw, writing about the same time, regretted that in the Union of Callan, in County Kilkenny, some 140 Protestants had lapsed into Catholicism since the mid 1790s. 'Ignorance and neglect have contributed too much to it ... this could not have been the case, were proper attention paid to instruction, from the want of which the lower orders have nothing to oppose to the arguments addressed to them [and] were easily induced to change their system of religious belief.'[28] This falling away from the reformed faith seems also to have been a class-specific phenomenon: poorer Protestants, particularly where heavily outnumbered, were more vulnerable and more subject to social pressures than their social superiors. Thus it was noted in relation to Killegney in County Wexford that 'among the observations that might be made is, that the Protestant religion declines among the lower classes, as the people of that description ... are apt to emigrate when opportunity serves, and to gain favour with the great majority, are apt to turn Roman Catholic'.

Table 6. Some correlates of Protestant settlement, c.1841

Relationship between	Correlation coefficient
No. of 'Big Houses' and density of Prots	0.26
No. of 'Big Houses' and RC/Prot. ratio	-0.26
Land value and density of Prots	0.58
Land value and RC/Prot. ratio	-0.20
Urbanization and density of Prots	0.80
Urbanization and RC/Prot. ratio	-0.50
Industry and density of Prots	0.70
Industry and RC/Prot. ratio	-0.42
No. of 'Big Houses' and land value	0.49

SOURCE: see note 23.

Revd Gordon continues, indicating a further mechanism liable to corrode Protestant numbers and community structures: 'A Protestant, male or female, married to a Roman Catholic, invariably adopts the Roman Catholic religion.'[29] While we have no detailed knowledge of the extent of mixed marriages in the Longford region, one might surmise that communal barriers against intermarriage were less tightly constructed in the eighteenth than in the nineteenth century. Certainly in the nearby diocese of Elphin such marriages were not uncommon in the 1740s,[30] while as late as the 1840s the occasional mixed marriage was being recorded by the assistant curate at Killashee, Revd James Strangeways.[31] However, a search through 780 households in the parish of Granard in 1911 revealed only one definite case of a mixed marriage.[32] The sole exception was a Protestant head of household, with the occupation of carrier, who had taken a Catholic wife.

But it is the large gap between the numbers of Protestants one might have expected in 1831 and the actual numbers recorded which prompts us to believe that a differential rate of emigration was the most potent factor responsible for Protestant decline. Thus, if the Protestant population had grown at the same rate as the population as a whole during the period 1766-1831, there would have been almost 4000 more Protestants than there were in County Longford in 1831. This is a shortfall, if expressed in relation to the Protestant total for that year, of more than a third. An alternative way of highlighting this divergence between the Catholic and Protestant demographic experience is to assume that the rates of natural increase for the two groups were the same and, using some plausible estimate of the rate,[33] project the 1766 totals forward to 1831. This gives a discrepancy of 50 per cent between actual and expected Protestant numbers in 1831, while the Catholic deficit turns out to be a mere 8 per cent.

The motives for Protestant emigration are likely to have been both complex and variable over time. Trade fluctuations in the late eighteenth century, particularly depression in the 1770s, may well have stimulated significant outmigration. The final quarter-century was, however, generally prosperous for farmers and landowners, the wave of economic expansion being prolonged until 1814 under the artificial stimulus of the French wars. Economic dislocation and problems of adjustment after 1815 ushered in a long period of deflation. Agricultural prices started to fall as early as 1814. Rent payments became increasingly burdensome, while population continued to rise.[34] There was widespread recourse to emigration, particularly from the more commercialized regions in the north and east of Ireland, in the decades before the Famine. Many middle-class Protestants, seeing wartime prosperity and rising expectations giving way to recession and despondency, feared a decline in living standards and status. In the voluminous petitions to the government for free passage to the colonies in the years after Waterloo, the most frequently cited motive for emigration was apprehension regarding economic prospects in Ireland.[35] Significantly also, the petitioners to the Colonial Office were disproportionately Protestant.[36] One particular type, 'an agrarian *nouveau riche*', appears to have suffered intense problems of adjustment and relative deprivation. 'During the war, and in consequence of what were called the *war prices*,' observed Maria Edgeworth with barely concealed contempt, 'graziers, land-jobbers, and middle-men had risen into comparative wealth.'[37] Unable to sustain the airs and graces they had assumed, it seems that many of these aspiring squireens or, 'half-gentlemen' emigrated during the pre-Famine years.[38]

More serious, though, was the loss of surplus sons from farming families and the displacement of many engaged in textile manufacturing. Compounding problems in agriculture, and of particular significance for Protestants (see Table 6), the domestic textile industry faltered in the 1820s. The production of linen yarns had been widespread in Longford and Westmeath, counties which formed part of a greater spinning region situated in the north midlands and south Ulster. Competition from mill-spun yarn, however, led to a rapid contraction of the hand-spinning industry, thereby destroying the livelihood of thousands of female outworkers. Handloom weaving, more a male preserve, was also adversely affected by the increasing concentration of the linen industry in north-east Ireland.[39] In Longford the trade was mainly associated with the districts centring on Granard in the north of the county.[40] The parish priest of Granard, Revd Farrell Sheridan, complained in 1835 that economic conditions in the area had deteriorated during the previous two decades as a result of 'the failure of the linen trade, rack rents, reduction in the price of agricultural produce, and want of employment'.[41] In Clongesh, to the west, it was reported that wages and living standards were falling due to underemployment and 'the total decay of the linen trade'.[42] Depressed conditions in the region and a growing awareness of opportunities in the United States combined to produce a stream of emigrants. Patterns of chain migration helped to perpetuate the flow of people across the Atlantic. According to Revd Thomas Farrelly, intending emigrants received assistance 'from their relatives in America, many of whom encouraged their friends to emigrate, by paying the expenses of the passage'.[43] As the cost of the voyage was a major barrier to emigration, it is likely that Protestant communities were better placed, initially at any rate, to avail of such opportunities and build up emigrant pathways and networks.[44] Arguably also, the cultural restraints on emigration were embedded more deeply in the consciousness of Catholic as compared to Protestant society in the eighteenth and early nineteenth centuries.[45]

There were other pressures, less anonymous than purely market forces, which were pushing Protestants out of the Longford region. In Ballymahon, for example, the middleman family of the Johnstons found itself crushed in the late 1830s under the combined weight of landlord displeasure and the ambitions of a rising Catholic bourgeoisie.[46] Four of the children had already emigrated to North America, most of the remaining seven children following soon after this crisis. The elderly Johnston parents withdrew northwards and, in a move which signified a severe decline of fortune, took over a waterlogged farm in an overwhelmingly Protestant parish near Enniskillen in County Fermanagh, thus reversing the earlier migrations of their ancestors from south Ulster in the early 1700s. Landlord policy generally in this period was to clear middlemen from their estates, thus abolishing economic niches which had hitherto sheltered Protestants of middling wealth and rank. Further down the social scale there are indications that Protestant tenant farmers, who might previously have expected preferential treatment from their landlords, were becoming victims of leasing policies which sought to maximize rent. The staunchly Protestant and Tory *Westmeath Guardian and Longford News-Letter* admitted that 'Gentlemen of the county have hitherto taken their lands out of the hands of Protestant tenants,' adding, though, that these tenants had only themselves to blame 'in expecting to get land upon a very reduced value'.[47] The *Guardian* offered its services in securing positions for 'our Protestant brethren' but it cautioned 'in all instances, to bid a liberal and fair value for the lands they propose for'. That at least some readers felt betrayed by the landed Ascendancy as a result of these policies is revealed in a letter to the same paper soon afterwards. The writer, a 'poor Conservative', upbraided landlords for their rapacious leasing arrangements and neglect of the Protestant cause.

When farms are out of lease, to what description of persons do you mean to let them? What kind of rents do you mean to ask for them? Will you demand what the land is really worth, or will you swell your nominal Rental by taking advantage of that ruinous spirit of competition which has been so fatal to the true prosperity of both landlord and tenant? Will you refuse a moderate, reasonable rent from a respectable Conservative, and take a Rack-rent from a man who at the bidding of a Priest would perjure himself, and help to overthrow that Church and Constitution you profess to love?[48]

What we appear to be seeing is the dissolution of earlier patterns of paternalism and preference in favour of free-market principles of maximizing the returns to land ownership, even at the expense of straining the social bonds that extended upwards through Protestant communities.[49] These bonds, rooted in the original colonial settlements, drew sustenance from shared religious and constitutional affiliations. The organizational and symbolic expression of these values, promoting a sense of Protestant community, was to be found in Church meetings and ceremonial as well as in loyal fraternities such as the lodges of the Orange Order and the Brunswick Constitutional Clubs. But conflict of interest along class lines cut across community solidarity, forcing out Protestant tenants, some of whom would have had little option other than to emigrate. Under the likely conditions of sectarian hiring practices, a loss of Protestant farms would, in turn, have resulted in a contraction of labouring opportunities for the poorer categories of Protestants. The effect of this negative employment multiplier would not have stopped there, but would have extended also to shopkeepers, artisans and others servicing Protestant farmers and labourers.

It is difficult to know how extensive the displacement of Protestant tenants may have been. Moreover, some contrary tendencies, partly politically inspired and possibly short-lived, are reported for the late 1830s. The Conservative landlords of County Longford, it was claimed, had agreed to operate a system designed to crush 'the political tyranny of the Romish priesthood, viz., of not granting, under any circumstances, lands to Roman Catholics, and encouraging by every means a Protestant tenantry'.[50] Possibly there is a measure of wishful thinking in this, but Lady Rosse had begun selective leasing to Protestants a decade earlier following the Catholic and O'Connellite triumph at the famous Clare by-election of 1828. Lord Lorton later waged a bitter war against his unruly Ballinamuck tenants during 1835-9, involving mass evictions, destruction of the pauper village there and attempts to introduce new Protestant tenants.[51] But, while accepting variation in landlord-tenant practices, it is doubtful if many landowners persisted in sacrificing profit on the altar of religious preference.

The changing political environment contributed to Protestant insecurity. Little is known of the tenor of interdenominational relations over most of the eighteenth century, though it may be significant that the Volunteers in Longford in the 1780s were fully in support of removing the civil disabilities endured by both Catholics and nonconformist Protestants.[52] Furthermore, Longford was a minor centre for the United Irishmen, and the movement locally had some Protestant leaders.[53] However, the final decade of the century witnessed acute political and sectarian tension in the region and in Ireland generally. The widening of the parliamentary franchise to include Catholic 40-shilling freehold- ers in 1793 was a reform nervously conceded under British pressure. But it was the United Irish and peasant rebellions of 1798, and the associated conspiracies to induce a French invasion, that exposed the full vulnerability of the Protestant nation in Ireland. An intrinsic and increasingly visible aspect of this vulnerability was the relatively small size of the Protestant population over much of the island.

The Act of Union implied a new political arithmetic. Ireland became a region of the United Kingdom - it held about a third of the combined population of the two kingdoms in 1800 - and Irish Catholics were reduced to a minority within the new political unit.[54] This was reassuring for the predominantly An- glican social élite in Ireland and presumably was also a source of some confidence to lower-class Protestants situated in scattered communities throughout southern

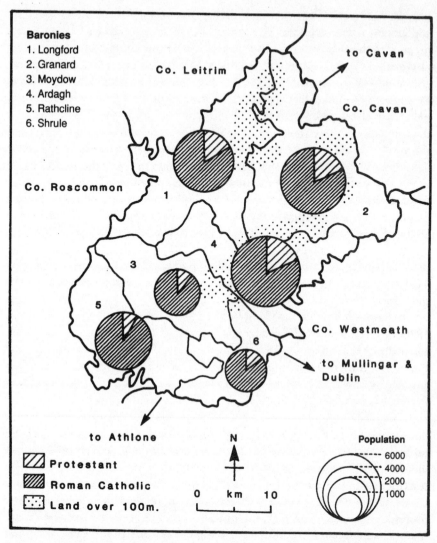

Baronies
1. Longford
2. Granard
3. Moydow
4. Ardagh
5. Rathcline
6. Shrule

Co. Leitrim

to Cavan

Co. Cavan

Co. Roscommon

Co. Westmeath

to Mullingar &
Dublin

to Athlone

N

Protestant
Roman Catholic
Land over 100m.

0   km   10

Population
6000
4000
2000
1000

Spacial Distribution of Longford Catholics and Protestants by Barony in 1732

Ireland. The localism of Irish parliamentary politics, as well as the coercive power of landlords over voters, also served to insulate the new constitutional arrangements from serious challenge. Yet, by the 1820s political agitation and interdenominational strife had surfaced in forms which were to alter fundamentally the course of Irish politics. The Rockite movement of 1821-4, with its anti-Protestant and millenarian tendencies,[55] was the most serious challenge to the established social order since the rebellions in east Ulster and south Leinster in the late 1790s. But the most enduring challenge emanated from O'Connell and the movement for Catholic Emancipation, discussed below by Fergus O'Ferrall. The Tithe War of the early 1830s and the campaign to repeal the Act of Union in the 1840s were natural if not wholly organic extensions of the first Catholic mass movement in Irish history. A complex historical dialectic linked these processes to Tory reaction, evangelical Protestant crusades in the 1820s and 1830s, and propertied fears regarding the encroachment of the lower orders on existing wealth and privilege. The various phases of agitation were well represented in Longford-Westmeath, and the fact that many landlords were high Tory and anti-Catholic ensured that the malign dialectic had particular force in the region.[56]

Political conflict was at its most visible at election time. During the 1820s and 1830s the electorate split fairly consistently along Liberal-Catholic and Conservative-Protestant lines. Because of the restricted franchise, the numbers of Catholics and Protestants entitled to vote were fairly evenly balanced.[57] This excited a rivalry that frequently boiled over into violence. But, while the more affluent Protestants were unfairly advantaged by the franchise qualifications, Catholics enjoyed overwhelming superiority when it came to massed confrontations during periods of electioneering and voting. In the 1830s Longford had the misfortune of hosting no less than six parliamentary elections. Following the violent summer election of 1837 when the White brothers took both Longford seats for the Liberals, and a reforming Whig administration was in place in Dublin Castle, Protestant fears concerning their lives and property reached levels probably unprecedented since the 1790s,[58] as Tom Dunne shows below.

A sense of powerlessness and betrayal fed these apprehensions. By 1840 much Protestant privilege had been stripped away. The process of political reform, initiated in 1793 but resumed only with the passing of a Catholic Emancipation bill in 1829, gathered momentum over the next decade with changes to the magistracy and police, the tithe system and, finally, municipal government. The beneficiaries had been not the Catholic masses but an aggressively aspiring *petite bourgeoisie* which successfully combined service to Catholic Ireland and its own collective interests in the spheres of economy and patronage. Set-backs and defeats in the arena of high politics are in themselves unlikely to have driven out many Protestants. But the low politics of communal conflict, religious intolerance and agrarian violence was an intrinsic element of the socio-political evolution of the region. In combination, these took their toll. 'There is a great deal of contention between the Two religious Parties ...

between the Persons called Orangemen and the persons called Ribandmen,'
observed the crown solicitor for the north-western circuit, Edward Tierney. 'In
fact,' he added, 'the lower Population who are Protestants are generally
denominated Orangemen by the other Party, whether they are so or not.'[59]
These antagonisms were structured by economic and ideological conditions. Falling
prices and contracting employment opportunities after 1814 adversely affected
relations. Land hunger was rife in the pre-Famine decades, Longford being one
of the most heavily populated of the Irish counties. In 1841 the density of
population was 361 persons per square mile of arable land, much higher than the
corresponding ratio of 247 for Leinster counties generally, but rather similar to
population pressure in parts of south Ulster.[60] On the ideological plane, the recent
memories of massacre and reprisal at Granard and Ballinamuck during 1798, as
well as more diffuse notions of dispossession in ancient times, conferred a
politico-sectarian coherence on the mass mobilizations of the 1820s and 1830s.
Reflecting both the struggle for existence and poisoned communal relations,
Longford county ranked as one of the most disturbed in Ireland.[61] Tierney,
drawing on his experience of the north-western counties, believed that only
Cavan approached Longford in terms of agrarian outrages, while Fermanagh,
Tyrone, Donegal and Londonderry were considerably more peaceful.[62] This is
not to suggest that most serious agrarian crime involved inter-communal
violence - and the experience of the four Ulster counties above indicates that a
religiously mixed population was not a sufficient condition for high levels of
outrage - but the sectarian dimension was important in Longford. During the late
1830s the *Westmeath Guardian* carried numerous accounts of not only the
boycotting of Protestants through 'exclusive dealing' but also more brutal assaults
in the form of beatings and killings.[63] Robert Dunlop, an RIC man stationed at
Bawnmore, recalled that in the years preceding the Famine, 'outrages of a
dangerous character were being perpetrated almost nightly' in north Longford
and the neighbouring counties of Leitrim and Roscommon.[64] Among a number
of cases, he cites that of a farmer, Joe Scott, 'a Protestant and a most inoffensive
man, and yet, I suppose because he was a Protestant, someone fired through his
bedroom window and wounded his wife severely in the breast, from which with
difficulty she recovered'. Even the local historiography carries echoes of these
passions. J.P. Farrell, writing in the 1890s, spoke approvingly of a secret society
which 'wreaked its vengeance on yeomen, denouncers, and exterminating
landlords, as opportunity occurred'.[65] A later historian of the region exulted that
in the thirty years after 1798 a new and more aggressive generation of Catholics
emerged in the Ballinamuck area. 'Brought up with vengeance rankling in their
breasts, they were determined to remove the Planters; and remove them they
did.'[66]

There is little doubt that pre-Famine Longford was a cauldron of sectarian
animosity. The evangelical Protestant crusade to the Catholic peasantry, described somewhat presumptuously as the 'New Reformation', deepened divisions based on religion. South Longford was particularly affected, Ballymahon

Table 7. The Protestant Share of Population arranged by Parish for 1831, 1861, 1881 and 1911

PARISH	1831 (%)	1861 (%)	1881 (%)	1911 (%)
Abbeylara	5.9	7.2	7.7	3.3
Abbeyshrule	15.4	21.8	21.5	20.1
Ardagh	4.9	6.1	6.9	7.8
Clonbroney	21.0	19.5	20.3	18.3
Forgney	15.2	21.9	21.3	24.8
Granard★	6.3	5.2	4.0	3.3
Kilcommock	15.5	20.7	21.0	18.3
Kilglass★	12.7	13.3	11.3	12.5
Killashee	12.1	13.1	10.8	11.3
Mostrim	6.7	9.3	7.6	7.4
Rathcline★	2.1	2.9	3.7	2.6
Shrule	6.4	8.0	7.6	6.3
Taghshinny★	12.4	9.2	9.4	10.9
Templemichael★	10.6	10.0	9.8	8.0
'Other'†	7.3	11.5	10.6	10.1
	9.5	9.6	9.0	8.0
Russagh	9.4	7.0	6.1	4.9
St Mary's	14.7	14.1	13.1	13.4
	7.3	7.8	7.4	7.0

★ Group of parishes.
† 'Other' refers to those parts of the parishes of Mohill, Noughaval and Street contained in County Longford.
SOURCES: calculated from *The First Report of the Commission of Public Instruction, Ireland* (HC 1835 xxxiii), the *Census of Ireland for the Year 1861* (HC 1863[3204-III] lix), the *Census of Ireland 1881* (HC 1881 [3402-] [C2931] xcvii) and the *Census Returns for Ireland, 1911* (HC 1912-13 [Cd. 6049] cxiv).

emerging as an important theatre for religious disputation and conflict.[67] The proselytizers enjoyed the backing of a number of Longford landlords, especially that of the Lefroy family and Lord Lorton.[68] No doubt some landed support was animated by anti-Catholic sentiment, but it is also possible that it stemmed from a desire to erode the overwhelming numerical superiority of the Catholic population, particularly as in an age of incipient democracy O'Connell was demonstrating the potency of political numbers. Furthermore, against a backdrop of heightened communal and class tensions, the assumed relationship between Protestantism, progress and orderly behaviour must have commended the movement to some beleaguered property-holders. But, whatever the combination of motives involved, it is clear that the crusade added a further twist to strained interdenominational relations in the region.

A revealing glimpse of early education into the ways of adult conflict is furnished by H.D. Inglis, who visited Longford and Westmeath in the course of an extensive tour of Ireland in 1834. Having learned that 'much bad feeling existed, owing to a difference in religious belief', he records a specific instance which occurred during his stay in the neighbourhood of Ballymahon.[69] Lady Rosse had established several Protestant schools in the area. Reaching these entailed certain hazards. Catholic children 'were accustomed to post themselves on a bridge, across which the Protestant children were obliged to pass, and to spit upon them as they passed by'.[70] More generally, the minority position of Protestants throughout much of southern Ireland rendered them especially vulnerable to attack. This was particularly the case in relation to middle- and lower-class Protestants who, in addition to sectarian reasons for assault, might also prove convenient victims in the event of unpopular political or economic policies on the part of the landed Ascendancy or the local representatives of the state. Feelings of widespread insecurity are apparent in the petitions to the Colonial Office cited earlier, many of the Protestant applicants adding sectarian as well as economic pressures as reasons for quitting Ireland.[71]

In view of the varied forces eroding the Protestant population, it is possible that some of the smaller communities in the Longford region were experiencing an absolute decline in numbers in the decade or so before the Famine. Despite conversions and emigration, however, it is unlikely that this was true for Protestants in the region as a whole. While we have no firm evidence on the matter, it is probable that under the impetus of past population growth the numbers of Protestants in Longford-Westmeath West continued to expand (albeit at a reduced pace), reaching their highest levels ever on the eve of the Famine. But the secular trend towards a relative decline observed earlier is also likely to have persisted, quite possibly accelerating during the 1830s and early 1840s.

III

The Famine reversed more than a century of sustained population increase for both Catholic and Protestant communities. Starvation, disease and death, reinforced by a panic exodus from the land, were decisive in bringing about a major decline in numbers at the mid-century. (Population in County Longford in 1851 was 29 per cent below the 1841 level, while for County Westmeath the fall was 21 per cent.) Thereafter, a central feature of the demographic history of the region, and indeed of all Ireland, was persistent population decline. Recent estimates of famine mortality place counties Longford and Westmeath in the middle range of suffering, with excess death rates somewhat below the national average.[72] However, relative to Leinster counties generally the Longford-Westmeath experience was severe. Both counties had much more in common with a south Ulster county like Monaghan, where appalling conditions prevailed, than with other Leinster counties like Wexford or Carlow for example.[73] Because

Table 8. *Changing occupational structure in County Longford, 1871-1911: selected male occupations*

	1871		1911	
	ROMAN CATHOLIC (%)	PROTESTANT (%)	ROMAN CATHOLIC (%)	PROTESTANT (%)
Farmers and graziers	27	32	36	36
Farm servants	20	9	5	2
Farm and general labourers	32	12	22	6
Professional	3	10	4	12
Commercial	2	3	1	3
Textiles and clothing	4	5	2	3

SOURCE: calculated from *Census of Ireland*, 1871 and 1911.

of the superior economic status of the Protestant population it is virtually certain that Protestant communities were more resilient in the face of famine and disease. Perhaps a few Protestants even squeezed comfort from the calamity in the manner of James Acheson, an indebted grazier and self-proclaimed High Churchman and Tory. Acheson had been the intended victim of a number of assassination bids. However, 'God in his Wisdom had caused all these troubles to cease. Pestilence and famine has ... swept one-third of the population and our good wholesome law strung some more on the gallows, so that we can now raise our Ebenezer to the Lord and no man to make us afraid.'[74]

In some respects the post-Famine world was indeed a more congenial one for Protestants of all social classes in the region. True, there was a steep decline in numbers around the mid-century, indicating a heavy burden of emigration, probably not very different from that of their Catholic neighbours. But, within the surviving population their relative size increased.

Furthermore, pressure on land eased, rural districts lost some of their most turbulent elements, and economic conditions showed a sustained improvement from the early 1850s. There are also indications of a revival of landlord authority and political power.[75]

A detailed discussion of the course of Catholic and Protestant demographic decline in the later nineteenth and early twentieth centuries is not possible here. But the statistical anatomy of decline may be swiftly sketched. The essentially rural economy of Longford-Westmeath was incapable of sustaining pre-Famine population densities at levels of income acceptable to a people advantaged by easy access to the more remunerative labour markets of Britain and North America. By 1911 the population of County Longford had contracted to 61 per cent of its 1861 size. For Westmeath West the story was much the same, the corresponding proportion being 67 per cent.[76]

The religious composition of the population tilted gradually in favour of

Table 9. Catholic and Protestant households: Granard 1911

	ROMAN CATHOLIC	PROTESTANT
Gender and age		
% male household heads	79	83
mean age of head	55	57
Household structure		
% nuclear families	60	58
% extended families	15	14
% solitaries	9	11
% households with children	43	39
Marriage behaviour		
% ever married (heads only)	82	77
% widowed (heads only)	22	26
% non-local wives	18	71
% mixed marriages	0	3
mean age at marriage (male farmers)	36	34
mean age at marriage (female farmers)	29	27
Wealth indicators		
% households with servants	16	29
no. of coach-houses per 100 households	14	41
no. of stables per 100 households	57	97
no. of outbuildings per 100 households	270	594
Occupational status		
% heads in professions	2	17
% heads farmers	44	49
% heads traders or artisans	8	20
% heads labourers	23	6
% heads with other occupations	14	6
% heads with no occupations	10	3

NOTE: The sample consists of all households in Granard parish in 1911 and is composed of 745 Catholic and 35 Protestant households. However, because of the small size of subgroups within the Protestant population, mean age at marriage for Protestant farmers has been calculated from an expanded sample (201 households) that takes in Protestants in neighbouring parishes as well as Granard itself.

SOURCE: P.R.O.I., census enumerators' returns for Granard, 1911.

Catholics, but only after 1871, thereby re-establishing the earlier pre-Famine trend. The process was a gentle one, with the 1870s and the opening decade of this century being periods of mildly accelerating relative decline for Protestants. Interestingly, these were also decades in which emigration from Ulster quickened, due in part to difficulties in the urban-industrial economy of the north-east.[77] By contrast, the rate of emigration from the other, predominantly Catholic provinces of Ireland slowed in these periods. This raises the intriguing possibility that not only did northern Protestant and southern Catholic communities possess different emigration patterns, but that emigration by southern Protestants formed part of a Protestant response distinct from that of their Catholic neighbours. Table 8, which contains information on the changing distribution of occupations over time, offers only perverse clues as to the economic causes of the disproportionate Protestant decline.

The collapse of farm servanthood and the erosion of labouring jobs are to be expected, given the course of employment change in Ireland in the later nineteenth century, but Protestants happened to be under-represented in these declining occupations. Comparing rates of decline within specific occupations is more revealing. Thus while the number of Catholic farmers was virtually static between 1871 and 1911, the number of Protestant farmers fell by a hefty 40 per cent. Similarly, the decline of labourers, farm servants and even professionals was more dramatic within the Protestant work force.[78] This suggests, firstly, the disappearance of vulnerable niches in the Protestant, and indeed general, social structure. But, secondly, it indicates a more generalized process of attrition, affecting sectors such as farming whose relative importance was expanding. Thirdly, in view of these steep declines, particularly among farmers, one might wonder if family as well as individual movement was a feature of Protestant outmigration.

Decayed demographic vitality, rather than outmigration, is of course an alternative explanation for both the mild relative and large absolute decline in Protestant communities. To explore this possibility and also to construct a profile of Catholic and Protestant communities on the eve of the decade of momentous change, 1911-21, we have availed of the rich household data contained in the census enumerators' returns for 1911. The parish of Granard was selected as a case-study.[79] The key points to emerge from this comparative analysis are sufficiently self-evident to require little further elaboration.

The superior economic status of Protestant households is confirmed both by the various indirect measures of wealth and by the respective occupational structures. There were, for example, virtually no Protestant labouring households. This stratum of Protestant society had been stripped away in the course of the nineteenth century, seemingly to a greater extent than in Catholic society. Similarly, only a narrow range of industrial occupations survived. Further up the social scale, middlemen families - once important brokers of economic and political power in the countryside - had disappeared altogether. The gentry still survived at the head of Protestant society, though much weakened economically and politically. The Protestant community of Granard had, therefore, undergone internal restructuring in the century before 1911. The residual population was now more specialized, dependent largely on farming, ancillary occupations and the professions. In terms of household types what is perhaps most surprising is the degree of similarity between the two communities. They differ, it is true, on certain demographic indicators, but the differences are not pronounced. Certainly there is no strong basis in these or other structural features of the Protestant community to suggest the traumatic decline that lay ahead.

In the decade 1911-21 the Great War cast a mortal shadow over Ireland generally, and Protestant Ireland in particular, while the secession of most of the island from the United Kingdom in 1921 delivered a psychological blow of fundamental proportions. Most southern Protestants were still unionist in political sympathy despite their isolation in a sea of Irish nationalism. In the fifteen-year interval between 1911 and 1926, allowing for natural increase, the Protestant communities of County Longford lost over 40 per cent of their members.[80] The Protestant share of population fell by 28 per cent. These changes can not, as we have seen, be put down to atrophied reproductive capacities. A number of processes were at work, but heightened political and sectarian tension accompanying the drive for and creation of a new Irish state must be central to any explanation for the Protestant exodus. The precise forms of insecurity and alienation affecting households at a local level may remain forever obscure. The childhood recollections of a Methodist minister, born into a strong farming family at Trillick-a-Temple, near Longford town, in December 1910, affords a glimpse of one of the mechanisms serving to deplete Protestant numbers. The Fee household was raided for arms and money by the IRA in late August 1921. The next incident carried more serious consequences.

Raiders again visited us in March 1922. This time they made no demands but gave instructions that in future we were not to supply farm produce to Protestant homes in Longford town, neither were we to purchase any goods except from Roman Catholic shops. My parents accepted these restrictions - they had no alternative, but they considered there were little prospects of making farming a paying proposition in the future, and so our farm was put up for auction and sold in March 1923.[81]

The experience of the Fee family, who, like the Johnstons several generations earlier, moved north to join relatives in a Protestant district near Armagh, is one detail in the unravelling of the patchwork of Protestant communities in southern Ireland.

IV

Viewed in long-term perspective, the Protestant communities of the region expanded (though in uneven fashion) during the seventeenth century, and continued to increase in absolute size up to the mid nineteenth century. The Protestant population peaked probably in the 1840s, when it is likely to have numbered 14,000 people.[82] The Great Famine inaugurated a long era of decline, this being particularly marked during the first quarter of this century. By 1981 Longford-Westmeath West held fewer than 1500 Protestants. Though mediated by local circumstances, secular decline was the outcome essentially of wider historical forces, located in Ireland, Britain and the Atlantic economy. For that reason the experiences of Longford-Westmeath Protestants probably had much in common with those of other small, scattered communities in southern Ireland.

Change in the *relative* strength of the minority religious population followed a somewhat different chronology. The Protestant share of the overall population increased substantially between the late seventeenth and mid eighteenth centuries, and then underwent decline until the Famine intervened in 1845-6. The relative position of the minority stabilized during the mid-Victorian period – an artificial and temporary respite – but went into continuous decline in the later nineteenth and twentieth centuries. The first population census of the new Irish state showed that by 1926 the Protestant share had fallen back to the minimal level established in the time of Cromwell. This was striking confirmation of its long-term decline.

Nevertheless, among the more enduring features of the Protestant presence in Longford-Westmeath is the stability of settlement patterns. Thus, from 1911 back to 1766, and possibly 1732, the ranking of districts by reference to size of Protestant population suggests considerable geographical persistence. The rural economic base of many of the communities no doubt accounted for much of this continuity. Within each district Protestants were not distributed evenly or at random over the land area. For 1911 at any rate, the impression formed from a sample of north Longford parishes is that Protestant households tended to cluster in a comparatively small number of townlands and were totally absent from most others.[83] Such patterns, which helped compensate to some extent for the numerical weakness of Protestants in the region as a whole, had important implications for social intercourse both within and between the two socio-religious groupings. Spatial segregation, at least of a limited kind, facilitated mutual aid, exclusive forms of sociability and, more generally, the reproduction of Protestant community structures through time. It is noticeable though that most Protestants in Granard, by contrast with Catholics, married non-local women, testifying to difficulties in recruiting suitable spouses locally and possibly signifying also a more cosmopolitan world view. The elaboration and maintenance of wider but exclusive social networks served to reduce dependence on neighbouring Catholics and tended to deflect the threat of eventual absorption into the majority population.

But decline there inevitably was. And it could be that the segregative and supralocal devices which preserved Protestant communities had the unintended effect of facilitating or even provoking some of those developments which ensured their eventual decline. The corrosive forces acting on the fabric of Protestant society extending from the economic and demographic to the political and sectarian have been treated in some detail. Among the mechanisms at work we have included the political and sectarian aggression directed against Protestants, a set of influences usually ignored or played down by historians and other commentators. Indeed, reading history backwards it would seem that the 'troubles' surrounding the formation of the Irish state, the political and sectarian disturbances of the early nineteenth century, and the tumult of the 1680s and the 1640s coincided with a weakening of the Protestant demographic position. These associations suggest that in general there may be a direct causal link between political tension and sharp relative declines among minority communities (perhaps Catholic as well as Protestant) in Ireland during recent centuries.[84] This hypothesis might be usefully explored in relation to other regions on the island, since the sapping of Protestant power and numbers constitutes one of the most significant and dramatic stories of modern Irish history.

Still, the likelihood is that socio-economic rather than political forces were primarily responsible for Protestant decline. Between 1766 and 1831, for example, Protestant communities in Longford 'lost' perhaps as many as one-third of their potential constituents. Although political and religious tensions were acute during the 1790s and the 1820s, in general that era was characterized by Protestant ascendancy and confidence. While we are unsure of the distribution in time of these losses, it seems significant that in other regions, such as Kilkenny, some Protestant communities were experiencing marked relative and even absolute decline in the later eighteenth century: that is, before the onset of political crisis. Likewise, much if not most of the contraction of the Protestant population in Longford between the Famine and the Great War is not obviously associated with disturbed conditions. However, rather than seeing socio-economic and political factors as separate, these are perhaps best understood as mutually reinforcing. Thus the key to Protestant attrition may lie in the complex interactions between economic processes, social structure, shifting class relationships within Protestant communities, and external political pressures. The comparatively high socio-economic status of many Protestant households and their over-representation in commercial and industrial occupations, coupled with landlords' leasing policies, may have made southern Protestant society particularly susceptible to class-specific pressures for emigration (and, perhaps, to restrictive practices respecting marriage, household composition and inheritance) which characterized the development of Irish capitalism from the mid eighteenth century on. A consciousness of wider opportunities, as well as developed migrant pathways, facilitated recourse to emigration. The consequent demographic decline and distortion of an already truncated social structure made southern Protestants increasingly vulnerable to Catholic political, economic and physical pressures. This was all the more true, of course, since the fundamental demographic reality was that most Protestant communities were minority ones throughout their long histories.

By the eve of the Great War, the more fully articulated Protestant class structure which had emerged by the late eighteenth century had virtually disappeared. Social stratification within Protestant communities was less marked than a hundred years earlier, with a rural and urban bourgeoisie predominating. This ensured that striking socio-economic differences between the two religious groupings persisted from the seventeenth through the early twentieth centuries. However, the superior status and exclusive character of southern Protestant society continued to incite Catholic resentment and assault and the absence of a dense and fully articulated social structure made the exposed remnants of the former Ascendancy acutely vulnerable to such external pressures.

We have already indicated that there were some similarities between the Longford region and Ulster counties. Unlike Ulster, by the second quarter of the twentieth century there was no longer an ethnic or religious minority problem in Longford-Westmeath. The key to this apparently happier state of affairs did not lie in benign social processes of accommodation and acculturation. There was no minority problem because there was virtually no minority. Rather as the phenomenon of the vanishing agricultural labourer resolved major issues of rural conflict in post-Famine society, so the 'vanishing Protestant' brought ethnic and sectarian confrontation to a close over much of Ireland.

NOTES

1. Examples of the genre, which also possess outstanding aesthetic merit, might be taken from the novels and short stories of Somerville and Ross, Elizabeth Bowen and Molly Keane (J.M. Farrell). An historical study of major importance for the understanding of Protestant society in post-Independence Ireland is Kurt Bowen, *Protestants in a Catholic State: Ireland's Privileged Minority* (Dublin 1983).
2. *Calendar of Patent Rolls Ireland, James I*, p. 432. For an overview see Brian Mac Cuarta, 'Newcomers in the Irish Midlands', M.A. thesis, U.C.G., 1980, ff. 88-183.
3. *Cal. pat. rolls Ire., Jas I*, p. 500.
4. There were connections also in terms of the personal fortunes of individual grantees. Frances Aungier, for example, was made Baron Aungier of Longford on the basis of, among other services, his work on the plantation of Ulster. *Cal. pat. rolls Ire., Jas I*, p. 502.
5. J. C. Beckett, *The Making of Modern Ireland, 1603-1923* (London 1981), pp. 54-5.
6. Admiral J. Forbes, *Memoirs of the Earls of Granard* (London 1868), p. 33.
7. Quoted from J.P. Farrell in his partisan *History of the County Longford* (Dublin 1891). Farrell, a journalist and newspaper proprietor, was first elected as a nationalist member of parliament for West Cavan in 1896. Between 1900 and 1918 he was returned continuously as MP for North Longford. An outline of Farrell's career is contained in *75 Years of Longford:* The Longford Leader, *1897-1972* (Longford 1972).
8. R. L. Edgeworth, *Memoirs of Richard Lovell Edgeworth, Esq.*, i (London 1820), p. 7.
9. S. Pender (ed.), *A Census of Ireland, circa 1659* (Dublin 1939).
10. W. J. Smyth, 'Society and settlement in seventeenth century Ireland: the evidence of the "1659 Census"' in W.J. Smyth, Kevin Whelan (eds), *Common Ground: Essays on the Historical Geography of Ireland* (Cork 1988), p. 56.
11. The demographic sources and methodology which underpin this essay are discussed at length in a sister paper; suffice it to say here that all population estimates prior to the mid nineteenth century must be treated with caution.
12. Forbes, op. cit., p. 66. On the attitudes and apprehensions of a Protestant Jacobite landlord during this period see the letters of the Earl of Longford reproduced in *Analecta Hibernica*, no. 15 (Nov. 1944).
13. D. Dickson, *New Foundations: Ireland, 1660-1800* (Dublin 1987), p. 105. For a discussion of landlord-sponsored immigration, and the limits of landlord powers in this regard, see L.M. Cullen, *The Emergence of Modern Ireland, 1600-1900* (London 1981), pp. 36-7, 52-4.

14. A settlement of Scottish tenants appears to have been established near New-townforbes as early as the 1620s. Townlands lying to the south-west of the village were known as the 'Scots' Quarters'. See *Centenary of St Mel's Cathedral, 1840-1940* (Longford 1940). The 1641 depositions also indicate the presence of small numbers of Scots in the county prior to that date. See Cullen, op. cit., p. 57.
15. T.J. Barron, 'Presbyterian exodus from County Longford in 1729' in *Breifne*, v, no. 18 (1977-8), p. 253.
16. Presbyterians accounted for just under 3 per cent of the Protestant population of Longford county in 1831. Possibly the proportion was larger in the eighteenth century but had been eroded through relatively high rates of emigration. See *First Report of the Commission of Public Instruction, Ireland* (H.C. 1835 xxxiii). Despite a number of visits to the county by John Wesley, it seems that Methodism had made few inroads into the Church of Ireland membership. The census of Ireland for 1861, for example, records only 95 Methodists as compared to 6200 members of the Established Church. It is likely, nonetheless, that Wesley prepared the way for later manifestations of evangelical fervour, these being contained within the framework of orthodox Church organization. See also E. MacCormaic, 'Rev. John Wesley, A.M., and Methodism in Co. Longford', in *Teathbha*, i, no. 2 (1971), pp. 128-30.
17. The evidence is indirect, being from a later period. The bulk of estates in the 1860s consisted of those of the lesser gentry, a condition which was unlikely to have been of recent origin. See R.F.B. O'Ferrall, 'The Growth of Political Consciousness in Ireland, 1823-1847: A Study of O'Connellite Politics and Political Education', Ph.D. thesis, T.C.D., 1978.
18. Some indirect evidence for this supposition is provided by Table 6 which shows a statistical relationship between the numbers of gentry houses and the presence of Protestant population. See also Edgeworth, op. cit., i, p. 331.
19. On depressed economic conditions in the 1720s and 1730s see Dickson, op. cit., p. 102.
20. Barron, 'Presbyterian Exodus', pp. 253-7.
21. K. A. Miller, *Emigrants and Exiles: Ireland and the Irish Exodus to North America* (Oxford 1985), pp. 152-3.
22. O'Ferrall, 'Growth of Political Consciousness', p. 458; Edgeworth, op. cit., ii, pp. 205-8. Note also the information in Tables 7 and 8 for later periods.
23. The measure of association used is Pearson's product-moment correlation coefficient (r). Depending on the availability of information, the number of cases varies between 13 and 16. In most instances it is 16, corresponding to the number of geographical units into which we have subdivided the region. Despite the small number of cases, five of the nine relationships turn out to be statistically significant at the 90 per cent confidence level (i.e. in those instances where r equals or exceeds 0.49).

The data sources are as follows. The number of Big Houses in each unit has been derived from S. Lewis, *A Topographical Dictionary of Ireland* (London 1837). Land values have been taken from the 1851 census of Ireland, while the degree of urbanization and dependence on industry have been constructed from Lewis's *Dictionary* and the 1841 census of Ireland respectively. Urbanization is measured relative to Irish conditions and is defined as the proportion of the population living in settlements of more than 100 inhabitants. The variable industry is defined as the proportion of families engaged in industrial pursuits.
24. P. Ó Duigneáin, 'Ballinamuck and '98: A Talk to the Society', in *Teathbha*, i, no. 1 (1969), p. 43.

25. J. P. Farrell, *Historical Notes and Stories of County Longford* (Dublin 1886).
26. For a detailed case-study of these links in the neighbouring county of Cavan see K. O'Neill, *Family and Farm in Pre-Famine Ireland: The Parish of Killeshandra* (Madison 1984).
27. W. S. Mason, *Statistical Account; or, Parochial Survey of Ireland*, ii (Dublin 1819), p. 323.
28. Ibid., ii, p. 631.
29. Ibid., i, p. 458.
30. P.R.O.I., *Census of the Diocese of Elphin*, 1749.
31. P.R.O.N.I., C.R.I./14/1, *Speculum Gregis for the Parish of Killashee from the year 1847*. Thus, for example, of a waiter at Sutcliffe Hotel, Longford, it is noted: 'His wife a papist and the children suspected of going *both* ways.'
32. Census enumerators' returns for Granard parish in 1911, held at P.R.O.I. This is likely to be an underestimate, of course, as traces of hitherto mixed couples may have disappeared due to the conversion of one or other of the spouses before or soon after the marriage ceremony. Nonetheless, there is little indication, from this source at any rate, of social mixing across the religious divide.
33. J. Mokyr, *Why Ireland Starved* (London 1983), p. 35.
34. L. Kennedy, 'The rural economy' in L. Kennedy and P. Ollerenshaw (eds), *An Economic History of Ulster, 1820-1939* (Manchester 1985), p. 37.
35. Miller, op. cit., chapter 6.
36. Ibid., loc. cit.
37. Edgeworth, op. cit., ii, p. 205.
38. E. MacCormaic, 'South County Longford: Its Farming Patterns and Customs', in *Teathbha*, ii, no. 1 (1980), pp. 61-2.
39. Kennedy, 'The Rural Economy', pp. 4-6.
40. W. H. Crawford, *Domestic Industry in Ireland* (Dublin 1972), pp. 5-6. Significantly, the coat of arms of Granard depicts a flax stalk and an ear of corn. See J. Burns & B. Grier (eds), *Granard: Its History, Our Heritage* (Granard 1987).
41. *Poor Inquiry (Ireland): Appendix E*, H.C. 1836 xxxii, p. 205.
42. Ibid., p. 206.
43. *Poor Inquiry (Ireland): Appendix F*, H.C. 1836 xxxiii, p. 204.
44. On Protestant emigrant networks see the pioneering work of B.S. Elliott, *Irish Emigrants in the Canadas: A New Approach* (Montreal 1988).
45. Miller, op. cit., pp. 235-8.
46. K. A. Miller, 'No Middle Ground: The Erosion of the Protestant Middle Class in Southern Ireland during the Pre-Famine Era', in *Huntington Library Quarterly*, xlix (1986), pp. 295-306.
47. *Westmeath Guardian and Longford News Letter*, 28 Sept. 1837.
48. *Westmeath Guardian*, 2 Nov. 1837.
49. The Edgeworth *Memoirs* (ii, pp. 16-42) contain an interesting statement and defence of the principles of political economy as well as advanced sentiments on the subjects of merit and equality of treatment.
50. *Westmeath Guardian*, 5 Apr. 1838.
51. F. O'Ferrall, 'The Ballinamuck "Land War" of 1835-39', in *Teathbha*, ii, no. 2 (1983), pp. 104-9.
52. Edgeworth, op. cit., pp. 45-51.
53. Ó Duigneáin, 'Ballinamuck and '98', p. 44.
54. Calculated from B.R. Mitchell & P. Deane, *Abstract of British Historical Statistics* (Cambridge 1962), p. 8.
55. J. S. Donnelly, jr, 'Pastorini and Captain Rock: Millenarianism and Sectarianism in

the Rockite Movement of 1821-4' in Samuel Clarke, J. S. Donnelly (eds), *Irish Peasants: Violence and Political Unrest, 1780-1914* (Manchester 1983), pp. 102-37; F. O'Ferrall, *Catholic Emancipation: Daniel O'Connell and the Birth of Irish Democracy* (Dublin 1985), pp. 46-8, 73.

56. F. O'Ferrall, 'The Struggle for Catholic Emancipation in County Longford, 1824-29' in *Teathbha*, i, no. 4 (1978), pp. 259-69.

57. O'Ferrall, 'Growth of Political Consciousness', pp. 642-9.

58. Miller, 'No Middle Ground', p. 299.

59. *Minutes of Evidence before the Select Committee on the State of Ireland in Respect of Crime*, H.C., House of Lords, 1839.

60. *Census of Ireland for the year 1841.*

61. According to Lee, Longford ranked alongside Limerick, Clare, Tipperary and Roscommon as among the most disturbed counties in pre-Famine Ireland. See J. Lee, 'Patterns of Rural Unrest in Nineteenth-Century Ireland: A Preliminary Survey' in L. M. Cullen and F. Furet (eds), *Ireland and France, 17th-20th Century* (Paris 1980).

62. *Select Committee on the State of Ireland, 1839.*

63. See, for example, the issues of the *Westmeath Guardian* during the summer and autumn of 1837.

64. P.R.O.N.I., T2815/1, *Reminiscences of Robert Dunlop, Clough, County Antrim, 1825-75.*

65. Farrell, *History of ... Longford*, p. 171.

66. J.F. Lenehan, 'Memories of Ballinamuck', in *Teathbha*, i, no. 1 (1969), p. 48. This 'land war' claimed some seven murder victims, mostly Protestant farmers and agents. See O'Ferrall, 'Ballinamuck', 104-9.

67. F. O'Ferrall, *Catholic Emancipation*, p. 165.

68. O'Ferrall, 'Growth of Political Consciousness', pp. 557-71.

69. H.D. Inglis, *Ireland in 1834: A Journey throughout Ireland, during the Spring, Summer and Autumn of 1834* (3rd ed., London 1835).

70. Ibid., i, pp. 340-1.

71. See, for example, the petitions of R. Talbot *et al.*, 29 Dec. 1817, P.R.O., C.O. 384/1, and J. Tully *et al.*, 17 Feb. 1830, C.O. 384/23.

72. Mokyr, op. cit., p. 267.

73. The death rate due to famine in counties Longford and Westmeath during the period 1846-51 was over twenty per thousand; in Carlow and Wexford it was in the region of five per thousand. See Mokyr, op. cit, p. 267.

74. James Acheson to his daughter, 27 Dec. 1848 (letter in the possession of Dr K.A. Miller).

75. K. Theodore Hoppen, *Elections, Politics and Society in Ireland ,1832-1885* (Oxford 1984).

76. Calculated from W. E. Vaughan & A. J. Fitzpatrick, *Irish Population Statistics , 1821-1971* (Dublin 1978).

77. Miller, *Emigrants and Exiles*, pp. 370-1.

78. The rates of decline experienced by Protestants in selected occupational groups between 1871 and 1911 were as follows: agricultural labourers -71% (-19%), general labourers -78% (-69%), farm servants -97% (-82%), professionals (excluding military) -56% (-15%), and textiles and clothing -59% (-65%). The corresponding Catholic rates are shown in brackets.

79. P.R.O.I., census enumerators' returns for Granard, 1911.

80. Calculated from census data for 1911 and 1926.

81. J. and D. Fee, *Happy Landings: The Perils and Pleasures of a Missionary's Life: Experiences in China, Malaya, England and Ireland* (Belfast 1988). We are grateful to Dr Brian Walker for drawing this source to our attention.

82. This estimate is based on the assumption of a very low Protestant growth rate of 0.1% per annum between 1831 and 1845.

83. Based on census enumerators' returns for five Longford electoral divisions.

84. This and related issues in the 'politics of demography' have been discussed with reference to the modern conflict in Northern Ireland by Liam Kennedy in *Two Ulsters* (Belfast 1986), pp. 26–35.

The Catholic Church in the Diocese of Ardagh, 1650–1870

The sixteenth-century Counter-Reformation prompted dramatic structural change in the Catholic Church throughout Europe, though the pace at which the reforms laid down by the Council of Trent were implemented varied from country to country and region to region. In Ireland, a series of provincial synods between 1614 and 1631 formally promulgated the decrees of the Council of Trent, but the mere enactment of Counter-Reformation legislation did not create a Counter-Reformation Church.[1] Political events and recurrent organizational and personnel difficulties in the seventeenth and eighteenth centuries interrupted or delayed this process, with the result that the establishment of a Tridentine Church in many rural and comparatively ill-endowed dioceses in Ireland was not completed until the mid nineteenth century. Ardagh fits this pattern, though the history of the Catholic Church in the diocese is not always clear because of the fragmentary nature of the surviving records. This problem is compounded by the fact that the diocese embraces parts of six different counties – Longford, Leitrim, Sligo, Roscommon, Westmeath and Cavan. Its core and greater part, comprising 32 of its 42 parishes, includes virtually all of County Longford (22 parishes) and half of County Leitrim (10 parishes); four parishes lie in County Cavan, three in Westmeath, two in Sligo and one in Roscommon.[2] It is a small diocese, and since 1756 it has been united with the still smaller diocese of Clonmacnois. The latter lies almost totally in County Offaly and is not considered in this study.

Despite these problems, the main features of the history of the Ardagh diocese from 1650 to 1870 can be established. Between the mid seventeenth and the mid eighteenth centuries the diocese was beset by a host of political, ecclesiastical and pastoral problems that weakened the Church organizationally and pastorally. The Catholic population was inadequately ministered to and parts of the diocese were seriously neglected. This improved in the second half of the eighteenth century, but it was not until the nineteenth century that the diocese underwent the sustained pastoral and structural reorganization that signalled the triumph of Tridentine Catholicism and the establishment of the modern Catholic Church. We can trace these trends, and assess the contribution of the five vicars and twelve bishops who had charge of the diocese during these two centuries, despite problems of source material. However, little is known about such subjects as the relationship between priests and people, the intensity of public devotion and the strength of popular religion. It is not possible, therefore, to write a total history of the Catholic Church in the diocese of Ardagh in this period, but a broad outline can be provided.

I

Though the Catholic Church in seventeenth-century Ireland had to endure repeated bouts of repression, the most severe attack began in 1649 with the arrival of Oliver Cromwell and his army. Cromwell was deeply hostile to Catholicism, and his brisk and efficient conquest heralded a sustained period of repression culminating in an edict, published in January 1653, expelling all Catholic priests and ecclesiastics from the country. Approximately a thousand clerics went into exile, while those who stayed behind were forced to conduct their ministry surreptitiously to avoid imprisonment or transportation.[3] We do not have precise information on the number of priests that suffered as a result, but the 1653 proclamation deprived the Church of many priests and undermined the structural and pastoral reforms effected in the early seventeenth century. The Church was obliged to assume a missionary form and, with only one bishop in the country, responsibility for ministering to the population devolved upon those secular and regular clergy who avoided exile.[4]

In the diocese of Ardagh, as elsewhere, the Cromwellian conquest took a heavy toll, and both the Catholic Church and the native landowners, on whom the Church relied for support, were dramatically weakened. Sixty-one per cent of the land of County Longford was confiscated and 174 'papist proprietors' were deprived of their patrimonies as a result of confiscation, although it is difficult to know how many of these confiscations were permanent. This greatly reduced the base from which the Church drew its financial support, as is revealed by the 1660 poll money returns which put the taxable population of the county at only 5392.[5] At the same time, the weakening of the Church's leadership and the fall in clerical numbers prevented the Church from fulfilling its basic sacramental obligations. The bishop, Patrick Plunkett, had chosen exile in 1651 and, while it is not possible to assess the number of clergy that followed his example, those who stayed behind were too ill-circumstanced to maintain even a functional Church. In the absence of Plunkett, who remained in France until 1665,[6] the diocese was administered by Cornelius Gaffney - one of its most senior and experienced pastors - who was appointed vicar-general. Gaffney was an appropriate choice; he had already served the diocese as vicar capitular in the interregnum between the vicar apostolicship of John Gaffney (1622-37) and the elevation of Patrick Plunkett to the episcopacy in 1647, a position for which he himself had been considered. According to Archbishop Edmund O'Reilly of Armagh (1657-69) Gaffney was a 'zealous pastor'. Pastoral excellence was not the only criterion necessary for elevation to the hierarchy, however, and in 1647 Gaffney had lost out to Patrick Plunkett, brother of the influential Earl of Fingal, because he lacked connections.[7] The decision was unfortunate; Plunkett was without pastoral experience. Worse still, he was not interested in Ardagh and his flight in 1651 left Gaffney with the daunting responsibility of leading the diocese through one of the most difficult periods in its history. It proved a harrowing experience and, like most of the clergy that chose to stay in the country, Gaffney was obliged 'to sleep in the open country, sometimes in the woods, and sometimes in the caves' and to minister as circumstances allowed. He evaded capture until 1660 when, with the worst of the anti-Catholic repression over, he was apprehended and condemned to death. This sentence was commuted and he was subsequently released, but other priests of the diocese did not fare so well. Donough O'Ferrall was martyred in Dublin; John O'Muldoon was transported; Eugene MacGauran died in prison in Galway; Patrick Travers was imprisoned on Aran, and John Micham in Athlone. Francis Farrell, who was Guardian of the Franciscan house at Ballinasagart near Edgeworthstown, was captured and imprisoned in County Cavan in 1658. Farrell, a gifted and learned priest, had been recommended to the bishopric of Ardagh in1637 by Emperor Ferdinand of Austria, and to the see of Meath in 1648; he received neither, but unembittered he went on to play an important role in revitalizing the Church in the midlands with the gradual easing of repression after 1658.[8]

Bishop Plunkett was kept informed of developments by Cornelius Gaffney, but he showed no eagerness to return to his see.[9] The administration of the diocese continued to be the responsibility of the vicar-general, who oversaw such efforts as were made to reanimate the Church organizationally and spiritually in the late 1650s and early 1660s. Indeed, the diocese of Ardagh pointed the way for the rest of the country in these years. In 1658 priests were ordained for the diocese, while the successful convening of a provincial chapter by the Franciscans at Ballinasagart in October of the same year and at Jamestown, County Leitrim in 1660 paved the way for a provincial synod of the archdiocese of Armagh at Clonelly in north Longford in October 1660.[10] The object of the synod was to reaffirm the doctrines and disciplines of the Council of Trent. Although a majority of the synod's resolutions must be described as aspirational rather than realizable, they do attest to the determination of those exercising ecclesiastical jurisdiction to revitalize the Church in the wake of the devastation of the 1650s.[11]

If it had proved possible to enforce the statutes agreed at Clonelly, the adherence of Irish Catholics to the doctrines laid down at Trent would have been palpably strengthened. This was Archbishop O'Reilly's objective but the Church as a whole, and especially that in Ardagh, was too severely undermanned and short of revenue to embrace such a radical programme. Gaffney's commitment at Clonelly to contribute £1 annually to the provision of grants for overseas students attests to the latter, but the former was even more disquieting. It is not possible to establish what, if any, improvement in clerical numbers occurred between 1658 and 1660, or to ascertain the effect of the statute promulgated at Clonelly giving clergy who had fled during the Cromwellian regime five months to return to their parishes, because there is no information on clerical numbers for these years. Archbishop O'Reilly's claim that there were only 18 secular clergy in the diocese in 1662 indicates a very slow recovery. O'Reilly maintained that no diocese possessed even one-third of the required number of clergy. Though some dioceses, Meath and Clogher, for example, with 60 and 29 clergy respectively, did not fare too badly, others, Dublin with 10 and Ferns with 9, were clearly in a very weak position indeed.[12] In these circumstances, it was hardly surprising that O'Reilly and Anthony MacGeoghegan of Meath, the two bishops active in the country in the early 1660s, grew impatient with the failure of exiled bishops like Patrick Plunkett to return to their dioceses.

In July 1660, Plunkett signalled to *Propaganda Fide* in Rome his intention of concluding his exile, but three years later he was still in Seez in Normandy where he had settled in 1657.[13] He clearly did not wish to return to the impoverished and unimportant diocese of Ardagh, which, his nephew Oliver claimed hyperbolically, was 'completely in the possession of non-Catholics and ... [without] three Catholics who possess fixed property'. With appointments to the more lucrative and prestigious sees of Meath and Dublin in the offing, he calculated that he could best achieve his ambition of promotion to one of these dioceses by lobbying from Seez.[14] With this end in view, he presented a series of petitions to Rome between 1660 and 1664, but they brought him no closer to his goal.[15] Indeed, their most tangible result was to alienate Archbishop O'Reilly who, despairing of Plunkett's return, suggested that Cornelius Gaffney should be made vicar apostolic of Ardagh, if he was not given a full bishopric. More contentiously, he also claimed that Plunkett was unworthy of promotion to the diocese of Meath because he had abandoned the diocese of Ardagh, fomented dissension in Dublin while abbot of St Mary's Abbey, and opposed the papal nuncio, Rinuccini, at the Confederation of Kilkenny. Moreover, his elevation was likely to make the regular clergy 'even more insolent than they are now'.[16] Realizing that his continued absenteeism was doing his chances of ecclesiastical promotion more harm than good, and pressed by Rome which took a dim view of his non-residence, Patrick Plunkett concluded his exile and returned to Ireland in the latter half of 1665 after nearly a decade and a half abroad. He did not settle in Ardagh, however, but instead chose to live in Dublin from where he continued to lobby for promotion.[17]

Once established in Dublin, Plunkett, as an aspirant for the archbishopric, quickly took stock of the problems facing the Church in the archdiocese, and contrived as best he could to respond to their needs. Dublin demanded close attention; it had suffered particularly severely in the 1650s and there were signs in the early 1660s that the devotional commitment of the Catholic population was wearing thin.[18] The diocese of Ardagh also required urgent episcopal care, but since he had no residence there and no friends or relations to support him such as he had in Dublin and Meath, Plunkett gave it little attention. He had evidently concluded that he would best serve his case by concentrating his energies on the urgent tasks of ordaining priests and reducing the backlog of people in the archdiocese awaiting confirmation rather than on Ardagh. With Bishop MacSweeney of Kilmore still indisposed and Archbishop O'Reilly in Rome and unable to risk returning to Ireland, Plunkett was 'the only active bishop' in the country in the late 1660s, and he made his presence felt by ordaining two hundred priests and by confirming thousands between 1665 and 1669. Meanwhile, there was no let-up in his campaign for ecclesiastical promotion,[19] but though his endeavours in Dublin won him praise, he was not deemed worthy of promotion to the see of Dublin. Part of the reason for this was the memory of his opposition to Rinuccini in the 1640s, but more influential was his intimacy with the Duke of Ormond[20] and his involvement with Peter Walsh's Remonstrance in the 1660s which activated old fears about his doctrinal orthodoxy and his commitment to maintaining Rome's status and authority.

The Irish Remonstrance or Loyal Formulary arose from the wish of the clergy to affirm their loyalty to the crown on the restoration of Charles II. This was not in itself controversial, and anticipating that an appropriate affirmation would encourage a more tolerant attitude towards their Church, the country's leading ecclesiastics, led by O'Reilly and MacGeoghegan and supported by Cornelius Gaffney, drew up an instrument of procuration in January 1661 directing Peter Walsh, a Franciscan who was their agent at court, to congratulate the King on behalf of the Irish clergy and to request greater toleration. This document was rejected by the Lord Lieutenant, the Duke of Ormond, who demanded a new declaration of loyalty and a more supplicatory request for toleration. A formula along the desired lines was drafted in the winter of 1661-2; but it ran into difficulty because the inclusion of a clause denying that the pope had the right to depose temporal princes laid it open to the charge of Gallicanism. Undaunted by this, Walsh sought to rally support for the Remonstrance but without much success, since it soon became clear that it was doctrinally suspect and disliked by Pope Alexander VII. The issue did not die. Encouraged by Ormond, Walsh persisted in seeking support for the Formulary in 1663 and 1664 but it was not until the debate on the Act of Explanation and the outbreak of war with the Dutch in 1665 that the subject became a matter of vivid controversy once again.[21]

Patrick Plunkett had resisted Walsh's overtures to sign the Remonstrance when he was urged to do so in Seez in 1662. He was not opposed in principle, however, as Archbishop O'Reilly observed, and he was not long in Dublin when his name appeared on a summons dated November 1665 requesting the attendance of all clerics exercising ecclesiastical jurisdiction at a national synod in Dublin in June 1666 to decide on a formula affording the King 'all reasonable assurance of their loyalty in all temporal matters'.[22] Plunkett had been put under enormous pressure by Ormond, who allowed him to perform his ecclesiastical functions undisturbed, to sign this requisition, but it was received with alarm in Rome which held that the synod threatened 'much danger to the Catholic religion'. In order to ensure that the papal position was made absolutely clear, the internuncio at Brussels, Rospigliosi, sent a Dominican, Christopher O'Ferrall, with letters to Dublin informing Plunkett and others of the papal objections. Instead of taking advantage of this to distance himself from Ormond, Plunkett plunged himself deeper into difficulty by transmitting the papal nuncio's letters unopened to the Viceroy who promptly had the friar imprisoned.[23] As it happened, the resolutions of the synod were not to Ormond's liking, but Plunkett's attempt to walk a tightrope between Rome and Dublin Castle convinced many in positions of ecclesiastical authority that he was not suitable for the archdiocese of Dublin. Rospigliosi was especially critical of what he perceived as Plunkett's complicity in the imprisonment of Christopher O'Ferrall, and urged that he should 'be treated with caution' in future.[24] Such advice was not unwarranted. Less than two years later Plunkett again demonstrated the fallibility of his judgment: he authorized the bogus credentials presented by the Franciscan James Taaffe as part of a mission in 1660 to persuade the clergy to reject Walsh's Remonstrance. Plunkett managed to extricate himself from this by persuading the unhappy Taaffe to conclude his disruptive mission, but he was unable to deflect criticism. [25] The Jesuit Nicholas Netterville expressed the views of many when he described Plunkett as 'a good man rather than a good prince' and recommended Peter Talbot as a better choice for the archdiocese of Dublin. The internuncio at Brussels concurred; Plunkett's royalism, his 'lukewarm and timid' affirmation of papal authority, and his willingness 'to accept principles ... contrary to the purity of the faith' were unacceptable in an incumbent in the key bishopric of Dublin, he contended.[26] Plunkett, for his part, would not be disappointed with Meath, and when Rome decided in 1669 to transfer him there as part of its strategy to strengthen the Irish hierarchy, he was happy to accept. Though he claimed otherwise, he had not done much during his twenty-two years as bishop to sustain the Catholic Church in Ardagh.[27] His main legacy to his successor was of an undermanned and ill-organized diocese that needed attentive leadership and clear pastoral direction.

II

Plunkett was succeeded in Ardagh by a vicar apostolic. This was in accordance with current thinking which held that the Church in Ireland was too poor to maintain a bishop in every diocese.[28] But the choice of Gerard Farrell, the dean of the diocese, was uninspired and, as it turned out, unfortunate. Like Plunkett, Farrell had little pastoral experience. He had spent the preceding twenty years in Rome as representative of the priests of the archdiocese of Armagh and as a *gentilhuomo* in the service of Cardinal Albizi. It is probable that his appointment owed more to his friendship with the influential Albizi and his close connection with Bishop Plunkett's family than to his pastoral excellence. Farrell's appointment, coinciding with Oliver Plunkett's to the archbishopric of Armagh and Peter Talbot's to Dublin, was seen as heralding an era of ecclesiastical reform in Ireland, and Farrell gave some indication that he was the person to accomplish this task in Ardagh when one of his first acts was to request medals and *Agnus Dei*. He was to receive little encouragement, for no sooner had his appointment been announced than Cornelius Gaffney contested his eligibility, and plunged the diocese into controversy by refusing to yield control.[29]

Gaffney was understandably upset by the papal decision to appoint Farrell over him to the vicar apostolicship; he had been in charge of the diocese for all but four years since 1637, and had been repeatedly recommended by Archbishop O'Reilly. But if Gaffney's opposition was stimulated, in part at least, by his feeling that it was unjust that someone who had spent twenty years in the comfort of Rome should be promoted above one who had not abandoned his diocese 'even in the fierce persecution of Cromwell', he also challenged the legitimacy of Farrell's appointment. Farrell, he asserted, could not become vicar apostolic because he was illegitimate; because he had been imprisoned for 'falsification'; because he was 'not fit to rule a diocese'; and because a vicar capitular could be replaced only by a bishop. These were potentially grave allegations, but Farrell dismissed them as inaccurate and unsustainable. He had, he countered, received a dispensation from Thomas Dease, Bishop of Meath (1621-52), relieving him from the allegation of 'irregularity contracted by reason of illegitimate birth'; he had not been found guilty of falsification; Gaffney was not competent to assess his suitability to administer a diocese, while on the subject of precedence he pointed out that a vicar apostolic always took precedence over a vicar capitular.[30]

Cornelius Gaffney's decision to resist the appointment of Gerard Farrell threw the diocese of Ardagh into turmoil. Gaffney had considerable support among the population and clergy, and because Archbishop Oliver Plunkett, whose sympathies lay with the vicar capitular, was unwilling to bring his authority as metropolitan to bear until he received a ruling from Rome, the diocese split into two factions. Plunkett's wish, he informed Airoldi, the internuncio, was simply that justice should be done, but the cogs of the Roman bureaucracy ground slowly. It was not until May 1671 that a special meeting of the *Congregatio de Propaganda Fide* in Rome considered Gaffney's charges, and decided to grant Gerard Farrell a dispensation from the impediment of illegitimacy (he had not been able to produce that given him by Dease) and to affirm his right to administer the diocese.[31] Plunkett was reluctant to enforce the decision without a papal brief. He informed Airoldi in September that Gaffney was held in affection by the priests and people of Ardagh, and that he was unlikely to accept the ruling without 'due process'. The archbishop desired a compromise; he wanted Farrell to appoint Gaffney vicar forane and judge of matrimonial cases during his lifetime, but the vicar apostolic rejected this accommodation. By the spring of 1672, the diocese was so riven with divisions that when Farrell summoned a diocesan synod, Gaffney convened a rival meeting. There is no information on the support each garnered, but Plunkett's delay in enforcing the *Propaganda*'s decision was unquestionably prolonging the controversy. Eventually Rome tired of the archbishop's procrastination and in April 1672 directed him to give Farrell his brief appointing him vicar apostolic. Stung by this, Plunkett set out for Ardagh in June, and ordered Gaffney and his clerical supporters to surrender the diocese and to obey Farrell.[32]

Plunkett's intervention finally concluded this unedifying episode in the history of the diocese, but the controversial manner in which Farrell secured control hardly augured well. Such evidence as is available indicates that he was not a reforming pastor. Oliver Plunkett, certainly, continued to have a low opinion of his capacities; in March 1675 he described him as 'a very ignorant person' and three years later concluded that 'it would be a good idea if ... [he] were suspended'. [33] No attempt was made to initiate suspension proceedings, and Farrell continued to administer the diocese in the unpredictable environment of the 1670s and early 1680s. After the difficulties of the 1650s, the main problem was a lack of resources. The Church as a whole was severely straitened financially in the late seventeenth century, but the diocese of Ardagh was particularly impoverished. Farrell's income in the 1670s was variously calculated between 60 and 120 scudi (£16–£32), which put it firmly in the bottom half of the diocesan league of incomes, and was insufficient to permit any kind of administrative innovation. [34] Priests eked out an even more precarious livelihood, and with few middle- and upper-class Catholics to support them (there were only '4 Catholic gentlemen [with ... property]' in Ardagh in 1675, it was claimed) they charged fees for administering the sacraments. Oliver Plunkett disliked this practice, but in the absence of an alternative it became commonplace, though it did mean that clerical incomes remained modest and fell dangerously low when economic conditions were bad. [35] The vulnerable financial condition of the Church and the ever-present fear of repression made it difficult for priests and their superiors to effect either spiritual or structural reform. There is no specific evidence of repression in Ardagh in the Restoration period, but the fact that vicars apostolic were 'more hated than the Catholic bishops' and that a priest was imprisoned in nearby Mullingar in 1674 obliged circumspection and ensured that Church structures remained weak. [36] To compound matters, the mediocre quality of the clergy and recurring jurisdictional squabbles between seculars and regulars prevented the Church from making the most of the intermittent periods of toleration it was afforded. There were 24 secular clergy, and three friaries (one Dominican and two Franciscan) in Ardagh in 1675. This represented an increase of six in the number of secular clergy since 1662, and clearly reflects some improvement in the state of the Church, though things would probably have been even better if the diocese was not excluded from the Irish College in Bordeaux. Because of low clerical numbers, priests had to accept responsibility for more than one parish. We do not have sufficient evidence to establish how the 24 priests in the diocese in 1675 were distributed, but it is improbable that they received much support from either the Franciscan or Dominican friaries. There are no reports of quarrels between regulars and seculars in Ardagh, but since they were endemic elsewhere it is unlikely that the diocese escaped completely. [37]

By the second half of the 1670s, as old age took its toll, it was clear that Gerard Farrell was not the person to revitalize the Catholic Church in Ardagh. He did not attend the reforming provincial synod which met in County Louth at Ardpatrick in 1678. Indeed, his primary interest seems to have been to clear the way for Christopher O'Ferrall, who had carried Rospigliosi's letters to Ireland in 1666, to succeed him. Oliver Plunkett was determined that this should not happen, and though he was to die before Farrell, he did at least ensure that O'Ferrall was not to follow in his near namesake's footsteps.[38]

Except for some petitions indicating who was jockeying for positions, the 1680s and 1690s are an undocumented period in the history of the Ardagh diocese. MacNamee has conjectured that Patrick O'Ferrall took over the administration of the diocese on the death of Gerard Farrell in 1683, but there is no evidence to confirm this.[39] Indeed, it is more likely that the diocese was left vacant between 1683 and 1688 despite the increase in the power and influence of the Catholic Church in these years. An explanation for this may lie in the fact that Ardagh was low in the diocesan pecking order. Oliver Plunkett had constantly argued that poorer dioceses such as Ardagh did not warrant bishops and that neighbouring ecclesiastics, responsible for larger and wealthier dioceses, could administer small and impoverished sees. The people and clergy of Ardagh did not share this sentiment, however, for in 1684 32 notables and 17 clergy signed a petition requesting the appointment of Charles Tiernan as vicar apostolic.[40] Tiernan was not appointed and the diocese had to wait until 1688 when, at the instance of James II, Gregory Fallon was appointed to the see of Clonmacnois and given the responsibility of administering Ardagh. It was not a very satisfactory arrangement. Fallon had long been recommended for elevation to the episcopacy, but he was over eighty in 1688 and physically incapable of steering the Church in Ardagh through the repression that followed the defeat of the Jacobite armies. Indeed, Fallon went into exile shortly after the Williamite triumph, and the diocese was left unadministered until 1696, just before the ratification of the Bishops' Banishment Act which required all bishops to leave the country.[41]

III

The Catholic Church in the diocese of Ardagh was ill-prepared to withstand the Penal Laws and the anti-Catholic mood of Irish Protestants in the aftermath of the Jacobite Rebellion. Since 1597 it had been administered by either absentee bishops or vicars apostolic, none of whom had come to terms with the particular problems posed by a poor diocese and an inhospitable political environment. Indeed, the diocese was described as having been devoid of pastoral care for many years when the decision was taken to replace the ailing Dr Fallon. Fallon's successor, Charles Tiernan, was not to be given a chance to turn the diocese round, however, because his vicar apostolicship lasted a mere three years, and because the Bishops' Banishment Act came into force soon after his appointment.[42] We have no evidence of how Tiernan responded to the Banishment Act, but there can be no question but that the ordinary life of the Church was seriously undermined by the harassment which followed. At the County Longford Lent assizes in 1699, for instance, Patrick Farrell, Dean of Ardagh, was indicted for continuing to administer in defiance of the law.[43] Bernard Donogher, who succeeded Tiernan as vicar apostolic in 1699, was also liable to prosecution under the Act, but he contrived to avoid this by passing himself off as a parish priest. This was an obvious way of circumventing the Act, but in 1703 the Irish parliament strengthened its anti-Catholic arsenal by approving a measure requiring the registration of all clergy. The purpose of this Act was to pave the way for the suppression of the Catholic clergy since no replacements were to be admitted from the Continent and no new ordinands created at home. Realizing the precariousness of their position, 32 priests registered in the diocese of Ardagh. This was an unexpectedly large return considering the repressive circumstances of the 1690s, but since the alternative to registration was to remain in hiding or to go into exile, the Church contrived to register as many clergy as possible. With at least 33 priests (Fergus Lee of Granard could not register because he brought no securities, but he continued to minister nevertheless)[44] the Church was as well equipped as could be expected to survive the tense years of the early eighteenth century.[45]

Bernard Donogher chose to register himself for the parish of Fenagh in County Leitrim. We have little information about the man and his activities[46] during his long vicar apostolicship (1699-1718), but it was a particularly difficult time for ecclesiastics, who ministered under the constant threat of imprisonment and transportation. Despite this, Donogher did his utmost to provide pastoral care and to ensure leadership in the Church by appealing to Rome to appoint bishops to Ireland. Donogher's plea for bishops was partly satisfied by the appointment of Ambrose McDermott to Elphin in 1707.[47] The greatest problem faced by him and his priests was to avoid the watchful eyes of local Protestants who did what they could to impede priests from performing their duties. In 1706 the Sheriff of Leitrim George St George summoned all registered clergy to present themselves, while in Longford in 1708 a Jacobite invasion scare prompted Richard Auchmuty to take the registered clergy into custody. In the same year, Bryan McHugh, who was the registered parish priest for Cashel, found himself in hot water for officiating in a mixed marriage. It was illegal for a Catholic priest to assist in such a union and McHugh was dispatched to Newgate prison in Dublin for transportation, but he escaped and returned to Longford with a forged pardon. Rearrested, the ever-resourceful McHugh escaped once more but, with a £20 price now on his head, he was captured a third time and transported.[48]

The treatment meted out to McHugh was such as any Catholic priest found guilty of infringing the Penal code could anticipate in the early eighteenth century when Protestant reliance on the Penal Laws was at its most complete. In 1709 the Irish parliament closed the loopholes in the existing legislation, and introduced a new more threatening provision whereby registered priests could be obliged to take an Oath of Abjuration. This oath required a juror to profess allegiance to Queen Anne, but since it also entailed denying that the divine right of kings applied to the exiled James III, whom Rome and most Irish bishops and priests regarded as the legitimate monarch, and pledging 'perpetual loyalty' to the Protestant succession, it was regarded with deep suspicion by Irish Catholics. Bishop McDermott described it as 'abominable', and his worst fears seemed realized when a subsequent proclamation commanded all registered priests to attend the nearest quarter sessions before 25 March 1710 to take the oath. Meanwhile, Rome adjudged that the oath was neither lawful nor binding, and exhorted the bishops and clergy to refuse to take it. Only 33 priests and a small number of lay people, with the midlands and the diocese of Ardagh well represented, did not do so. Some of those, illustrating the strong sense of religious community that enabled the Catholic population to withstand the Penal Laws, subsequently sought absolution. Bernard Donogher was one of those who withstood intense pressure to abjure. He was arrested when he refused to abjure voluntarily, but his preparedness to 'suffer death' rather than subscribe frustrated his captors and he was subsequently released.[49] The refusal of the overwhelming majority of the clergy and population to subscribe to the oath meant that the measure was unenforceable, though its retention on the statute book gave the Protestant establishment another powerful weapon with which to harass the Catholic clergy.

In fact, Irish Protestants did not seek to use the Abjuration Oath to weaken the priesthood, but there was little sign of a permanent easing of repression in the 1710s. In 1712 in County Leitrim, local officials ordered 'all the popish clergymen that are registered for and reside in the county to appear and take the oath', but not one complied. Indeed, the usual effect of such actions was to drive the clergy underground and, when the Sheriff of Leitrim was unable to secure one priest during the 1714 invasion scare, the Grand Jury of the county drafted a presentment for the apprehension of the 23 priests known to be in the county. Among those listed was 'Bryan Donagher' who was described as 'a moderator over the popish clergy in the dioceses of Killmore and Ardagh'.[50] Donogher was not troubled on this occasion, but the contemporaneous and probably incomplete report on the Catholic clergy of Longford which put their number at 12, or 33 per cent down on the 1704 figure, indicates that the Penal Laws were taking their toll and that large areas of the diocese did not have a priest. These included the parishes of Kilglass, Killoe (Dromard), Ardagh and Moydow, Templemichael and Clongesh, and Clonbroney. The Leitrim part of the diocese fared better, for though the number of secular clergy had fallen from 15 to 12, seven Franciscan friars supplemented the depleted parish clergy in the parishes of Cloone, Mohill, Fenagh, Killtobrid and Annaghduff. The Franciscan friars at Ballinasagart and the Dominicans at Kilcommock may have performed similar duties in County Longford.[51] Overall, the numbers of priests active in the diocese had fallen little from the 1704 figure, but the fact that large parts of County Longford were without a resident priest must have been a cause of concern.

Bernard Donogher remained in charge of the diocese of Ardagh until 1718, when he was succeeded by Thomas Flynn, the parish priest of Cloone. Flynn was appointed bishop (the first episcopal appointee in forty-nine years)[52] but he was seventy-six years of age and, as it turned out, unsuited to the task of revitalizing the Church as it emerged that the Penal Laws would not be strictly enforced and that the Church could improve its physical fabric and its clerical numbers provided it proceeded discreetly. He began his episcopate confidently but things quickly turned sour, and as old age, illness and drunkenness took their toll, he became, Archbishop Hugh MacMahon of Armagh reported, 'deranged in mind'. The Church as a whole could have endured Flynn's eccentric conduct, and the diocese would have survived his maladministration if the bishop's disposition to ordain 'as many as come before him' had not threatened to flood the Church in Ireland with unqualified and unsuitable priests and to lower further the already poor clerical standards. Flynn, the internuncio Cardinal Spinelli reported to Rome in June 1729, ordained all who applied to him, whatever their origin, 'no matter what condition they are in, so long as they know a few words of Latin and give him some money'. His disregard for clerical and episcopal standards was such that he ordained even 'candidates ... accused of enormous crimes' though they caused the Catholic population to 'plunge themselves into a sea of wickedness and [to] treat with irreverence the most sacred principles of the Catholic faith'. Anxious to put an end to this appalling state of affairs, Spinelli advised MacMahon to gather evidence of Flynn's misconduct, but the archbishop declined lest it should attract unwelcome Protestant interest. Pope Benedict XIII (1724-30) was more decisive; in August 1729 he instructed MacMahon and two suffragans to investigate the charges made against the Bishop of Ardagh and empowered them to suspend him if the charges were well founded. The archbishop did as he was instructed, but Flynn countered the move to suspend him by appealing to Rome and by threatening 'to ignore the censures imposed on him'. An unedifying and long-drawn-out dispute seemed unavoidable, but Flynn's timely demise in January 1730, aged eighty-eight, finally concluded the matter.[53]

IV

Though the surviving evidence is tantalizingly thin, such as there is indicates that Thomas Flynn left the diocese of Ardagh in considerable disarray. His successor, Peter Mulligan, who was bishop for nine years (1730-9), was an Augustinian, and his most urgent task was to reduce the number of priests. He chose to do this by not ordaining any new clergy.[54] This was a blunt and unpopular way of respond-ing to the problem, but the proliferation of friars and priests in the 1730s was such that they were a burden on 'the poor of their persuasion'. It had also become a source of anxiety to Rome which was perturbed by the willingness of both the regular and secular clergy to cast 'insults and calumnies at one another'.

Though the available evidence is suggestive rather than conclusive, the diocese of Ardagh seems to have escaped the worst excesses of secular-regular friction. The Dominicans at Mollivorney in Kilcommock parish evidently worked well with the secular clergy for two of their number were listed as assistants in the nearby parish of Shrule in 1774. The Franciscans in Jamestown, County Leitrim, had long done the same, but there is no information on their friary at Ballinasagart, or on the Augustinian house on Holy Island, Lough Ree.[55] These communities were traditionally small, so it may be that they maintained few of Bishop Flynn's ordinands. Whether or not this is the case, Pope Benedict XIV (1740-58) was convinced of the need to control the clerical intake in Ireland. Rome decreed in 1742 that each bishop should be limited to 12 ordinations *titulo missionis* during his lifetime and in 1751 that the regular clergy should be prohibited from receiving novices in Ireland. The effort to reduce numbers continued uninterrupted during the episcopates of Mulligan's successors, Thomas Byrne (1740-7) and Thomas McDermott Roe (1747-51).[56] Byrne and McDermott Roe, then Dean of Ardagh, faced their severest test when a further upsurge in Jacobite activity in the mid 1740s excited intense Protestant disquiet and threatened to nullify the gains made in the relaxed years of the late 1730s and early 1740s. The decision of John Johnson, the seneschal of the manor of Granard, to order the closure of the local 'masshouse' in 1744[57] indicates how dependent the Church was throughout the eighteenth century upon the goodwill of Protestant landowners for permission to build and to maintain masshouses, and how powerless it was when this permission was arbitrarily revoked. Comparatively few landowners acted in this manner, and the Catholic Church in the diocese of Ardagh during the 1740s was much better placed to withstand this bout of repression than it had been during the Jacobite scare of 1714. Due in part to the ordinands of Bishop Flynn, the returns made by the High Sheriff, James West, reveal that there were at least 26 priests in County Longford in 1744, and that every parish (excluding Rathcline for which there is no return) had a priest. Indeed, the four parishes with the largest urban centres, Mostrim (Edgeworthstown), Shrule (Ballymahon), Templemichael (Longford) and Granard had one or more 'assistants' (curates).[58] Ordinary Catholics could generally attend church unhindered, and they did so in large numbers though the masshouses in which they worshipped were not always structurally sound. In Edgeworthstown in 1749 the collapse of a masshouse as a result of a fire panic resulted in at least one death and twenty serious injuries.[59]

Following McDermott Roe's demise in 1751, Augustine Cheevers, an Augustinian, guided the diocese for six years until he was transferred to Meath in 1756, while Anthony Blake's two-year spell (1756-8) was merely an interlude between his terms as warden of Galway and archbishop of Armagh. Neither man had much impact on the diocese, certainly not the uninterested Blake.[60] Cheevers, by contrast, was a decisive and energetic prelate, which accounts for his appointment as administrator of the diocese of Clonmacnois in place of MacEgan of Meath who was old and infirm. Cheevers was emboldened by his experience in Clonmacnois to petition Rome to unite it with Ardagh. While his argument was plausible - that the see of Meath was more than sufficient for any bishop and that it would greatly benefit the impoverished bishopric of Ardagh if the two dioceses were united - his petition was rejected. However, when he requested permission to continue administering Clonmacnois after his transfer to Meath, he was again turned down and the diocese was united with Ardagh in 1756.[61]

In the long term the unification of the diocese of Ardagh and Clonmacnois, allied to the expansion of the Irish economy in the second half of the eighteenth century, facilitated the reanimation of the Catholic Church in both dioceses. In the short term, however, episcopal preoccupations continued to centre on the campaign to reduce the number of regular clergy, to undermine the autonomy of the religious orders and to affirm the primacy of episcopal authority as decreed by Trent. Bishop Cheevers, who was an Augustinian, did not share these sentiments, as he demonstrated in 1756 when he acceded to the request of the Dominican provincial, Father Shanly, that Francis Farrell of the order's house at Mollivorney should be made parish priest of Kilcommock.[62] But James Brady, who guided the diocese for thirty years between 1758 and 1788, was fully convinced of their validity. As provisor in the Irish College in Paris between 1747 and 1753, Brady was a member of a reformist party, led by Archbishop O'Reilly of Armagh, which pressed for the suppression of Irish novitiates and for the application of stricter criteria in the appointment of bishops. Nor did his views mellow with time. When the regular clergy pressed in the mid 1760s for the relaxation of the prohibition on the admission to novitiates, he declined to support them. He was then embroiled in a row with the Franciscan provincial over his suspension of two friars, and was more convinced than ever that the papal decrees of 1751 were 'very wisely framed'.[63] Inevitably, the regular clergy did not prosper in this environment. The Dominican community at Kilcommock, for instance, had always been small, but having survived the Penal Laws and the destruction of its house in 1734, it seemed set to prosper. But this was not to be. By 1767, a decade after Brady's elevation, it contained only two priests, and though its numbers had doubled by 1800, its existence remained precarious.[64] The Augustinian house on Holy Island, Lough Ree, proved less enduring for it was abandoned sometime in the mid eighteenth century. The Franciscans proved better survivors; they successfully maintained their three small houses at Ballinasagart, Jamestown and Athlone, but with only 10 friars between them at the beginning of the nineteenth century. Indeed, Brady's refusal in 1774 to allow their request that they be afforded the exclusive right to quest in the parishes of Gallen and Rynagh in Clonmacnois, and his declaration that he saw no reason why diocesan priests should not also quest, reveals his determination to grant them no favours.[65]

Meanwhile, the 1760s and 1770s saw a perceptible dilution in religious antagonism, though interdenominational relations remained difficult, as is indicated by the modest number of Catholic conversions and the hostile response which they provoked. According to the convert rolls, 39 Catholics in Longford and 23 in Leitrim embraced Protestantism between 1706 and 1810. Of that total, and corresponding with the national trend, 18 in Longford and 20 in Leitrim recanted between 1760 and 1780. Those Catholics that embraced Protestantism usually did so at some personal inconvenience, and the social ostracism that sometimes followed recantation acted as an important disincentive.[66] One can gain some perspective on this and on sectarian tension in the diocese from the case of Patrick Sweeney, a priest - variously described as 'parish priest of Bornacoole County Longford' (sic) and a curate in Longford town - whose recantation in the local Protestant church in 1770 was interrupted by two local Catholics who cursed and damned the congregation as 'a set of hereticks'. The conversion of a priest was seen as an act of particular betrayal, hence this public display of anger, but the Protestant establishment did its utmost to foster this phenomenon by providing substantial sums for priests who apostatized. According to a 1703 act of parliament, reaffirmed in 1771, a 'popish priest' who 'duly converted to the Protestant religion' was eligible for an annual pension of £40. In County Longford, according to the Grand Jury records, 'Patrick Sweeney and three other priests', Francis McHugh, Michael Creed and Roger Boyce, each received this pension for most of the 1770s.[67] Taken with the acceleration in the rate of conversion and the repeal of Penal legislation in 1778 and 1782, this points to a reduction in the intensity with which religious convictions were held in the third quarter of the eighteenth century, but also to the need for a thoroughgoing reanimation of the Catholic Church. Bishop Brady did what he could to prepare the ground for this, but it is not possible to establish his impact on religious observance. He certainly avoided political involvement, and did not take the oath of allegiance when the question arose in 1782, unlike the dean of the diocese, Edward Meagher, and the parish priest of Shrule, John Cruise.[68]

Brady's long episcopate came to a close in 1788. In some ways the developments that had the greatest long-term impact on the Church took place despite him. The beginnings of the repeal of the Penal Laws and the expansion of the Irish economy left the way clear for his successors to embark on a process of organizational reform. The fact that he was able to leave £100 for 'the poor of my diocese' indicated that shortage of money was no longer an insuperable obstacle to change.[69]

V

If the Catholic Church in Ardagh struggled to provide even a basic pastoral service in the century after 1650, the hundred years following the demise of James Brady saw the establishment of an ordered and disciplined Church along Tridentine lines. This process began fitfully in the late eighteenth century during the episcopate of James Brady, and since the establishment of a systematic Church bureaucracy was one of its key features, the introduction of parish registers provides a convenient means of identifying its main phases. The parish of Granard was the first, introducing baptismal, marriage and death registers between 1779 and 1782. Two other parishes followed suit during the episcopacy of James Cruise (1788-1812), but it was not until James Magauran assumed charge (1815-29) that a firm pattern was established as no less than 10 parishes introduced registers during the fourteen years of his episcopacy. The lengthy episcopate of William O'Higgins (1829-53) saw a further 14 commence registers, while six others finally followed their example during the episcopacies of James Kilduff (1853-67) and Niall McCabe (1867-70). It is apparent from this that the establishment of a Tridentine structure throughout the diocese took the best part of a century. A closer analysis reveals that the parishes with the wealthiest agricultural base and the largest urban centres were usually first to adopt registers: Granard was followed by Ardagh and Moydow (1793), Templemichael and Ballymacormick (1802), Shrule (1820), Street (1820), Killashee (1826) and Clongesh (1829), while poorer rural parishes like Abbeylara (1854), Kilglass (1854), and Columbkille East (1870) proved much slower.[70]

The figure who guided the Catholic Church in the united diocese of Ardagh and Clonmacnois through the early stages of the long drive towards modernization was John Cruise, the former parish priest of Shrule, who had taken the oath of allegiance in 1782. Cruise was not the first choice to succeed James Brady in 1788, but when Peter Flood, the former professor of theology at the Sorbonne, decided that Ardagh was not 'worth his acceptance', Cruise was appointed.[71] He proved a committed pastor and, between 1788 and 1812, he laid the foundations for the rapid modernization effected by his successors. It was his practice, for instance, to distribute devotional works while on confirmation visitations. We can gain some idea of his impact and of the state of the Church in the diocese at the turn of the eighteenth century from the returns submitted to Lord Castlereagh in 1801 and from the *relatio status* sent by Cruise to Rome in 1804.[72] According to the 1801 report, the diocese of Ardagh and Clonmacnois contained 55 priests, 52 of whom were engaged in parish work, and three (out of a total of 14) regulars otherwise engaged. Subtracting priests listed for parishes outside Longford, which number 24, in order to compare the 1801 figure with the returns made by Sheriff West in 1744, we arrive at a figure of 28 priests, a modest improvement of two on the 1744 position. Fifty-two priests was certainly insufficient to minister to the 130,000 Catholics Cruise reckoned were in the diocese, though the fact that eight parishes in County Longford, or double the 1744 number, were now served by two or more priests reflected progress. By 1804 things had improved even further. In his report to Rome, Cruise noted that there were 70 priests in the diocese - an increase of fifteen on the 1801 figure. This was still insufficient to permit a comprehensive ministry throughout the diocese, though the fact that clerical numbers were on the rise, that every parish had at least one chapel and that the Eucharist was reserved in them all was cause for optimism. Moreover, there was wealth in the community to which the Church could appeal for funds for construction and other purposes. Total diocesan income was calculated at just under £3000 in 1800, £310 of which went to Bishop Cruise, and an average of £51 to each priest. These were modest sums compared with what was available in the richer dioceses of Munster and Leinster, but with full chapels and parishes like Mostrim, Templemichael, and Ardagh and Moydow able to support their priests to the tune of £100 per annum, conditions seemed ripe for a period of sustained reorganization.[73]

Cruise devoted most of his energy as bishop to diocesan affairs, but he also joined in episcopal calls for a Catholic seminary in the 1790s and signed the controversial resolutions agreed by the hierarchy in 1799 which, in principle, conceded the king the right of veto on the appointment of future bishops.[74] His successor James Magauran was also politically active, though the cause in his case was Catholic Emancipation. The foundation of the Catholic Association in 1823 dramatically altered the environment in which the Catholic Church operated. The 1820s are usually remembered for the triumphant agitation for Catholic Emancipation, but the politicization of the Catholic middle class and the Catholic clergy, as discussed by Fergus O'Ferrall in his essay in this volume, was arguably as important. It certainly had a significant impact on the Church in the diocese, creating a mood of confidence that contributed in no small way to the emergence of a dynamic and assertive Catholic Church in Ardagh in the early nineteenth century.[75]

Magauran's involvement with the Catholic Association did not distract him from his pastoral duties, however, and he proved a diligent and attentive bishop. From Ballymahon, where he resided, he spearheaded the reorganization of the Church, as the acceleration in the number of parishes maintaining parish registers reveals. His episcopacy also saw an acceleration in the pace of church-building. The construction of new, more structurally sound chapels in the place of the traditionally flimsy and unsophisticated 'masshouses' had begun in the 1780s, but much remained to be done. Most of the chapels in the diocese were, Magauran conceded in 1825, 'miserable enough', but under his direction parishes like Killashee and Ballymahon replaced the existing inadequate structures with buildings more in keeping with the needs of the Catholic population and the aspirations of the Church. There were, of course, many areas, like Tarmonbarry, where the masshouse had 'fallen into ruin' and the people were too poor to rebuild, but slowly and surely the Church put behind it the neglect and poor leadership that had characterized the period 1650-1780 and emerged a much more vibrant organization. Magauran's regular visitations to administer confirmation and his efforts to improve the standard of chapels attest to a sense of optimism and an awareness of opportunity that none of his predecessors had dared indulge.[76]

VI

With the way forward established, Magauran's successor, William O'Higgins, was ideally positioned to accelerate the reorganization of the Catholic Church in Ardagh. It was under O'Higgins, indeed, that the Church in the diocese can be said to have assumed its modern shape. But O'Higgins was too dynamic and imaginative simply to give effect to someone else's ideas and, while he built on the foundations laid by Cruise and Magauran, he brought his own vision and energy to bear. The diocese needed decisive leadership, for though much had already been achieved, overall church attendance was still perturbingly low and there were many administrative and religious problems.[77] O'Higgins wasted little time introducing structures to meet the current needs of the Church. With 90 priests, and 38 of the diocese's 41 parishes served by two or more priests (only three parishes had one priest, while four had three), the early 1830s were ripe for the affirmation of ecclesiastical authority and for the introduction of firmer disciplinary and spiritual guidelines. With this in mind, O'Higgins convened a diocesan synod in October 1834.[78] Eighty-one priests attended, and the result was a comprehensive *Statuta Diocesana* that affirmed the doctrines of the Church as laid down at Trent, provided explicit instructions to priests to ensure they administered the sacraments in a correct manner, and laid down a strict code of clerical conduct. Priests were reminded that they were subject to episcopal authority, were directed to dress in black or '*sub-negri*' at all times, and were prohibited from attending public demonstrations, horse-races or theatres. Over-indulgence in alcohol and undue familiarity with the opposite sex were also cautioned against. But the statutes were not confined solely to doctrinal and disciplinary matters, and the Church's thinking on moral issues was also affirmed: murder, abortion, fornication, crimes against the Church and inducements to moral turpitude were designated reserved sins; participation in clandestine marriages incurred automatic excommunication, while the effort to eclipse popular religion continued with the unequivocal condemnation of wakes as occasions of sin and moral turpitude.[79]

The *Statuta Diocesana* represented an important stage in the formation of the modern Catholic Church in the diocese of Ardagh, because it laid down a code of conduct for observance by priests and people. O'Higgins was determined to ensure it was complied with, directing the vicars general of the diocese to submit four reports annually on the conduct of the clergy and the state of the Catholic religion in their jurisdiction. In addition, every parish priest had to submit a comprehensive report on the Church in his parish two days before an episcopal visitation. [80] There is no evidence illustrating the effectiveness of this regimen, but organizationally it was a quantum advance on what had gone before and it ensured that O'Higgins was kept up to date on all developments in the diocese. One of the most important of these was the ongoing effort to upgrade the diocese's chapels - a task that was virtually complete in 1840 when all but two of the thatched chapels had been replaced by slated buildings. Each parish was also supplied with a small library of devotional literature. By 1845, when O'Higgins's active episcopate neared its end, the diocese of Ardagh had 68 churches and approximately 90 priests. With an estimated 195,000 Catholics, this represented a priest to people ratio of 1 to 2178, and a chapel to people ratio of 1 to 2868. Neither was ideal, but the Church was undeniably better placed to provide its population with a full sacramental service than it had been for centuries.[81]

But if the diocesan synod of 1834 was an important step towards creating a modern well-organized diocesan Church, O'Higgins had still larger goals in mind. His most ardent wish was to build a cathedral and a seminary for the preparation of priests in Longford - the largest, wealthiest and most centrally located town in the diocese - and to transfer the episcopal residence there from Ballymahon. O'Higgins was to be frustrated in his ambition to build a seminary, but the foundation-stone for St Mel's Cathedral - an immense, costly structure modelled on the Madeleine Church in Paris, the Pantheon and St John Lateran in Rome - was laid in 1840. O'Higgins was indefatigable in his efforts to raise the large sum (£40,000) needed to fund this expensive undertaking, and the walls and the pillars were in place by 1846. The Great Famine delayed matters at this point, and it fell to John Kilduff, who succeeded O'Higgins in 1853, to complete the cathedral.[82]

Though he was unable to proceed with his plans for a diocesan seminary because of the cost of building St Mel's Cathedral, O'Higgins did found classical schools at Longford, Athlone, Ballymahon and Drumlish. At the same time, he was implacably hostile to the government's national school system established in 1831, and he joined with his long-time friend, the outspoken Archbishop of Tuam John McHale, in condemning it in 1839.[83] Indeed, O'Higgins's commitment to revitalizing the Catholic Church in Ardagh was matched only by his enthusiasm for the causes of Catholic nationalism. In the early 1830s, when the Tithe War was at its severest, he bluntly informed his flock that the payment of tithes was 'contrary to reason and religion' and that it was 'the imperative duty of every sincere Christian to suffer any persecution, even death itself, rather than wittingly acquiesce in their payment'.[84] This was a quite extraordinary declaration, and it revealed clearly that O'Higgins's episcopal sympathies lay with the confrontational wing of the hierarchy led by McHale rather than with the cooperative wing led by Archbishops Daniel Murray of Dublin and William Crolly of Armagh.

Not unexpectedly, considering his friendship with McHale, O'Higgins was well inclined towards Daniel O'Connell, but it was not until the Liberator launched his campaign for the repeal of the Union in 1840 that the Bishop of Ardagh threw himself into political activity. O'Higgins was one of O'Connell's most devoted supporters and a frequent speaker at his political rallies in the 1840s. He even persuaded 74 of the priests of his diocese to follow his example and join the Repeal Association. However, O'Higgins's enthusiasm for repeal created difficulties with other, less committed members of the hierarchy, and he exposed these differences to public scrutiny when he declared at Mullingar in May 1843 'that every Catholic bishop in Ireland without exception is an ardent repealer'. This was untrue (two archbishops and nine bishops refused to join the Repeal Association), and it provoked such howls of protest that Archbishop Murray felt obliged to disavow the statement. This did not deter the ebullient bishop, however, and he continued to agitate vigorously for repeal and to support O'Connell though it was clear after October 1843 that repeal was no longer a realizable political aspiration.[85]

O'Higgins and O'Connell were also united in opposition to Robert Peel's 'nefarious' Charitable Bequests Act (1844) and Universities Act (1845). Indeed, O'Higgins was so opposed to what he termed the 'Infidel Colleges', that when he visited Rome in 1848 he lobbied Pope Pius IX to condemn them.[86] This had little direct impact on affairs in Ireland, but meanwhile the focus of O'Higgins's and O'Connell's attention had moved onto the Young Ireland movement. O'Higgins shared O'Connell's concern with the ambivalence of the Young

Irelanders' stance on the use of violence, but his ire was primarily excited by what he perceived as the anti-Catholicism of the *Nation* newspaper, which he condemned in characteristically forthright fashion as 'calculated to make fatal impressions on youthful minds'. He held their enthusiasm for interdenominational education in especially low esteem and, after O'Connell's demise, he remained a strong critic of what he regarded as their dangerous radicalism.[87]

By 1850, O'Higgins's best years as bishop were over. His episcopacy had seen the Catholic Church in Ardagh make rapid strides, though the incomplete shell which was St Mel's Cathedral attested to the fact that the diocese found it difficult to bear the financial burden of his ambitious pastoral design. Nationally, O'Higgins was better known for his outspoken political pronouncements and for his close attachment to O'Connell, and it was his political activities in tandem with his decisive diocesan administration which justified the reputation he forged as one of the country's leading prelates. He was the first bishop of Ardagh in two centuries to achieve such eminence, and if he was content on most national issues to follow McHale's lead, he and Magauran before him had transformed the diocese and the bishopric of Ardagh into a force within the Irish Church. O'Higgins's unvarnished pronouncements on education, tithes and repeal primarily reflected his own personal style but they also attest to the new-found confidence of the Catholic hierarchy in the wake of Catholic Emancipation. No eighteenth-century bishop would have dared to comment as O'Higgins did on the impossibility of Ireland's receiving justice from England, to fulminate against the tithe, or to describe the clergy of the Church of Ireland as 'useless persons' who calumniated the 'religion of the people'. Moreover, his use in correspondence of phrases like 'heretical monarch', 'heretical viceroy and his ecclesiastical abettors', and 'the proverbial treachery of heretical England' bear witness not just to his nationalist convictions, but also to the marriage of nationalist sentiment and religious righteousness which made the Catholic Church such a powerful force in nineteenth-century Ireland.[88]

<h2 style="text-align:center">VII</h2>

By the early 1850s O'Higgins's deteriorating health was a cause of concern, and the recently installed Archbishop of Armagh, Paul Cullen, recommended the appointment of a co-adjutor. The agreed choice was Peter Dawson, parish priest of Kiltoghert, and when O'Higgins died in January 1853 he was made *dignissimus* by the diocesan priests. However, Dawson did not become bishop, being deemed unacceptable by Cullen because of an alleged sexual impropriety with the maids in the bishop's house and his ownership of a racehorse that had accidentally killed a Protestant spectator in a collision at Bundoran races. The ease with which Dawson was dropped, and the efficiency with which Cullen ensured that his own nominee, John Kilduff, became bishop contrasted vividly with the unseemly altercation which followed the appointment of Gerard Farrell almost two centuries earlier. The Catholic Church was so tightly structured by the mid nineteenth century that there was little chance of a repeat of the unsavoury row which marked Farrell's appointment. Cullen favoured Kilduff, and ensured his appointment though he was only thirty-two and but six years a priest, because he shared the archbishop's ultramontane views on Church government.[89] There was some opposition within the diocese to Kilduff's appointment, notably from Dawson, but the new bishop's authoritarian style soon overrode all opposition. He was even able to persuade his priests to keep out of politics, a notable testimony to his authority in the wake of such active political prelates as Magauran and O'Higgins.[90]

Kilduff's religion like his rule was austere and stern, and he wasted little time in impressing this upon clergy as well as the laity. His first Lenten pastoral, for instance, dealt with the subject of fasting and, in the course of a long justification of the virtues of penance, he exhorted the faithful to:

use flesh meat at dinner only on Sundays, Mondays, Tuesdays, Thursdays and Saturdays (except the Saturday of the Quatuor Tenses) from the first Sunday of Lent, inclusive, to Palm Sunday, inclusive. Flesh meat is prohibited during the first and last weeks of Lent ... Eggs are forbidden on Fridays, and on the first four and last four days of Lent. Fish and flesh meats are never allowed at the same meal. Milk and white meats of every description are forbidden on Ash Wednesday and on Wednesday and Friday in Holy Week.[91]

An equally uncompromising attitude was manifest in Kilduff's 1865 pastoral letter outlining the main features of Pius IX's *Syllabus Errorum*. In this Kilduff dismissed the critics of the encyclical as 'infidels, revolutionists and heretics', cited England and the Church of England as proof of the accuracy of the Pope's observations and recommended the encyclical unreservedly as testimony of the 'vitality of the Church of God, and her irreconcilable hatred of every species of error, no matter how masked by false theology, false philosophy, false politics or any other garb by which the spirit of falsehood seeks to deceive poor souls and plunge them into perdition'.[92]

This rather abrasive pastoral attests further to the growing confidence of the Catholic Church in nineteenth-century Ireland. Kilduff was building upon foundations laid by his predecessors, literally in the case of St Mel's Cathedral to which he devoted much time and money between 1853 and 1856, when the cathedral was finally consecrated. Kilduff's attention then switched to O'Higgins's scheme for a diocesan seminary. The first appeal for funds was made in 1861, but with the financial resources of the diocese now on a par with those of Ferns, Armagh, Kildare and Leighlin, money proved no obstacle and the seminary, St Mel's College, was ready to receive its first students in 1865.[93]

With both the cathedral and the seminary in place, and the diocese well-stocked with obedient, if not always zealous, priests, the Catholic Church in the diocese of Ardagh had become a recognizably Tridentine Catholic structure.[94] It was now possessed of a vigorous and committed bishop who had enough priests and churches to ensure that comprehensive religious instruction was imparted in

every parish.[95] Moreover, though emigration and the Great Famine had taken a
heavy toll on the diocese's population, this worked to the advantage rather than
to the disadvantage of the Church. It strengthened the middle class on which the
Church primarily relied for donations, dramatically improved the ratio of priests
to people, and greatly weakened unorthodox popular religious practices, which
had been one of the most persistent barriers in the way of Tridentine Catholicism.
The reorganization of the Church effected by Cruise, Magauran, O'Higgins and
Kilduff, and the severe demographic rationalization effected by the Famine,
ensured that the Tridentine Catholicism which successive bishops and vicars
apostolic had contrived for nearly three centuries to implant held unchallenged
sway by the mid nineteenth century.

NOTES

I would like to thank Fr Patrick O'Donoghue, Fr Owen Devaney and Ms Judith Brady
for their help with this paper.

1. For the Counter-Reformation in Ireland see John Bossy, 'The Counter-Reformation and the people of Catholic Ireland, 1596-1641' in T.D. Williams (ed.),
   Historical Studies, viii (Dublin 1971), pp. 155-69; Colm Lennon, 'The Counter-
   Reformation in Ireland,1542-1641' in Ciaran Brady and Raymond Gillespie (eds),
   Natives and Newcomers: The Making of Irish Colonial Society, 1534-1641 (Dublin 1986),
   pp. 75-92.
2. James J. MacNamee, *History of the Diocese of Ardagh* (Dublin 1954), pp. 1-2. These
   calculations of the number of parishes in the diocese of Ardagh are based on the 1879
   diocesan map, and count unions such as Ardagh and Moydow as two parishes and
   not one. The 1879 map is reproduced in *Diocese of Ardagh and Clonmacnois Atlas ,1988*
   (Longford 1988), p. 44.
3. For an overview of the 1650s see P. J. Corish, *The Catholic Community in the Seventeenth and Eighteenth Centuries* (Dublin 1981), chapter 3; Benignus Millett, 'Survival and reorganization,1650-95' in P. J. Corish (ed.), *A History of Irish Catholicism*
   (Dublin 1968), vol. 3, part vii.
4. The bishop who remained was Eugene MacSweeney of Kilmore; he was incapaci-
   tated. One archbishop and ten bishops went into exile. According to John Burke,
   Archbishop of Tuam, there were 150 secular priests in hiding in Connacht in 1658,
   see B. Millett (ed.), 'Calendar of vol 13 of Fondo di Vienna, pt 2' (henceforth 'Vienna
   2'), in *Collectanea Hibernica* (henceforth *Col. Hib.*), xxv (1983), pp. 57-8.
5. K. S. Bottigheimer, *English Money and Irish Land: the 'Adventurers' in the Cromwellian
   Settlement of Ireland* (Oxford 1971), p. 215; John O'Hart, *Irish Pedigrees or the Origin
   and Stem of the Irish Nation* (Dublin 1881), pp. 257-60; S. Pender (ed.), *A Census of
   Ireland c. 1659* (Dublin 1939). The Longford returns are given in J. P. Farrell,
   Historical Notes and Stories of County Longford (Dublin 1886), pp. 47-9.
6. Plunkett's exile is usually put at 12 years. He is deemed to have left the country in
   1652 and to have returned in 1664. In fact, as shown below, he returned in 1665,
   and since it was maintained then that he had been in exile fourteen years, he must
   have left in 1651 (see Rationes quare Illustrissimus ... [1664/5] in B. Millett
   (ed.), 'Calendar of vol 13 of Fondo di Vienna, pt 3' henceforth 'Vienna 3'), *Col. Hib.*,

xxvi (1984), p. 31; E. Curtis, *Blessed Oliver Plunkett* (Dublin 1963), p. 35.

7. For Gaffney, see MacNamee, op. cit., pp. 297-9; O'Reilly to [ ], 22 Aug.1663 in Millett (ed.), 'Vienna 3', *Col. Hib.* xxvi (1984), pp.28-30; F. X. Martin, T. W. Moody, F. J. Byrne (eds), *A New History of Ireland*, ix (Oxford 1984), pp. 339-40; Farrell, op. cit., p. 62. For Plunkett, see below; E. Curtis, op. cit., pp. 14-15; P. F. Moran, *Memoir of Oliver Plunkett* (Dublin 1895), pp.1-2; Oliver Plunkett to Tanari, 30 Nov. 1669 in J. Hanly (ed.), *The Letters of Saint Oliver Plunkett* (henceforth *Plunkett Letters*) (Dublin 1979), pp. 536-7.

8. Plunkett to Baldeschin [mid-May 1670], *Plunkett Letters*, pp. 90-1; Gaffney to Congregatio, 4 Aug. 1660, in Millett (ed)., 'Vienna 2', in *Col. Hib.*, 25 (1983), pp. 42-3; B. Millett, *The Irish Franciscans, 1661-1665* (Rome 1964), pp. 42-5, 282-3, 524; Testimonial for Edmund O'Reilly, Dec. 1660, in B. Millett (ed.), 'Vienna 3', in *Col. Hib.*, xxvi (1984), p. 23.

9. Petition of Patrick, Bishop of Ardagh etc. [1657-8], O'Reilly to Congregatio, 27 July, 1658. A brief account of Irish hierarchy 1659, in Millett (ed.), 'Vienna 2', in *Col. Hib.*, 25 (1983), pp.40-1, 58-9, 61-2.

10. Enos to Propaganda, 18 Jan. 1658, A petition of some Irish bishops, 1658, in Millett, (ed.), 'Calendar of vols 12 and 13 of Fondo di Vienna' (henceforth 'Vienna 1'), in *Col. Hib.*, 24 (1982), pp. 56-7; Millett, *The Irish Franciscans*, p. 22.

11. For Clonelly see 'The Synod of Clonelly', in *J.A.C.A.S.*, i, no. 6 (1937), pp. 84-6; T. Ó Fiaich, 'Edmund O'Reilly, archbishop of Armagh, 1657-1669' in Franciscan Fathers (eds), *Father Luke Wadding Commemorative Volume* (Dublin 1957), pp. 196-7. The synod affirmed the decrees of the Council of Trent, extended them throughout the province of Armagh, decreed severe penalties for acts of treason and disloyalty towards Charles II, laid down a strict code of conduct for priests, urged greater decorum at wakes and funerals, adherence to Church law on matrimony, and fasting on Fridays.

12. 'Synod of Clonelly', in *J.A.C.A.S*, i, no. 6 (1937), pp. 85-6; Millett, *The Irish Franciscans*, pp. 317-18.

13. Plunkett to Alberizzi, 26 July 1660, Testimonial of François Rouxel de Mendany, Bishop of Seez, 5 June 1662, Memorandum by the internuncio, Flanders [1663], Edmund O'Reilly's State of the church in Ireland, 22 Aug. 1663, all in Millett (ed.), 'Vienna, pts 1-3 in *Col. Hib.*, xxv (1983), pp. 62, 45; xxiv (1982), p. 67; xxvi (1984), pp. 25, 30.

14. Oliver Plunkett's description of Ardagh can be found in *Plunkett Letters*, p. 19; see also 'A Report on the state of the church in Ireland by William Burgat' [1668] in B. Millett (ed.), 'Calendar of vol 1 of Scritture Referite nei Congressi, Irlanda' (henceforth 'Scritture'), in *Col. Hib.*, vi and vii (1963-4), p. 78; Plunkett to Propaganda [1664], in Moran, op. cit., pp. 30-1. Dublin was vacant, and MacGeoghegan of Meath was very old. O'Reilly and MacGeoghegan wrote to the Pope in October 1660 recommending Oliver Dease, vicar general of Meath, for the Archbishopric of Dublin (*Col. Hib.*, xxvi [1984], p. 22).

15. Calendars of a series of petitions and testimonials dating from 1658 to 1664 recommending Plunkett to the diocese of Meath and to the archdiocese of Dublin are to be found in *Col. Hib.*, xxv (1983), pp. 44-5. See also Oliver Plunkett to Propaganda, *c*.1664, *Plunkett Letters*, pp. 10-11.

16. Burgat and Conn's index ecclesiarum ... Hiberniae ... [1664], Decretum Congregationis [1664], Millett (ed.), 'Scritture', in *Col. Hib.*, vi and vii (1963-4), pp. 105-7, 128-37; Rationes quare illustrissimus [1664/5], in Millett (ed.), 'Vienna 3', *Col. Hib.*, xxvi (1984), p. 31. It was also claimed that Plunkett alienated the two

Franciscans, Patrick and Robert Plunkett, from obedience (Millett, *The Irish Franciscans*, p. 424).

17. In March 1665 the Pope was reported to be concerned about the non-residence of Irish bishops, and the nuncio at Paris was directed to seek out those bishops still in exile. See Roberti-Vittori to Propaganda, 16 Jan., 27 Mar. 1665, [Lynch] to Congregation, 25 Mar., Plunkett to Roberti-Vittori, 10 Feb. 1665, in Millett (ed.), 'Vienna 2', in *Col. Hib.*, xxv (1983), pp. 46-7; O'Reilly to Nuncio, 17 July 1665, in 'Vienna 3', in *Col. Hib.*, xxvi (1984), pp. 34-5.

18. In a letter to Oliver Plunkett, 27 Apr. 1661, Patrick Plunkett reported that 600 Catholics in Dublin had recently apostasized (*Col. Hib.*, xxiv [1982], p. 58).

19. For information on the state of the hierarchy in the 1660s see *Plunkett Letters*, pp. 22-3 and Burgat's Brevis Relatio ... [1668], in Millett (ed.), 'Scritture', in *Col. Hib.*, vi and vii (1963-4), pp. 71-9. For Plunkett's political endeavours, see O'Reilly to Congregatio, 5 Feb.1666 in Millett (ed.),'Vienna 2', in *Col. Hib.*, xxv (1983), p. 38; Millett, *The Irish Franciscans*, p. 424, note 4. For his lobbying for the archbishopric see *Plunkett Letters*, p. 19, *Col. Hib.*, vi and vii (1963-4), pp. 82, 16 (1973), p. 8.

20. For Plunkett, the Confederation and Rinuccini's censure see Oliver Plunkett to Father General of Capuchins, 14 June 1659, *Plunkett Letters*, p. 8; Testimonial of Robert Barry, Bishop of Cork and Cloyne, 1 May 1658 in Millett (ed.), 'Vienna 2', in *Col. Hib.*, xxv (1983), p. 45; Curtis, op. cit., pp. 14-15, 34-5. Plunkett had one niece married to a nephew, and a nephew (the Earl of Fingal) married to a niece of the Duke of Ormond (see *Plunkett Letters*, p. 16). For evidence of Ormond's protection of Bishop Plunkett, see White to Ubaldi-Baldeschi [1668], in Millett (ed.), 'Scritture', in *Col. Hib.*, vi and vii (1963-4), p. 90, and Oliver Plunkett to Tanari, 30 Nov. 1679, *Plunkett Letters*, pp. 536-7.

21. For the Remonstrance controversy see Ó Fiaich, 'Edmund O'Reilly ...', pp. 201-23; Millett, *The Irish Franciscans*, pp. 430-63.

22 Millett, *The Irish Franciscans*, 437, 461-7; O'Reilly to Propaganda, 30 Jan. 1665 in Millett (ed.), 'Vienna 2', in *Col. Hib.*, xxv (1983), p. 35; Curtis, op. cit., pp. 38-9. There is a copy of the summons signed by Plunkett, dated 18 Nov., in Millett (ed.), 'Vienna 3', in *Col. Hib.*, xxvi (1984), p. 41.

23. Ormond to Clarendon, 9 June 1666 in W. P. Burke, *Irish Priests in the Penal Times* (Shannon 1969), pp. 16-17; Rospigliosi to secretary of state, 15 May, O'Farrell to Rospigliosi, 25 May, 31 Aug., Stapleton to Rospigliosi [May], O'Kelly to Rospigliosi, 13 Aug. 1666, all in *Col. Hib.*, iii (1960), pp. 8-9, 11-12, 21, 16, 17.

24. Rospigliosi to secretariate of state, 9 Oct. 1666 in *Col. Hib.*, iii (1960), pp. 28-31.

25. For the Taaffe episode see B. Millett, 'The papal mission to Ireland of James Taaffe in 1668', in *Archivium Historiae Pontificiae*, iv, pp. 219-46; Eustace to Agretti, 21 Nov., Plunkett to Agretti, 30 Oct. 1668, in Millett (ed.),'Scritture', in *Col. Hib.*, vi and vii (1963-4), pp. 198-9; Plunkett to Propaganda, 22 June 1669 in Moran, op. cit., p. 3.

26. Netterville to Rospigliosi, 15 Sept., 25 Nov., Report on episcopal candidates [1668], in Millett (ed.),'Scritture', in *Col. Hib.*, vi and vii (1963-4), pp. 179-80, 200-1, 176-7. Another critic was Terence Fitzpatrick, vicar apostolic of Ossory, in Millett (ed.), 'Calendar of vol 2 (1669-71) of Scritture riferite' (henceforth 'Scritture 2'), in *Col. Hib.*, xvi (1973), p. 11.

27. Plunkett to Propaganda, 22 June 1669, in Moran, op. cit., pp. 2-3; Plunkett to [Barberini], 6 Aug. 1669 in Millett (ed.), 'Scritture 2', in *Col. Hib.*, xvi (1973), p. 38; Report on episcopal candidates [1668], in Millett (ed.),'Scritture', in *Col. Hib.*, xvi and xvii (1963-4), pp. 176-7.

28. See Burgat's Brevis relatio... [1668] in Millett (ed.), 'Scritture', *Col. Hib.*, vi and vii (1963-4), p. 74.

29. Plunkett to Baldeschi [July-Aug. 1669], 24 Jan. 1671, *Plunkett Letters*, pp. 34-6, 157; Gerard O'Farrell to Pope [1669] in Millett (ed.),'Scritture', in *Col. Hib.*, vi and vii (1963-4); Albertoni to Propaganda, 30 Aug., Farrell to [Propaganda], 17 Sept. 1669, in Millett (ed.),'Scritture 2', in *Col. Hib.*, xvi (1973), pp. 39-40.

30. Plunkett to Baldeschi [mid-May 1670], Plunkett to Brennan, 14 May 1670, *Plunkett Letters*, pp. 82, 89-91.

31. Plunkett to Airoldi, 1 Aug. 1670, *Plunkett Letters*, pp. 120-1. C. Giblin (ed.), 'A *congregatio particularis* on Ireland at Propaganda', in *Col. Hib.*, xviii and xix (1976-7), pp. 19, 22, 28-9; Baldeschi to Slusio, 27 June 1671 in Millett (ed.),'Scritture', in *Col. Hib.*, xvii (1974-5), p. 42.

32. Plunkett to Airoldi, 19, 22, 28 Sept., 15 Nov. 1671, 31 Jan., 2 April, Baldeschi to Plunkett and reply, 30 Apr., 19 July 1672, in *Plunkett Letters*, pp. 230-1, 234, 252, 276, 291-2, 309, 311; Brenan to [ ], 28 May 1672 in B. Millett (ed.), 'Calendar of vol 3 (1672-5) of Scritture Riferite' (henceforth 'Scritture 3'), *Col. Hib.*, xviii and xix (1976-7), p. 57, note 22.

33. Plunkett to Baldeschi, 19 July 1672, Plunkett to Tanari, 6 Mar. 1675, 2 Aug. 1678, in *Plunkett Letters*, pp. 309, 442-3, 507.

34. On income generally, and the inability of Catholic gentlemen to support the Church, see Plunkett to Baldeschi, 4 May 1670; for the Ardagh diocese see Plunkett to Falconieri, 28 Dec [1673], Plunkett to Creagh, 26 May 1674, Plunkett to Tanari, 6 Mar. 1675, 2, 28 Aug. 1678, *Plunkett Letters*, pp. 77-9, 393-5, 410, 443, 507, 511.

35. Plunkett to Airoldi, 2 Aug. 1671, Plunkett to Tanari, 5 Aug., Plunkett to Cerri, 13 Aug. 1675, in *Plunkett Letters*, pp. 446-7, 454-5, 495; Falconieri to Ravizza, 11 Aug., Falconieri to Altieri, 18 Aug. 1674, in Millett (ed.), 'Scritture 3', in *Col. Hib.*, xxi and xxii (1979-80), p. 61.

36. For repression see *Plunkett Letters*, pp. 386-436 *passim* and *Col. Hib.*, xxi and xxii (1979-80), pp. 62-4; for opposition to vicars apostolic, Plunkett to Tanari, 11 Aug. 1675, *Plunkett Letters*, pp. 452.

37. Since, according to Archbishop Plunkett (*Plunkett Letters*, pp. 29-30) there were 1000 seculars and 600 regulars in the country, Ardagh was clearly undersupplied with priests. There is abundant evidence of secular-regular disputes, see *Col. Hib.*, xxv (1983), pp. 55-6; xxiv (1982), pp. 72-5 and *Plunkett Letters*, pp. 43, 45-6, 87, 215-16, 237-8, 277, 292-3, 300, 373-4, 460-1. On the Bordeaux College see Plunkett to Airoldi, 30 Sept. 1671, *Plunkett Letters*, p. 262.

38. For the Synod of Ardpatrick see *Plunkett Letters*, pp. 516-22. The diocese of Ardagh was represented at the Synod by James Cusack, co-adjutor to the Bishop of Meath. For Farrell's advocacy of the case of Christopher O'Ferrall see P. F . Moran (ed.), *Spicilegium Ossoriense* (3 vols, Dublin 1874-84), ii, pp. 246-8, and for Farrell's response, Plunkett to Tanari, Plunkett to Cerri, 2, 30 Aug. 1678, *Plunkett Letters*, p. 507.

39. MacNamee, op. cit., pp. 355-6.

40. Oliver Plunkett recommended that the bishop of Kilmore should be made responsible for Ardagh (*Plunkett Letters*, pp. 355-6); Millett (ed.), 'Some lists of priests in Ireland, 1684-94', in *Col. Hib.*, xxvii and xxviii (1985-6), pp. 96-7 and notes.

41. For recommendations, dating from the 1660s, that Fallon be promoted to a bishopric see *Col. Hib.*, vi and vii (1963-4), pp. 108-9; xxiv (1982), pp. 65-6; xxv (1983), pp. 34, 36-7; xxvi (1984), pp. 31-4. For his appointment see Dean Monahan (ed.), *Records relating to the Diocese of Ardagh and Clonmacnois* (Dublin 1886), pp. 115-16, and

MacNamee, op. cit., pp. 357-9, and for his exile see *Spicilegium Ossoriense*, ii, pp. 307, 312; Burke, op. cit., pp. 135-6.

42. Martin, Moody, Byrne, op. cit., ix, p. 340, note 8; Maziere Brady, *The Episcopal Succession in England, Scotland and Ireland, 1400-1875* (3 vols, Rome 1876-7), i, p. 293.

43. Burke, op. cit., p. 156. Farrell was subsequently acquitted and discharged.

44. The information on Fergus Lee is taken from 'Parish priests of Granard since the seventeenth century', in *J.A.C.A.S.*, i, no. 1 (1926), pp. 98-9.

45. A list of those clergy that registered for the diocese of Ardagh can be found in MacNamee, op. cit., pp. 368-82 and P. M. O'Donohoe, 'The priests of County Longford in 1704' and 'Priests of Ardagh and Clonmacnois in 1704', in *J.A.C.A.S.*, i, no. 1 (1926), no. 2 (1929), pp. 96-8, 99-100. The figures given do not include the diocesan parishes in Westmeath, Cavan, Roscommon and Sligo.

46. Maziere Brady, op. cit., i, p. 293.

47. H. Fenning, 'Ambrose MacDermott, bishop of Elphin 1707-17', in *Archivium Fratrum Praedicatorum* (hereafter *A.F.P*), xl (1970), pp. 244-5.

48. Burke, op. cit., pp. 439, 332-5; MacNamee, op. cit., pp. 376-8.

49. For the Abjuration Oath and Donogher's experience see M. M. McRory, 'The life and times of Dr Patrick Donnolly', in *Seanchas Ardmhacha*, v (1969), pp. 24-6; Fenning, 'Ambrose MacDermott', pp. 257-9; C.Giblin (ed.),'Catalogue of the Nunziatura di Fiandra, parts 3 and 4' (henceforth 'Fiandra'), in *Col. Hib.*, iv (1961), pp. 118-19, v (1962), pp. 12-13, 25-7, 28-9; Burke, op. cit., p. 441.

50. Burke, op. cit., pp. 439-44. Donogher was not, in fact, administrator of Kilmore.

51. The figure for 1704 is taken from *Spicilegium Ossoriense*, ii, pp. 380-1; those for 1714 are from Burke, op. cit., pp. 442-4, 333.

52. Attempts were made in 1709 and 1711 to appoint a bishop in the place of Donogher. See Maziere Brady, op. cit., i, pp. 293-4; Monahan, op. cit., p. 37; J. MacNamee, 'Ardacha Dominicana', in *J.A.C.A.S.*, ii, no. 12 (1951), p. 25.

53. There is no mention of the attempt to suspend Flynn in the hagiographic account provided by MacNamee, *Ardagh*, pp. 383-6. The account provided here is based on the correspondence of the nuncio at Brussels, see Giblin (ed.),'Fiandra', parts 5, 7 and 10, in *Col. Hib.*, ix (1966), p. 14, xi (1968), pp. 87-9, xiv (1971), p. 44.

54. Maziere Brady, op. cit., i, p. 294; J. Brady (ed.), *Catholics and Catholicism in the Eighteenth Century Press* (Maynooth 1966), p. 60; H. Fenning, *The Undoing of the Friars, A Study of the Novitiate Question in Eighteenth Century Ireland* (Louvain 1972), p. 41.

55. Burke, op. cit., p. 337; J. Brady, op. cit., p. 60; Spinelli to Lercart, 3 Feb. 1730 in Giblin (ed.), 'Fiandra 7', *Col. Hib.* xi (1968), p. 87. For the Dominican friary in Longford see Fenning, *The Undoing of the Friars*, p. 86; H. Fenning, 'The Irish Dominican province, 1721-45', in *A.F.P.*, xlii (1972), p. 353; H. Fenning (ed.), 'Some problems of the Irish mission, 1733-74', *Col. Hib.*, viii (1965), pp. 80-1; H. Fenning (ed.), *The Fottrell Papers* (Belfast 1980), p. 73; J. MacNamee, 'Ardacha Dominicana', pp. 25-6. According to Galbraith Holmes, the High Sheriff, there were 'no fryerys or nunnerys' in Longford in 1731, but this is clearly inaccurate ('Report on the state of Popery, 1731', in *Arch. Hib.*, i [1912], p. 27).

56. For the papal decisions on ordinations see H. Fenning, *The Undoing of the Friars*, *passim*; for Byrne and McDermott Roe, see H. Fenning (ed.), 'John Kent's report on the state of the Irish mission, 1742,' in *Arch. Hib.*, xxviii (1966), p. 96; Maziere Brady, op. cit., i, p. 294; J. Brady, op. cit., pp. 74, 79.

57. Burke, op. cit., pp. 336-7.

58. West's return of the Longford clergy is in Burke, op. cit., pp. 335-6, and MacNamee, *Ardagh*, pp. 389-91. The Leitrim returns can be found in the same sources, pp. 444-5 and 392.

59. J. Brady, op. cit., p. 78.

60. For Blake see MacNamee, *Ardagh*, pp. 398-9; P. Whelan, 'Anthony Blake, archbishop of Armagh, 1758-1787', in *Seanchas Ardmhacha*, v (1970), pp. 294-5.

61. For Cheevers and the unification of the dioceses of Ardagh and Clonmacnois see A. Cogan, *Diocese of Meath Ancient and Modern* (3 vols, Dublin 1862-70), ii, 163-5; Monahan, op. cit., pp. 125, 133; Martin, Moody, Byrne, op. cit., ix, pp. 340-1 especially note 20; Fenning, *The Undoing of the Friars*, pp. 196-7, 215, note 4; H. Fenning, 'The Irish Dominican province, 1721-45', in *A.F.P.*, xlii (1972), pp. 269-71. MacEgan had been appointed bishop of Clonmacnois in 1725, and he continued to administer it after he transferred to Meath in 1729.

62. H. Fenning, 'The Irish Dominican province, 1745-61', in *A.F.P.*, xlv (1975), p. 462; id. (ed.), 'Some problems of the Irish mission, 1733-74', in *Col. Hib.*, viii (1965), pp. 80-1; id., *The Undoing of the Friars*, p. 275.

63. Fenning, *The Undoing of the Friars*, pp. 52, 160, 177, 232, 274.

64. Fenning, *The Fottrell Papers*, p. 73; id., 'The Irish Dominican province, 1765-78', in *A.F.P.*, xlix (1979), pp. 279-80, 287; id., 'Some problems of the Irish mission, 1733-74', in *Col. Hib.*, viii (1965), p. 99. For evidence of Brady's continuing disinclination towards regulars see F. J. McKiernan, 'Kilmore priests', in *Breifne*, vi (1986), p. 317.

65. For the Augustinians see H. Fenning (ed.), 'Clerical recruitment 1735-83', *Arch. Hib.*, xxx (1972), pp. 18-19; and for the Franciscans see id., 'The Irish Dominican province, 1765-78', in *A.F.P.*, xlix (1979), pp. 339-42; Marquess of Londonderry (ed.), *Memoirs and Correspondence of Viscount Castlereagh* (4 vols, London 1848), iv, p. 116.

66. These figures are based on Eileen O'Byrne (ed.), *The Convert Rolls* (Dublin 1981).

67. J. Brady, op.cit., pp.138-9; S. F. O'Cianain, 'In the days of the planters: gleanings from the records of the Grand Jury of County Longford, 1760-1800', in *J.A.C.A.S.*, i, no. 5 (1935), pp. 70-1.

68. 'A list of ecclesiastics who took the Oath of Allegiance', in *Arch. Hib.*, i (1912), p. 71.

69. Canon Carrigan (ed.), 'Catholic episcopal wills in the P.R.O. Dublin, 1683-1812', *Arch. Hib.*, i (1912), pp. 161-2.

70. The above is based on the parish register list in N.L.I. The number of parishes cited as having adopted registers does not correspond with the number of parishes cited at the outset because unified parishes are counted as one, and because the N.L.I. list does not include Cashel and Rathcline. For a wider context see Kevin Whelan, 'The regional impact of Irish Catholicism, 1750-1850', in W. J. Smyth, Kevin Whelan (eds), *Common Ground: Essays on the Historical Geography of Ireland* (Cork 1988), pp. 235-77.

71. Caulfield to Troy [Jan. 1788] (D.D.A., Troy Correspondence 1).

72. Monahan, op.cit., p.138; *Castlereagh Correspondence*, iv, pp. 114-16; Cruise to Borgia, 26 April 1804 (Archives of Congregation of Propaganda Fide, Rome, Scritture Riferite nei Congressi, Irlanda, vol. 18, pp. 227-8ff). I would like to thank Fr Patrick O'Donoghue for this reference.

73. The figures on clerical income are taken from *Castlereagh Correspondence*, iv, pp. 114-16. For church attendance see the comment by Edward Wakefield, *An Account of Ireland, Statistical and Political* (2 vols, London 1812), p. 615; and C. R. Cornwall, *Excursions through Ireland* (3 vols, London 1820).

74. Monahan, op. cit., pp. 151-6; *Spicilegium Ossoriense*, iii, pp. 614-15; T.Wyse, *Historical Sketch of the Late Catholic Association of Ireland*'(London 1829), ii, appendix.
75. For Catholic emancipation in County Longford see F. O'Ferrall, below, p. 123; 'The struggle for Catholic emancipation in County Longford, 1824-29', in *Teathbha*, i, no. 4 (1978), pp. 259-69; id., *Catholic Emancipation: Daniel O'Connell and the Birth of Irish Democracy* (Dublin 1985), pp. 69-71, 96, 106-7.
76 Monahan, op. cit., pp. 138-9; S. J.Connolly, *Priests and People in Pre-Famine Ireland, 1780-1840* (Dublin 1982); P. Whelan, *History of St Matthew's Church Ballymahon* (Ballymahon n.d.), p. 3; 'Extracts from old Parish Registers', in *J.A.C.A.S.*, i, no. 2 (1929), p. 102.
77. For a perspective on church attendance see D. W. Miller, 'Irish Catholicism and the Great Famine', in *Journal of Social History*, ix (1975-6), pp. 81-91. According to Miller the attendance at four Catholic chapels near Virginia was about 40 per cent (p. 86).
78. These figures are taken from the appendix to *Statuta Diocesana in Diocesi Ardachensi ...* (Dublin 1834). They are to be found in a more convenient form in *J.A.C.A.S.*, i , no. 1 (1926), pp. 100-2.
79. *Statuta Diocesana ...*, *passim*; Connolly, op cit., p. 163. For some information on the place of holy wells in the religion of the people see 'Some wells in the parishes of Abbeylara and Granard', in *J.A.C.A.S.*, ii, no. 12 (1951).
80. A schedule of the forms to be filled in by the vicars general and parish priests is printed in appendix 1 of *Statuta Diocesana*.
81. D. Keenan, *The Catholic Church in Nineteenth Century Ireland: A Sociological Study* (Dublin 1983), pp. 118, 140; D. Kerr, *Peel, Priests and Politics: Sir Robert Peel's Administration and the Catholic Church in Ireland* (Oxford 1982), p. 33.
82. Monahan, op. cit., pp. 161, 167-9; M. J. Masterson, 'Centenary of St Mel's Cathedral', in *J.A.C.A.S.*, ii, no. 7 (1940), pp. 53-60; MacNamee, *Ardagh*, pp. 502-6.
83 Masterson, as note 82, pp. 53-4; Monahan, op. cit., pp. 168-9; Kerr, op. cit., pp. 60-1. For a perspective on schooling in the Ardagh diocese previous to 1831 see the abstracts published in *J.A.C.A.S.*, ii, no. 9 (1943), pp. 69-70; vol. 2, no. 10 (1945), pp. 80-3; vol. 2, no. 11 (1946), pp. 86-9.
84. Monahan, op. cit., p. 207.
85. K. B. Nowlan, 'The Catholic clergy and Irish politics in the 1830s and 1840s' in John Barry (ed.), *Historical Studies*, ix (Belfast 1974), pp. 122, 125; Kerr, op. cit., pp. 76, 78, 81, 84-5, 88-9; S. J. Broderick, *The Holy See and the Irish Movement for Repeal of the Union* (Rome 1951), pp. 117-18, 121, 132-9; O'Connell to O'Higgins, 10 Apr.1841 in M. R. O'Connell (ed.), *The Correspondence of Daniel O'Connell*, vii (Dublin 1974), pp. 35-7; L. J. McCaffrey, *Daniel O'Connell and the Repeal Year* (Kentucky 1966), pp. 64-70; E. Larkin, *The Historical Dimension of Irish Catholicism* (Washington 1982), pp. 125-6, n. 17.
86. Kerr, op. cit., pp. 212-13, 154, 142, 149, 175, 322-3, 354; MacNamee, *Ardagh*, p. 444.
87. Broderick, op. cit., p. 216; Richard Davis, *The Young Ireland Movement* (Dublin 1987), pp. 104, 190; O'Higgins to O'Connell, 31 July 1846, in *O'Connell Correspondence*, viii, p. 94, n. 9.
88. MacNamee, *Ardagh*, pp. 457-8; Broderick, op. cit., pp. 213-14; O'Higgins to Maginn, 14 Sept. [Sept], 1848 in Monahan, op. cit., pp. 164-7.
89. E. Larkin, *The Making of the Roman Catholic Church in Ireland, 1850-1860* (Chapel Hill 1980), pp. 161-8; for Kilduff's background see Monahan, op. cit., pp. 208-10.
90. P. J .Corish (ed.), 'Irish College Rome: Kirby papers', in *A. H.*, xxxi (1973), pp. 15,

45, 46, 47-8; Larkin, *The Making of the Catholic Church*, p. 217. For further evidence of Kilduff's authoritarian tendencies see Corish, op. cit., p. 18 and P. Conlan (ed.), 'A short title catalogue of material of Irish interest in … the general archives of the Friars minor, Rome', in *Col. Hib.*, xviii and xix (1976-7), pp. 161, 165; xx (1978), pp. 112, 113, 114.

91. First Lenten pastoral of Dr Kilduff, 17 Feb. 1854 in Monahan, op. cit., pp. 220-7. The quote is from p. 225.

92. Monahan, op. cit., pp. 246-50, especially pp. 246-8.

93. Ibid., pp. 217-19; Monsignor Langan, 'Nine years in St Mel's College', in *J.A.C.A.S.*, i, no. 4 (1935); Keenan, op. cit., pp. 228-9.

94. See the comment of Primate Dixon in Keenan, op. cit., p. 68.

95. See Cullen's comment, cited in Larkin, *The Making of the Catholic Church*, p. 255.

III
STUDIES IN TRANSITION 1760–1880

'A gentleman's estate should be a moral school':[1] Edgeworthstown in Fact and Fiction, 1760–1840

TOM DUNNE

Recent investigations of the records of individual estates have contributed much to our understanding of the complexities of the Irish land system, and of landlord-tenant relations in the eighteenth and nineteenth centuries.[2] Such records normally tell us more about the social and economic realities than about the landlord's perception of his position and role, but a remarkable series of texts, ranging from legal documents to novels, records the views and reflects the psychology of three generations of the Edgeworth family in Longford between the 1760s and the 1840s.

The first layer of text is the collection of documents put together by Richard Edgeworth in 1768, and known to the family by its binding as 'The Black Book'. Having rescued the estate from the ruin threatened by generations of neglect and improvidence, Richard Edgeworth compiled this record as a practical handbook, an abstract of Letters Patent, surveys and title deeds, giving 'a clear and honest title to my son' and a guide to the family in future legal disputes and difficulties.[3] He added an account of the family history, telling the story of a 'New English' family with a legal and ecclesiastical background who came to Ireland in the 1580s and built up an estate in Longford, with a grant from James I in 1619 and later purchases of confiscated land. From the beginning, however, the Edgeworth achievement was threatened as much by improvidence and absenteeism as by successive attacks on the land settlement. 'The Black Book' thus offered a warning to the family about threats to their position from both within and without, and as the Edgeworths fled in 1798 to escape the peasant insurgents, who had risen to greet the invading French army, they paused only to bury it in the garden in a tin box.[4]

The family history was also the starting-point for Richard Lovell Edgeworth, son of the author of 'The Black Book', when he began his *Memoirs*[5] (a second layer of text), towards the end of his life, most of which had been spent as a resident improving landlord on his estate. Earlier, he too had been an absentee in England, more interested in experiments in applied mechanics and his friendships with fellow members of the Lunar Society and with the eccentric Thomas Day. With the latter he shared an interest in educational theory and practice, which he began to apply to the education of his own large family from four marriages - with the help of his daughter, Maria. Her fascination with Ireland began as an impressionable fifteen-year-old when she returned with her father in 1782, and was shaped above all by her role as his assistant in both the creation of a model estate and the education of the younger children. In the latter role she began her career as a writer, notably with *The Parent's Assistant: or Stories for Children* (1796) and (with her father) *Practical Education* (1798). These set the tone of all her later works, which aimed at moral improvement and the provision of didactic models of behaviour. Four of her novels (*Castle Rackrent* [1800]; *Ennui* [1809]; *The Absentee* [1812]; *Ormond* [1817]) dealt with aspects of Irish landlordism, projecting into fiction the lessons of her family history, and the experiment in 'moral' landlordism by her father.

These form a third layer of Edgeworthian texts[6] and the use of fictional forms by this talented writer makes it possible to explore the family experience in ways which transcend the more conventional histories and memoirs. Maria also made a distinctive contribution to the earlier texts: completing her father's *Memoirs* after his death in 1817, with a glowing account of his stewardship of the estate; and adding a long manuscript 'Appendix' to 'The Black Book'. This gives an account of her own contribution as agent for her brothers Lovell and Sneyd successively, during which time she emulated her grandfather and saved the estate from threatened financial ruin.[7]

These different texts show remarkable patterns of continuity and interaction. In particular, the theme of colonist insecurity in the face of the native threat recurs: 'The Black Book' is an influential subtext for all that follows, but is substantially recast in Richard Lovell Edgeworth's *Memoirs* and in Maria's fiction. As the first volume of the *Memoirs* was being written Maria was producing a fictional version of the same events in *Ennui*, and father and daughter were reading each other's work. The second volume was written by Maria eight years later, after her father's death, and was a commentary on her own Irish fiction, as well as on his life. Such interactions and the patterns of thought which they reveal are the concern of this paper, rather than some chronologically based blend of 'fact' and 'fiction'. Nor, despite (or perhaps because of) this writer's training as an historian, is it the intention to become involved in 'the unusual business of checking fiction against fact', as W.J. Mc Cormack and Kim Walker describe an aspect of their valuable introductory essay to the World's Classics edition of *The Absentee*.[8] Instead, it is suggested that 'fact' and 'fiction' can also be seen as inextricably mixed or confused, with 'histories' and 'novels' containing elements of both. The focus, therefore, is on the versions or narratives of the 'facts' of their history which the Edgeworths composed, the relationships of these to Maria's Irish novels, and what, taken together, the three layers of texts can tell us of the fears and concerns of these particular representatives of the Irish ruling class during a period of revolutionary change.

I

Marilyn Butler's excellent biography of Maria Edgeworth pointed to the fact that not only were the Rackrents, the landlord family of her first Irish novel, based on the first four generations of Edgeworths, being 'sportsmen, litigants, drunkards, gamblers, duellists, adventurers in marriage', but that even the novel's structure was based on that of 'The Black Book'. However, the influence of her grandfather's text on *Castle Rackrent*, and also on the later Irish novels, goes much deeper, to the levels of insecurity and ambivalence which characterized the family's perception of its colonist role. In a 1792 letter to his sister, defending his advocacy of Catholic Emancipation, Richard Lovell Edgeworth acknowledged that this was 'adverse to my own interest, possessed as I am now of landed property by rights of Conquest. [That] right has hitherto been sufficient for the common purposes and common sense of mankind – upon [what] foundation is another matter.'[9]

The legal foundations were itemized in 'The Black Book', beginning with the 'Copy of Letters Patent granted by King James the First to Francis Edgeworth Esq' in 1619. A striking feature of this and later Letters Patent is the absence of any reference to the original owners of the land – although titles to land granted by the crown at the same time to various 'Irish Papist' Ferralls and Nugents are included, as their lands were added to the Edgeworth estate over succeeding decades, some being 'forfeited ... on account of the Irish Rebellion' of 1641.[10] These were the dominant Gaelic Irish and Old English families of the area, with some branches holding on to land into the nineteenth century, and their names make interesting appearances in the later texts. It was 'a menial servant and a papist' named Ferrall who saved the Edgeworth family home and the life of the heir in 1641. Lady Edgeworth was helped by 'a Mr Nugent' after fleeing her home in 1690, while one of her Williamite sons was arrested 'by Colonel Nugent of Coolamber, who was governor of Longford in the interests of King James'. In *Castle Rackrent*, Sir Murtagh is in dispute with Nugents over land. The hero of *The Absentee*, Lord Colambre, is in love with Grace Nugent, a name taken from the title of the well-known song by Carolan, reputedly a visitor to Edgeworthstown in the early eighteenth century. Mc Cormack and Walker have uncovered a fascinating range of reference points for Grace Nugent and other characters in this important example of 'antiquarianism transformed into historical fiction'. Their argument is that the Jacobite associations of the Nugent name are central to *The Absentee*'s 'acknowledgement and denial of rival worlds and divided values'; many also support the view that the insecurities of the family's colonial experience, detailed in 'The Black Book', continued to find echoes in Edgeworth's fiction.[11]

In the legal documents that make up much of 'The Black Book', the native world is most clearly evoked in the repeated listing of townlands, beginning in 1619 with 'Cranelaghmore, Craunelaghbeg, Lissard and Goorte (translated into English)'.[12] The list of these often crude or garbled versions of Gaelic place-names was a constant reminder of the origins of their lands, a fact reflected in Maria's fiction, most memorably in *Castle Rackrent*, where the Gaelic origins of the subversive servant, Thady Quirk, are emphasized by his role as interpreter of the meaning of similar place-names to the Jewish wife of Sir Kit. When at the end the Quirks take over the estate, its Gaelic townlands are listed in a manner reminiscent of 'The Black Book' ('the lands of O'Shaughlinstown, and the lands of Gruneaghvolagha and the lands of Crookanawaturgh') as if to underline the collapse of the colonial land settlement.[13]

Recent research has drawn attention to the complex interaction between the early-seventeenth-century settlers and the Gaelic world,[14] and this is also reflected in 'The Black Book'. The recipient of the original 1619 grant, Francis, married first a 'daughter of one of the great O'Cavanaghs', and later a Catholic named Jane Tuite, who converted on her marriage but after becoming estranged from her husband returned to her original religion, later founding a convent of nuns in Dublin. Her portrait, however, continued to feature in successive family homes, and was credited with a key role in saving the property in both 1641 and 1689, its clear Catholic character deflecting rebel vengeance. Her son was known to 'the common Irish' as 'Shaen More or Great John', and the family history preserved that name and recorded his traditional Gaelic life-style of open house, which was 'to the great joy of the common Irish and to the great detriment of his fortune'. While the next two generations were headed by staunch Protestants and soldiers in the Williamite cause, they also included younger sons; one 'conversed more with Papists than with Protestants'; another 'became a Jacobite out of Principle'; a third became a Catholic and the father of Abbé Edgeworth, the priest famous for his ministrations to Louis XVI on the scaffold and venerated by the family.[15]

In Maria Edgeworth's fiction the Gaelic world again combines threat with fascination. In this she is also in a colonist tradition, most famously exemplified by Edmund Spenser's *A View of the Present State of Ireland*, written in 1596.[16] She had been given this work by her father shortly after her arrival in Ireland, as a guide to the country's history and condition, and she in her turn recommended it to her fictional returned 'absentee', in the novel of that name.[17] She wrote the first half of *Castle Rackrent*, as Spenser wrote the *View*, in the midst of a major Irish rebellion, which drove her from her home. A sense of being under siege from the native Irish world underlies all her Irish novels. It is signalled in the first footnote to *Castle Rackrent*, when she not only compares the greatcoat of the subversive narrator, Thady Quirk, to the cloaks of the Irish rebels castigated by Spenser, but amends her Spenser quotation on the usefulness of such cloaks to the disaffected, by having the Irish emerge from the 'black bogs' rather than from the 'thick woods' - as the 1798 rebels had done in Longford.[18]

Like Spenser, she presented a stereotype of the native Irish, which suited her recipe for the anglicization of all aspects of Irish life - in her case, a benevolent improving landlordism. This stereotype reflected the major Spenserian theme of the seductive as well as the hostile and degraded nature of native society, together with her greater optimism about the possibility of exploiting its surviving mores in the interests of loyalism and social deference. It was what she perceived as the quasi-feudal nature of that society which constituted for Maria 'its dangerous seductiveness' and its real potential. In *Ennui* it excites the imagination of the hero, who has to resist and then exploit the traditional expectations of his vassals in order to become a good improving landlord.[19] In *Ormond*, the classic colonist fear of the native world as morally corrupting focuses on the archaic Gaelic backwater of 'Black Island', and is countered by the influence of a modernizing landlord. This landlord becomes the ultimate model for the hero who returns to exploit the native trait of deference to their hereditary lords, which had earlier threatened his ruin. His ambition is expressed in Spenserian terms as that of 'further civilising the people'.[20]

Maria Edgeworth's understanding of the nature of hereditary loyalty in Gaelic society was evident even in *Castle Rackrent*, where Thady Quirk's explanation that while he didn't 'belong' to Sir Condy, 'I live under him, and have done so these two hundred years and upwards, me and mine,' has parallels in Irish poetry.[21] Thady's definition further highlights the fact that the Rackrents, however much based on the Edgeworths, were a native Irish family rather than a colonial one in origin. The first Rackrent was an O'Shaughlin and 'related to the kings of Ireland', but forced into the double apostasy of changing his name and (probably) his religion in order to gain the estate.[22] Similarly in *Ennui*, the hero, Lord Glenthorn, is told that his family name, 'before they stooped to be lorded', was O'Shagnesee, and there are hints that the Clonbronys in *The Absentee* have a similar background. The theme of the apostasy of Sir Ulick O'Shane is discussed openly and at length in *Ormond*, where it is regarded, not only by his Gaelic Catholic cousin 'King' Corney, but also by the author, as basic to his moral degeneracy.[23] This repeated pattern suggests Edgeworth may have regretted that some way had not been found of combining modernization with the traditional loyalty given by the people to the old native families, even when they changed religion. Such a combination was an important feature in the resolution of all three of her Irish novels after *Castle Rackrent*, as her anglicized heroes returned to 'reign over' their hereditary fiefs.[24]

While there are many echoes of the Gaelic elements of 'The Black Book' in Maria's fiction, its main influence as a shaping text was on *Castle Rackrent*. Scholars are now less willing to accept her own description of her first novel as 'the plain round tale of faithful Thady', and have come to regard it as a deeply ironic and pessimistic story, dominated by an ambivalent, subversive narrator - its theme being as much the rise of the Quirks as the fall of the Rackrents. Such a reading raises the difficult questions of how a young, inexperienced, English-educated woman, living on a remote estate, could have produced such a richly layered and subtle first novel, and why she never repeated its experimental form. The answers lie in the circumstances of the composition of *Castle Rackrent* and in the use made of its historical subtext, 'The Black Book'. Edgeworth's own account of the origins of this novel stressed her fascination with the speech of her father's steward, John Langan, her main interpreter of the strange and exotic world of Edgeworthstown in the early years. Her family's urgings that she should commit her fond mockery of that speech to paper started her writing, but she also claimed that Langan was not only the model for Thady, but the virtual dictator of what she wrote.[25]

However, there are major difficulties with this explanation. The narrator's language is very different from the examples of peasant speech given in the 'Glossary' and from the scanty records we have of Langan's conversation.[26] It is, instead, a heavily modified and easily comprehensible version of peasant language, which allows for a very sophisticated and nuanced commentary. Awareness of the danger that the English reader might completely misunderstand the book, and above all its revolutionary device of a peasant narrator, led her to add successive layers of explanation - a preface, glossary, footnotes and an endnote - all of which gave a clear interpretative framework, that of the educated liberal Ascendancy commentator on Ireland's exotic and dangerous peasant world. In this authoritative subtext the key to the ironic 'loyalty' of Thady and to the novel's warning about the fragility of the colonial settlement is clear, but these elements are also signalled in the main text through her adaptation of the family history - shot through with a deep pessimism and black humour which reflected the threatening circumstances of the novel's composition.

The Rackrents were clearly modelled on the earlier family black sheep - Sir Patrick on the over-hospitable Shaen Moore, Sir Kit and Sir Murtagh on the litigious gambler, Sir John, and Sir Condy on the ultimately penurious Francis - but the novel reversed the theme of the history. Instead of the story of a family's salvation from ruin by diligent legal work and economic prudence, she wrote the story of a similar family's ruin through failure to take such action, allowing instead a trusted servant and his lawyer son to take over the estate. In terms of its shaping text, the family history, *Castle Rackrent* - as the story of what *might* have happened the Edgeworths - was both a tribute to her grandfather and a warning to her class to follow the Edgeworth lead, now turned into a model landlord system by her father.

The novel also has a basis in another reversal of a recurring theme in the family history - that of the loyal servant saving the house during the rebellion, as had happened when the family faced extinction in the upheavals of 1641, 1690 and 1798. In 1641 the heir was saved by a Catholic servant, Edmund MacBrian Ferrall, who pretended he wanted to kill the child, and then saved the house from being set on fire by telling the rebels 'that the castle had formerly belonged to some of the Ferralls who might choose to live in it'.[27] In *Castle Rackrent*, instead of a loyal servant pretending to be a rebel and having an ancient claim to the estate, Edgeworth has a dominant servant figure, endlessly protesting his loyalty while promoting the takeover of the estate by his son. In the historical record the Edgeworths are threatened by a combination of personal weaknesses and the recurring threat of native revolt. In the novel, the threat of rebellion is masked by the figure of the subversive servant, who achieves what successive rebellions had failed to do. Later, in *Ennui*, set in the period around 1798, another dissimulating personal servant is discovered to be a rebel leader, while the theme of a peasant takeover is masked by the literary device of having the heir to the estate brought up as a member of a peasant family called Donoghue and taking over when the truth is revealed. His immediate response to the news is to believe 'your honour's jesting me about them kings of Ireland that they say the O'Donoghues were once, but that's what I never think on, that's all idle talk for the like of me, for sure that's a long time ago, and what use going back to it'.[28] He is quite sincere, but his protestation involves the admission that there was a widespread belief among the peasantry in their historical right to the land confiscated and colonized in the sixteenth and seventeenth centuries. Despite the general absence of such claims in the notices of secret societies, or the rhetoric of Catholic politicians, they were often felt by Irish Protestants to be a factor in agrarian unrest and in the demand for the repeal of anti-Catholic legislation. A major aim of the novels of Edgeworth's contemporary, Lady Morgan, was to demonstrate that such fears were groundless, and that Catholics accepted the colonial settlement.[29] It was understandable that the work of Edgeworth, the leading 'Big House' novelist of this period, should have continued to mirror these fears. When Christy Donoghue has taken over the Glenthorn estate, his wife claims descent 'from one of the kings of Ireland', and they quickly reduce the estate to a caricature of the traditional barbarous Gaelic life-style. Clearly, the achievement of what Spenser had called 'civilite' was seen as superficial and fragile, and the Gaelic threat no less real in being conducted through legal and economic means rather than open warfare.[30]

Maria Edgeworth's fictions, therefore, project the fears of earlier generations of her family into the era of landlord and tenant, and extend the lessons of her grandfather's 'Black Book' beyond those of prudent estate management to the underlying realities of the colonial project, to which she and her father were still committed. His *Memoirs* form the second layer of these remarkable family chronicles, and interact in interesting ways with the Irish novels of his daughter.

II

Richard Lovell Edgeworth's interest in his family history was limited and lay mainly in the eccentricities of his forebears and in the lessons it provided in 'the formation of character'.[31] In the first volume of his *Memoirs* he is concerned with his experiences in England *before* the decision to return to Ireland in 1782. Illness interrupted his narrative, and his failure to resume it during the remaining and otherwise active eight years of his life is interesting, probably indicating a reluctance to relive his more radical political past and a time when he was an isolated figure in Longford gentry society.

His brief account of the earlier Edgeworths, written from memory rather than from the text of 'The Black Book',[32] softens his father's description of them as a besieged colonist family. In 'The Black Book', for example, the family of Sir John, living in Lissard Castle (he bought 'Edgeworthstown', then Mostrim, in 1670 but the family didn't make their home there until 1700), is under siege from rapparees and a hostile local population and protected by armed servants. In the *Memoirs* the emphasis instead is on Sir John's wife whose belief in fairies is used by the locals to scare her by showing lights in the 'fairymount' opposite the castle.

There are also some interesting glosses on his father's account, which offer further clues to the composition of *Castle Rackrent*. Commenting on the story of the 'faithful servant ... Bryan Ferrall' who saved the family home and the heir in 1641, he adds: 'His last descendant died within my memory, after having lived and been supported always under my father's protection.' The fact that the Quirks had likewise lived as privileged servants and tenants under the O'Shaughlin/Rackrents 'these two hundred years and upwards', makes their connection with the Ferralls more clear-cut. Another element of Thady's narrative may have its origins in the story Richard Lovell tells of his father's successful legal battles to save the estate, one of which involved showing up as fraudulent a deed which had been sworn to by 'an antient servant of the Edgeworth family', who 'had been accustomed to transcribe papers for the gentlemen who had executed the deed'.[33]

The first volume of the *Memoirs* was written in the same year, 1809, as *Ennui* was published. The two texts had features in common; for example, the story of the suddenly ennobled O'Donoghue wife in the novel filling the castle with her relatives and ruining the estate echoed that of a relative whom Richard Lovell remembered visiting as a child, whose fortune was dissipated by the relatives of a wife 'of inferior station'.[34] Indeed the basic story of the novel - a languid young Anglo-Irish landlord comes to live on his Irish estate and learns how to cope with the manipulative cunning and bad habits of his Irish tenants in order to reform the estate on English lines - is contained in Edgeworth's few comments on his early experience as a landlord.[35] Edgeworth himself had even more in common with the principled and serious-minded Lord Colambre, hero of *The Absentee* (published three years later), who decided to return to Ireland out of a sense of duty - 'because it is the country in which my father's property lies, and from which we draw our subsistence'. This was clearly based on Richard Lovell's account of his decision in 1782 'to remain at Edgeworth-Town and to improve my estate, and thus to sacrifice my tastes to my duty. I had always thought that, if it were in the power of any man to serve the country which gave him bread, he ought to sacrifice every inferior consideration and to reside where he could be most useful.'[36] The account of how he fulfilled this 'duty' was left to Maria, in her addition of a second volume to his *Memoirs*.

The 38-year-old 'absentee' who felt duty-bound to return to Ireland in 1782 was a complex man. From his father he had learned habits of sobriety and thrift and a sense of obligation to preserve his patrimony. Educated in both Ireland and England (as schoolboy and undergraduate) he experienced acutely the Anglo-Irish sensation of being an outsider in each country. In his own account, this was focused particularly on accent. As an eight-year-old schoolboy in Warwick he was 'sufficiently tainted with Irish accent and Irish idiom to be the object of much open ridicule and much secret contempt'. Later, at school in Drogheda, he found himself 'as ridiculous for my English accent as I had been at Warwick for my Irish brogue'. This sense of insecurity persisted all his life, and was indicated by his daughter's repeated insistence in the second volume that he sounded English in 'accent, style and manner of speaking'.[37]

It had some positive consequences, leading to a lifelong sensitivity to and fascination with varieties of speech, especially their role in the creation of damaging national stereotypes. He shared with Maria an understanding of the role of language in both the Anglo-Irish colonial relationship and that of landlord and tenant. Together they wrote *An Essay on Irish Bulls*, which attacked the linguistic basis of the negative view of the Irish in England. Likewise, her view of the peasantry in her novels is developed mainly through analysis of their language.[38]

What most marked Richard Lovell Edgeworth out from other young Anglo-Irishmen of similar background living in Britain was his passion for science, especially as applied to practical mechanics. He was a talented inventor and might have been recognized as such had he remained in the English midlands. In the very different Irish midlands he inevitably appeared an eccentric, although he successfully developed machines to suit this terrain, including a light wooden railway which laid its own track as it moved forward. He remained in contact with members of the Lunar Society and transplanted to Ireland their belief in progress and in rational approaches to social and political problems.

An important friendship - with the eccentric English philanthropist, Thomas Day - began his interest in educational theory and practice, though he abandoned Day's Rousseauistic philosophy and instead applied scientific principles to the learning processes of young children. His work with his own large family, helped mainly by Maria, led to a remarkable spate of publications which won them both a European reputation. Thus, although 'remote in the middle of Ireland', in what appeared to Richard Lovell in a moment of despair in 1794 as 'a dreary, unsociable, puritanical abode',[39] Edgeworthstown under this returned absentee had much of the character of an experimental laboratory, whether in the mechanics of bogland reclamation, in estate management or in the acquisition of reading skills. Its ambience was intellectual and liberal.

All of this sharply differentiated the Edgeworths from the great majority of their fellow Longford Protestant gentry, whose 'desperately tiresome long formal dinners' they sometimes suffered, listening to talk of 'claret, horses and dogs' from the men and 'dress and scandal' from the women. As the larger landowners were non-resident, county society was dominated by a 'kind of half-gentry or mock-gentry', despised by the Edgeworths as '*middlemen* who relet the lands and live upon the produce, not only in idleness, but in insolent idleness'.[40] These 'journeymen gentlemen' were generally also ultra-Protestant in politics and increasingly dominant in the magistracy and yeomanry. In Maria's opinion they were totally unsuited to such roles, being 'men without education, experience or hereditary respectability' so that 'in these new characters they bustled and bravadoed: and sometimes from mere ignorance and sometimes in certainty of party support or public indemnity, they over leaped the bounds of law'.[41] Everything about Richard Lovell Edgeworth was an affront to this dominant group - his paternalistic estate, his scrupulous fairness on the bench, and above all his seemingly radical politics.

Maria never fully shared his libertarian ideology and the reflection of her father's views in the novels had always been mediated through an innately conservative cast of mind.[42] Before his death he had come closer to her position, and in a memorandum 'on the political part of my life' regretted that 'my opinions then went further than I can now approve'. His claim that he had never supported those who 'were led further away from the influence of aristocracy than was prudent' seems to be borne out by his daughter's account, which stresses his role in defusing the crisis of 1783 by opposing the more radical Volunteer proposals. Maria, however, exaggerated his role in this crisis, and omitted all mention of his continued involvement with the increasingly radical reform movement during the following years.[43] This silence was in line with her father's final thoughts on the matter, but there are similar, if less obvious, silences in the novels, whose Edgeworthian heroes lack any overt political dimension. Nothing obscured Richard Lovell Edgeworth's comparative radicalism in the eyes of his Longford neighbours, however, at the time of his arrival in the year of seeming reform triumph, 1782. Immediately caught up in 'the public enthusiasm' for Grattan, he issued an address to the Volunteers of Longford, stressing his support for further reform and above all for Catholic relief.[44]

Edgeworth's isolation in the county became more marked and dangerous for the family in the heightened atmosphere of the early 1790s, with, on the one hand, the growth of sectarian peasant violence in the Defender movement, and on the other, in consequence of the wartime economic boom, the increased power and influence of the *arriviste* 'mock-gentry', made up of 'graziers, land-jobbers and middlemen'. In 1793, the major reform giving Catholics the vote, forced on the Irish parliament by the British government, destabilized Irish society.[45] In a letter from Clifton in England, where the family were temporarily resident, Edgeworth had sent an address to the Catholics of Longford in 1792 offering to serve their cause while regretting their failure to support the wider cause of parliamentary reform - precisely the position of United Irishmen like Tone a year later.[46] In 1793, the disturbances in Ireland made it a matter of 'duty' to return and he was soon immersed in 'the glory of commanding a squadron of horse' against the '*sans cullotism*' of the local Defenders.

His correspondence with Erasmus Darwin in this period shows a wish to dissociate the reform movement from what was happening. Sympathy for 'the lowest order of the people' who had 'been long oppressed' and 'are ignorant', was balanced by fear that 'the most horrid calamities may ensue'. He feared 'an insurrection of such people must be infinitely more horrid, than anything that has happened in France'. Even in Maria's deliberately light-hearted and politically neutral letters to her favourite aunt, Ruxton, some of the local horror of Defenderism and the state of siege in which the family ultimately lived, is apparent. Her fear of having 'my throat cut ... by a man with his face blackened with charcoal' was matched by her contempt for the ultra-Protestant Granard Rangers, whose activities only made matters worse. Her father's decision in the midst of all of this to contest Longford county in the 1797 election may have been politically naïve but it represented an attempt to cash in on his well-known championship of their cause with the new Catholic electorate. In fact that vote, in so far as it existed in 1797, was firmly controlled by the dominant landlord interests, and in seeking it, Edgeworth confirmed his political isolation in the county and ensured that the danger to his family in 1798 came as much from the ultra-Protestants as from the rebels.[47]

The rebellion first appears in the *Memoirs* as a background to her father's fourth marriage, which takes place in Dublin in the grip of panic, after the discovery of a widespread 'conspiracy'; the journey home was 'through a part of the country that was in actual insurrection'. The emphasis of the *Memoirs* is initially on the difference between her father's even-handed approach and the violent Protestantism of the majority of magistrates and yeoman commanders in the county, which alienated the people from 'the authority ... on their obedience to which the safety of all ranks depends'.[48] By September, symptoms of rebellion were evident 'even in the county of Longford', in anticipation of the arrival of the French, and Edgeworth focused more on the problem of the peasantry.

Those around Granard were believed to be 'leagued in secret rebellion', and while Edgeworth's own tenants were thought to be trustworthy, undoubtedly 'there were disaffected persons in the vicinity'. Despite continued lack of arms the Edgeworthstown corps remained active and loyal even after the 'dreaded news' of the arrival of the French. When the time had come for the family to take refuge in Longford, they had a fortunate escape in refusing the escort of an ammunition wagon, which blew up shortly afterwards on the road. A few hours later, as Maria recounted to her aunt,

We were obliged to fly from Edgeworthstown. The pike men, three hundred in number, actually were within a mile of the town. My mother, aunt Charlotte and I rode; passed the trunk of the dead man, bloody limbs of horses ...[49]

Simply because there was no room for her in the wagon, their English housekeeper remained behind, and this accident was to save the family home. The leader of the rebel group which laid waste the village protected the house because of a kindness the housekeeper had once done his wife. This, however, added to the suspicion and dislike of Richard Lovell among the ultra-Protestant faction, and the relief felt at the news of the defeat of the French at Ballinamuck and the virtual end of the rebellion, was manifested partly in Orange violence against Edgeworth in Longford town, from which he was rescued by the army. Maria in the *Memoirs* used the same term for his attackers as she had used for the rebels - 'the mob'. Returning through the shattered village, they found the house untouched. The same day, Maria wrote to her cousin:

The scenes we have gone through for some days past have succeeded one another like the pictures in a magic lantern and have scarcely left an impression of reality upon the mind. It all seems like a dream, a mixture of the ridiculous and the horrid.[50]

Neither her understated and unemotional account in the *Memoirs*, written nearly twenty years later, nor the reassuring tone of the family correspondence, should obscure how closely and personally the horrors of 1798 touched Maria and her father. His first instinct after it was over was to abandon the country, telling his father-in-law that he preferred to live in England 'among men, instead of warring against savages' – an epithet which embraced the 'sanguinary party' of both sides.[51]

Instead he satisfied himself with trying to have the yeoman sergeant who incited 'the mob' in Longford court-martialled, and with getting rid of those few tenants of his own 'on a remote estate' who had joined the rebels and were 'never readmitted'. However, he found some means of rewarding the rebel leader who had saved the house, Maria noting how this man's conduct showed 'Irish acuteness and knowledge of character' in understanding the sense of obligation created. Despite a reassuring visit to the English camp at Ballinamuck, the threat to Edgeworthstown did not lift at once. On 2 October, Maria is concerned that if her father carries out his threat to return to England, 'the R.C.'s in this neighbourhood, who are now kept quiet by my father's example and influence, will inevitably rise when he is gone' – and a letter of the following day records rumour of another outbreak in Granard, as a result of which 'all the windows in this house are built halfway up, guns and bayonets dispensed by Captain Lovell in every room'. Her sense of the continuity between their harrowing experiences of native Irish revolt and those of earlier generations is clear in a characteristically humorous letter of 1800. She describes to Letty Ruxton a walk

to see the old Castle of Cranalagh from which Lady Edgeworth was in the time of the last rebellion (but one) turned out naked, I should say without clothes to a lady of your delicacy – God save that we may never be turned out in the same way – especially as this is very raw weather for Lady Godiva's and peeping Toms of Coventry.[52]

This fear, so expressive of vulnerability, also points to a recurring motif in many colonist accounts of rebel atrocities, ever since the time the Edgeworths first came to Ireland.

It has been argued above that this state of siege from a hostile peasant world was reflected in the novel which was begun before the storm of 1798 broke and finished after it subsided – *Castle Rackrent*. The Edgeworths' experience of the rebellion was to receive more overt treatment in her next Irish novel, *Ennui* (1809). This not only anticipates many of the details and much of the language of the account in the *Memoirs* (1820), it also initially domesticates the rebellion, both in the sense of focusing the threat on yet another house servant, and in making it relatively harmless by the employment of humour and anecdote. Here again the family history is reversed as the English man-servant of the lethargic and uncomprehending Lord Glenthorn, the returned absentee, leaves at the outbreak of the rebellion, and is replaced by 'that half-witted Irishman, Joe Kelly, who had ingratiated himself with me by a mixture of drollery and simplicity'. Glenthorn is slow to appreciate the reality of the threat, in part because (as in Edgeworthstown) 'my tenantry had not yet been contaminated by the epidemic infection'. When he is finally roused to take part in suppressing the uprising, he does so in a manner that gains him the enmity of 'the violent party of my neighbours'.[53] Glenthorn treats the whole episode as rather a joke, regretting the initial suppression of the rebellion, which had been the best cure he had found for his boredom!

The account in *Ennui* of the post-rebellion situation was to be reused by Maria a decade later in completing her father's *Memoirs* - a remarkable example of correspondence between literary and historical texts. The tone of aristocratic disdain towards the lower-class Protestants who were prominent in quashing the uprising is clear in both accounts, almost to the point of making their upstart pretensions the real threat to the social order.[54]

By contrast, the peasant threat, largely suppressed in the *Memoirs*, becomes dominant in *Ennui*, when, as had happened in Edgeworthstown, the danger of rebellion returns. The supposedly half-witted Irish servant, who by now has 'secured considerable influence over my indolence', is discovered by a loyal servant to be not only 'a *united man* and stirring up the rubbles [rebels] again here', but also the leader of a plot to kidnap the hero, and ultimately to 'give the castle to Joe Kelly, and the plunder all among them entirely'. The plot is foiled in a standard melodramatic manner, but the castle and estate do indeed fall to 'peasant' ownership, when the blacksmith, Christy Donoghue, is discovered to be the real Glenthorn. The theme of colonist insecurity thus reverberates throughout the novel, more clearly than in the later account in the *Memoirs*. In Joe Kelly, the threat of subversion from below, covert in Thady Quirk, was made overt and given dramatic contemporary form. The line connecting the United Irish rebels with the Gaelic rebels of Spenser's account, suggested in the first footnote to *Castle Rackrent*, is finally made clear in *Ennui*. Edgeworth's fictional account of 1798, therefore, combines many elements of her own experience of the event with the underlying fears of her class, but it does so in a semi-comic manner which reduces the sense of trauma and horror.[55]

Instead of carrying out his threat of returning to England, Richard Lovell Edgeworth decided that the lesson to be learned from his experience in 1798 was 'that he ought to mix more with society and make himself more generally known in Ireland'. He had already become an MP for the pocket borough of St John's Town, with the intention of campaigning for better education for the poor. Inevitably, he was also caught up in the debate on the main government measure to deal with the aftermath of 1798, the Union. His attitude was characteristically idiosyncratic:

I am a unionist, but I vote and speak against the union now proposed to us ... It is intended to force this measure down the throats of the Irish, though five-sixths of the nation are against it. Now I think such a union as would identify the nations so that Ireland should be as Yorkshire to Great Britain, would be an excellent thing; yet I also think that the good people of Ireland ought to be *persuaded* of this truth, and not to be dragooned into submission.

Assimilation to English models was central to the whole Edgeworthstown experiment, and the Union offered the possibility of a more stable environment for the reforming public man and landlord, and of reducing the threat to the colonial settlement. 'The hope of establishing the Catholic religion and Catholic claims to antient forfeitures must be radically destroyed by melting the people of both countries into one mass,' he wrote to a correspondent during the debate.[56]

That he had worries about the negative possibilities of the new system was evident in the tentative discussion of the Union in the preface and afterword which he encouraged Maria to add as part of the explanatory framework to *Castle Rackrent* - the main text of which was completed during his absence at the Dublin parliament. In the 'Preface' Maria seemed to welcome the time 'when Ireland loses her identity with an union with Britain', if only because it may wean Irish Protestants from 'attachment to their identity' as this was defined by their dissolute ancestors. In the brief epilogue, however, raising the question of whether the Union 'will hasten or retard the amelioration of this country', she seems to fear the latter, declaring that 'the few gentlemen of education' would go to England and be replaced by 'British manufacturers', whose influence no one could predict.[57] By the time *The Absentee* appeared twelve years later, a more determined optimism is brought to bear on the basic problem of increased aristocratic absenteeism, although the damage it inflicts is also depicted with a savage irony. The Clonbronys represent the new breed of post-Union absentees, who not only dissipate their rent-rolls in England and neglect the proper administration of their property in Ireland, but also make themselves ridiculous by an affectation of fashionable manners and accents. Their idealistic son, Lord Colambre, although brought up to despise Ireland and grateful for the education which made him 'a British nobleman', has retained some commitment to 'his native country' and returns to judge it for himself.

Dublin is a revelation, a city of commercial vitality, great elegance and good society; his guide, the English officer Sir James Brook, explains that after the Union there had been a great deterioration, as a gross class of entrepreneurs had replaced the fleeing nobility, but things had settled down and the social mix of returning gentry and the more talented survivors of the new business class was superior to the corrupt pre-Union society. While the novel proceeds to make fun of the absurdity and bad taste of the *nouveau riche* grocer's wife, Mrs Rafferty, this is put in perspective as a middle-class version of Lady Clonbrony's equally absurd pretensions, and the main emphasis of the novel is on the potential of the new system as an environment for an enlightened anglicizing landlordism.[58] Paralleling her father's disengagement from the political arena after 1800, the three later Irish novels of Maria Edgeworth focus on contrasting models of good and bad landlordism, in line with the Edgeworthstown experience which she was later to describe in the second volume of the *Memoirs*. While modifying its political organization, the Union had not changed the underlying colonial basis of Irish society, and this basis persists as central to both the 'fictional' and 'factual' representations of Edgeworthian landlordism, to which we finally turn.

III

The fictions came first in this instance – three highly schematic and didactic novels, whose main purpose was to present contrasting models of good and bad landlordism as vital factors in the moral education of their heroes. The *Memoirs* summarize the lessons developed in the novels, and are less concerned with an *account* of her father's experience than with 'the facts and principles upon which he acted'. While her father's ideas seem to dominate the novels as much as the *Memoirs*, Maria's depiction of these ideas was very much her own, and coloured by both a more conservative cast of mind than his and a more romantic sense of the exoticism of Irish life. She never altogether lost the sense of wonder with which her return to Ireland was invested – a fifteen-year-old liberated from the horrors of boarding-school in England and suddenly the constant companion of an idolized but hitherto remote father. Her initial excitement is echoed years later in the novels – in the classic colonial scene in *The Absentee* when Lord Colambre, stepping off the boat in Dublin, finds himself 'surrounded and attacked by a swarm of beggars and harpies, with strange figures and stranger tones', and in the hero's moonlight arrival in *Ennui* to a welcome which 'gave me an idea of my own consequence beyond anything which I had ever felt in England', and where 'my imagination was seized by the idea of remoteness from civilised society'.[59]

Their house, as the Edgeworths found it, is clearly the model for that in *Castle Rackrent*: in an awkward angle at the end of the village street and characterized by 'damp, dilapidation, waste! … Painting, glazing, roofing, fencing, finishing – all were wanting.' To the end of her life, however, she also recalled her delight at finding snow on the roses outside the door, although it was June,[60] and Edgeworthstown always retained a magical quality for her. This focused above all else on the eloquence of peasant speech, which threatened to overwhelm the hero in *Ennui* as it had her father, with 'such a perplexing and provoking mixture of truth and fiction, involved in language so figurative and tones new to my English ears'.[61] Her main concern was the way in which their speech reflected the moral condition of the peasantry. Its calculated fluency and false servility were the consequences of a harsh exploitative landlordism: peasant speech in Edgeworth's fiction was the defence mechanism of a vulnerable people and a barometer of the moral evils of their alienation from social superiors. It represented the climate which the model landlordism of her father had to overcome, the psychological barrier to improvement, as well as a rich source of amusement and study.

The critique of traditional landlordism in *Castle Rackrent* concentrated on the evils of the middleman system, and Jason Quirk's ultimate victory was that of the agent-middleman who exploits the non-residence and indifference of successive landlords to take over the estate. Defining, in an explanatory note, 'the characteristics of middlemen' as 'servility to his superiors and tyranny towards his inferiors', Edgeworth emphasizes how this was indicated in the language of the poor:

In speaking to them, however, they always used the most abject language, and the most humble tone and posture - 'Please your honour - and please your honour's honour', they knew must be repeated as a charm at the beginning and end of every equivocating, exculpatory or supplicatory sentence ...

Indeed, the ironic subversiveness of Thady's language throughout the main text is an example of similar manipulation of language, learned from a succession of masters. Sir Murtagh was a resident, hard-working landlord, but of the old tyrannical sort, endlessly exploiting the law to squeeze more money from his unfortunate tenants. The result was detrimental to peasant morality; in Thady's words, 'so he taught 'em all, as he said, to know the law of landlord and tenant'. This had an effect on peasant language also. A note in the 'Glossary' explains how 'almost every poor man in Ireland ... is ... occasionally a lawyer' - and the returned absentees in *Ennui* and *The Absentee* are surprised by their tenantry's knowledge of legal terms and their employment in the language of servile supplication with which they bombarded their new masters.[62]

In *Ennui*, Lord Glenthorn's early indiscriminate generosity, which had such ill effects, is due to the fact that 'the rhetoric of my tenants succeeded in some instances'. This great flood of peasant speech, which all but overwhelms him in his first days on the estate, is related to the 'power seemingly next to despotic' which he could exercise over people who 'altogether gave more the idea of vassals than of tenants and carried my imagination centuries back to feudal times'. A major theme of the novel is the way in which such power could be used by the modern enlightened landlord or agent for both the material and moral welfare of the tenants, but only if he counteracted the damage done by traditional landlord perspectives, which were essentially rooted in a more abrasive colonial mentality. Thus the bad agent in *Ennui*, Hardcastle, shows the real basis for his tyrannical regime in his attack on the proposal that the poor should be educated. By contrast the good agent, M'Leod, makes an appeal to the enlightened self-interest of the tenants, on the principles of Adam Smith.[63]

In *The Absentee*, Edgeworth presents the reader with two different examples of the evils of traditional landlordism. In the first of these, the ramshackle quasi-Gaelic Killpatrickstown, the emphasis is again on the moral degeneracy of the tenants as reflected in their language. The idealistic Lord Colambre is brought there by Lady Dashfort, an Englishwoman who regards the Irish as 'Barbarians' who must be taught 'manners and fashions' by 'the civilised English'. In selecting the worst examples of 'the old uneducated race', she was guided 'by the first sound of the voice, the drawling accent on your "honour", or "my lady"'. Their 'habits of self-contradiction' could then be exposed: 'their servility and flattery one moment, and their litigious and encroaching spirit the next'.[64]

The Killpatricks are well-meaning, but ineffectual; by contrast, the second example of a badly run estate in this novel is given as

the picture ... of that to which an Irish estate and Irish tenantry may be degraded in the absence of those whose duty and interest it is to reside in Ireland, to uphold justice by example and authority; but who, neglecting this duty, commit power to bad hands and bad hearts; abandon their tenantry to oppression and their property to ruin.

The villain of the piece is Garraghty, the Irish agent to whom half of the estate had been entrusted, a 'perfect picture of an insolent petty tyrant'. His systematic abuse of the law and injustice to his tenants have demoralized the latter to 'wrangling, brawling, threatening, whining, drawling, cajoling, cursing and every variety of wretchedness'. When Garraghty is exposed and dismissed by the hero, the language of the peasant response is again emphasized, but this time it offers hope for the success of the returning, reforming absentee - 'the true thing ... and the *rael* gentleman'. The novel ends with Larry Brady's delight that 'The master's come home - long life to him,' and his belief that, as 'he knows the *natur* of us', he will be able to 'do what he pleases with us'.[65] Good resident landlords could replace the false language of servility with the 'true' language of traditional deference.

In *Ormond* the varieties of landlordism to which the young hero is exposed are central to his education in correct moral principles. The estate of his apostate anglicized guardian, Sir Ulick O'Shane, is depicted in the opening chapter as being in a state of siege, sheltering behind locked gates from a 'revengeful' people at the behest of his English wife. Relations with the tenants are also soured by Sir Ulick's 'haughty and tyrannical' son, Marcus, who is made worse by a brief inglorious residence in England. Considering himself to be 'more than half an Englishman ... he vented his ill humour on his countrymen, on the poor Irish peasants - the natives, as he termed them in derision. He spoke of them always as if they were slaves; he considered them as barbarians and savages.' Such discredited colonial attitudes provoke the only act of peasant retaliation in Edgeworth's fiction, but for the most part, the tenantry learned that 'cringing and flattery easily won his favour'. Sir Ulick, more interested in his political career as a Dublin Castle hack than in his estate, corrupts peasant morality in a different way, encouraging them to make up their rents illegally by plundering the wrecks on the coast. These tenants were 'an idle, profligate, desperate set of people', whose relationship with their landlord is again defined by the language they use - praising him as 'the kind gentleman that understands the law for the poor'.[66]

While Sir Ulick thus operated by 'bribery, favour and protection', his cousin 'King Corney' preserves the traditional Gaelic system on the isolated Black Islands, where Ormond next stays. Archaic farming practices such as ploughing by the tail are followed, but the real evil of his system is 'the life of lawless freedom' which it allows Ormond, and especially the temptations which flow from the excessive loyalty of the people, accorded to him as Corney's heir. In return, they expected 'there'd be fine hunting and shooting and carousing continually'. However, while the life-style of this 'barbarian mock-monarch' may be undermining of that of 'civilised society', and involve much 'ingenious casuistry', it is preferable to that of Sir Ulick; and the hereditary loyalty of the people to their chief could be exploited in the interests of an Edgeworthian experiment in

improving landlordism, typified in *Ormond* by Sir Herbert Annally. He becomes
the ultimate role-model of the hero, who chooses to return to the Black Islands
at the end of the novel with the intention of

further civilising the people of the islands, all of whom were warmly attached to him.
They considered Prince Harry as the lawful representative of their King Corney, and
actually offered up prayers for his coming again to reign over them.

The manipulation of language was also a feature of Annally's approach. He
'governed neither by threats, punishments, abuse, nor tyranny', and treated his
tenants 'neither as slaves subject to his will, nor as dupes, nor objects on which
to exercise his wit or his cunning'. Instead 'he treated them as reasonable beings.
… He spoke sense to them; he mixed that sense with wit and humour, in the
proportion necessary to make it palatable to an Irishman.' Given that he is the
character in her novels most clearly modelled on her father, it is interesting how
shadowy a figure he is - the emphasis is all on the general principles upon which
he operates and the effect that his approach has on peasant character, so that even
'their countenance had changed from the look of desponding idleness and
cunning to the air of busy, hopeful independence'.[67] The only specific feature on
his estate which parallels the Edgeworthstown experience is the non-denominational school in which the bright peasant boy gets a chance of advancement, to
the dismay of another set of middle-class Protestant bigots, the McCrules. The
two earlier novels which feature Irish landlordism contain more impressive
fictional representations of the Edgeworthstown experiment.

In *Ennui* the initial enthusiasm of the hero for his 'feudal' power is dampened
by the stolid, efficient Scots agent, M'Leod, who quotes Adam Smith in a
successful campaign to stop Glenthorn's indiscriminate charity, especially the
granting of high wages and long leases. M'Leod gives the standard economic
analysis of the evils of the Irish land system, and on his own estate, after twenty-
six years of patient endeavour and good example, has produced spectacular
results. This novel was published twenty-six years after her father had returned
to reside at Edgeworthstown, and M'Leod's estate (which also featured a model
non-denominational school) is clearly how Maria would like a visitor to perceive
her father's achievement. Glenthorn's comment is particularly revealing: 'There
was nothing wonderful in anything I saw around me, but there was such an air
of neatness and comfort, order and activity, in the people and in their cottages
that I almost thought myself in England, and I could not forbear exclaiming,
"How could all this be brought about in Ireland?"'[68] The anglicization of the Irish
countryside was the aim of modern improving landlords, as it had been, in
Spenser's account, of the earlier colonization projects.

It had also been the objective of Glenthorn's initial generosity to his tenants,
and in his disappointment at the failure of this experiment he makes the
comparison with the Elizabethan experience. When his old nurse Ellinor turns
the English cottage he had built for her into 'a scene of dirt, rubbish and

confusion', he calls her in anger 'a savage, an Irishwoman and an ungrateful fool' and decides 'it was in vain to attempt to improve or civilise such people as the Irish'. On cooler reflection, he realizes that the current state of Ireland paralleled that of Elizabethan England, and that he was wrong to expect 'to do the work of two hundred years in a few months ... as if any people could be civilised in a moment'.[69] The project was still what Spenser had called 'civilite' - the reshaping of every aspect of Irish life and society on English lines. This was now to be informed by the principles of the Enlightenment but the colonial project still had to cope with the traditional problem of Irish resistance and rebellion.

This project is emphasized less in *The Absentee*. While the hero is encouraged to read Spenser and Sir John Davies's *Discovery of the true causes why Ireland was never entirely subdued* (published in 1612), on his arrival in Dublin, he is also pointed in the direction of Arthur Young's 1780 classic, *A Tour in Ireland*.[70] This detailed survey of the Irish land system, focusing on estate management and agricultural practices and prices on a wide variety of Irish estates, was the bible of improving landlords and it is an important subtext in *The Absentee*. Here, as in Young, a range of estates are represented, although in moral rather than economic terms: the ramshackle traditionalism of Killpatrickstown, with its degraded clan ethos, balanced by the brief description of the Oranmore estate, an example of 'what had been done by the influence of great proprietors residing on their own estates and encouraging the people by judicious kindness'. The device of the good and bad agent is reused in the description of the absentee's own estate, the management of which is divided between the rack-renting immoral Garraghty, and the exemplary Mr Burke, respected by all classes 'from the brogue to the boot'.

This is the verdict of the local innkeeper, who also blames the depredations of Garraghty on the absentee landlord, who 'might as well be a West Indian planter and we negroes, for anything he knows to the contrary'. The comparison is revealing - absenteeism was a discredited form of colonialism. The resident enlightened landlord, by contrast, would not only bring prosperity and justice to his tenants, but would give them an English education. This is the feature of Burke's system most stressed in the novel, his model non-denominational school, run on modern Bell and Lancaster lines. As later, in *Ormond*, such a school is seen as the solution to the sectarian conflict which, especially since the early 1790s, had come to the fore in landlord-tenant relations.

Like Mr Burke, Richard Lovell Edgeworth tended to see himself as 'a plain man, [who] made it a rule not to meddle with speculative points, and to avoid all irritating discussions; he was not to rule the country but to live in it, and make others live as happily as he could'.[71] Despite his wide reading and intellectual interests, he saw his social and (after 1800) his political role as being that of offering a practical example and a moral lesson to his fellow landlords. This is a key element of his portrayal by his daughter in the second volume of the *Memoirs*.[72] On one level, the *Memoirs* detail her father's reforms and their effects, and offer important evidence of his experiment in model landlordism; on another level, there are equally important insights into the enduring colonist attitudes that could still lie behind such experiments.

Richard Lovell's father may have saved the estate from ruin and placed it on a sound legal footing, but, as Marilyn Butler puts it, 'he was a typical Anglo-Irish landlord in everything except his excellent book-keeping'.[73] He had no interest in agricultural improvement, and followed the conventional patterns of estate management, allowing long leases and subdivision. Under the agent who ran the estate after his death, while his heir lived mainly in England, the economic situation became perilous, the rents declining during a period when the Irish agricultural economy was showing steady improvement. The returned absentee of 1782, therefore, had pressing economic reasons for reforming the management of the estate. How he went about the task is described in general terms by his daughter: taking the direction of affairs directly into his own hands, getting rid not only of the agent but of 'petty tyrants' like the 'drivers', who had enforced rent collection. Instead he received his own rents directly, got to know all his tenants personally, and became 'master of the value of the different land on his estate'. When leases fell in he replaced them with shorter terms and favoured industrious tenants. He respected 'his *tenants' right*, as it is called', but ignored the mere plea of 'I have lived under your Honour, or your Honour's father or grandfather.' He devised an 'alienation fine' to prevent subletting, and abolished 'any oppressive claims of duty-fowl-of-duty work'. He tried, with less success, to abolish the 'cottager system' for labourers, which produced 'a state of dependence too nearly approaching to slavery'. As a magistrate, he administered the law impartially, favouring neither his own tenants nor his own religion.

By this means, Maria concludes, he did 'succeed altogether beyond his most sanguine hopes in meliorating the condition of the people. Especially in the last twenty years, his tenantry, and the whole face of his estate, strikingly improved in appearance and essentially in reality.'[74] He also achieved a substantially increased rent-roll, although not much above the general level of increase and, with the agricultural depression which succeeded the end of the Napoleonic Wars in 1815, not enough to pay the generous legacies to his children in his will. Add to all of this his encouragement of modern agricultural methods and his reclamation of bogland, and Edgeworth emerges as the very model of the improving, paternalistic, resident landlord advocated by Arthur Young. There was also, however, an important colonial element to Edgeworth's second volume of *Memoirs*, which echoes some of the themes and concerns of the first volume, and of the novels.[75]

Maria, in several places, describes her father in 1782 as 'coming to settle in Ireland',[76] a phrase implying perhaps an attitude and commitment akin to that of his Elizabethan ancestor. This is reinforced by the manner in which his main problem (like that of the returned absentees of the novels) is depicted as that of coping with the habits and psychology of the natives. Reforming the middleman system was relatively easy compared to the challenge offered by the peasantry in any attempt to promote 'the passage from one state of civilisation to another'. He had to confront the ingrained habits of mind and speech which the corrupt traditional system had taught them. Thus, 'he often "rated them roundly" when they stood before him, perverse in litigation, helpless in procrastination, detected in cunning or convicted of falsehood'. Alternatively he exploited 'their prejudices', including their love of 'eloquence' and their 'instinct for the *real gentleman*', or the fact that 'they really are more attached by what touches their hearts, than by what concerns their interests'. Thus, the traditional stereotype of the native Irish was confirmed by experience, and offered the key to reform. It necessitated, above all, guarding

against his own good nature and generosity ... If the people had found or suspected him to be weak, or, as they call it, easy, there would have been an end to all hope of really doing them good. They would have cheated, loved and despised a mere easy landlord; his property would have gone to ruin, without either permanently bettering their interests or their morals. He, therefore, took especial care that they should be convinced of his strictness in punishing, as well as of his desire to reward.

By such means did her father show that 'he was fit to live in Ireland'. A major motivation in taking estate management out of the hands of middlemen was to gain the power 'to encourage and reward' his tenants. This 'keeps up the connexion and dependence, which there ought to be between the different ranks, without creating any servile habits, or leaving the improving tenants insecure'.[77] However, even when the language of analysis was that of class, the tenants were always viewed as 'lower Irish' (an important implication being that the Edgeworths were not Irish) whose peculiarities had always been the basic problem for colonial control in Ireland.

Colonist perspectives likewise informed Richard Lovell Edgeworth's support for a state educational system, which would integrate the poor into society, and his plan for a model school at Edgeworthstown as the best means of tackling the fundamental question of the moral character of the peasantry.[78] His was an optimistic analysis, but even as she presents it in the *Memoirs*, Maria feels obliged to distance herself somewhat from it, commenting especially on his 'important mistake' in believing that education in itself would improve conduct, and taking too little account of the weaknesses of human nature, the effects of passion, and 'the hurricane of the soul'. She was, however, proud of his achievement at Edgeworthstown, and shared his sense of it. A letter of 1819 to her sister-in-law describes a visit of some English friends - now a regular occurrence.

Another morning we took a tour of the tenants. Hugh Kelly's house and parlour and gates and garden, and all that should accompany a farmhouse, as nice as any England could afford. James Allen, though grown very old, and in a forlorn shag wig, looked like a respectable yeoman ...

Thus an anglicized Edgeworthstown fulfilled the Spenserian dream, but she was always aware that it resembled an oasis in a hostile environment. On a visit in 1822 to Lord Dillon's estate in the neighbouring county of Roscommon, she recorded the contrast - the 'gaunt famine-struck tenants', their 'absurd' and archaic Jacobitism and the fact that 'most of them talk more Irish than English'.[79] This traditional view of native encirclement was, however, about to be superseded by fear of its new phase, in the guise of O'Connellite democratic politics. Education, in the broad sense, was to prove a two-edged weapon, and the Edgeworthstown estate could not be isolated from danger. By the mid 1830s the blight of sectarian politics had destroyed the patterns of paternalism and deference which her father's reforms had established. Her response to this process can be found in her letters, but not in her fiction, nor in her long manuscript appendix to her grandfather's 'Black Book', written mainly in 1839. The emphasis in that document is on her success in keeping together the family's lands, and her pride that all those her grandfather had listed still featured in the rent-rolls. Her successors must, above all, ensure that such lands 'will not go out of the family'.[80]

This perspective also shaped her response during this period to the rapidly changing 'public scene', and a detailed analysis of this can be found in Butler and Hurst.[81] Her support for Catholic Emancipation owed less to the liberal principles her father had championed in the 1780s and 1790s than to a pragmatic assessment of its potential for diffusing crisis. It would make 'the people ... contented and quiet. English capital ... will flow over here, set industry in motion all over this country, and induce habits of punctuality, order, economy.' Above all, 'the safety of the Protestant Establishment in Ireland requires Catholic Emancipation'. Balancing such optimistic calculation was her fear of 'democracy ... the monstrous, the disgusting absurdity of letting the many-headed, the greasy many-headed monster rule. The French Revolution gave us enough of the majority of the people.' This fear was not made public, however, and the Edgeworths were regarded as whole-hearted supporters of the Emancipation cause, as Fergus O'Ferrall's account in this volume shows. That the incipient threat involved could be seen as the latest in the long series endured by this colonist family since the early seventeenth century is reflected in the remarkable fact that among those most active in the Catholic cause in the area were a Nugent and several O'Ferralls - members of the original Old English and Gaelic Irish families whose dispossession was the basis of the Edgeworthstown estate.[82]

The Emancipation campaign effectively polarized Longford politics along sectarian lines, and as this worked through in successive elections in the 1830s, Maria's optimism disappeared, and her letters and those of her family were full of the danger posed by 'the mob' led by O'Connell to 'the Protestant aristocracy of this county', who may be driven out 'between the danger from armed mobs, nightly depredators and daily insults'. Maria particularly disliked the new political priesthood, and when the contagion finally spread to her own estate, the local priests were active in urging the tenants to vote against the landlord interest. The defection of three of the longest-established tenants (one of them a Langan) in the 1835 election led to her momentarily giving in to pressure to punish them, by calling in the customary 'hanging gale', or arrears of rent. She found the episode 'shameful' and agonized about it in a letter to her brother, wondering what their father would have done. In the end she concluded that, even though landlord influence was vital to 'the real balance of the British Constitution', it was wrong to meet priestly intimidation in kind. Other means 'to stop, if possible, the power of democracy' should be found.[83]

In subsequent elections an uneasy truce operated – further punishment was not threatened, and the majority of tenants followed the Edgeworth lead. But the damage was done: her father's experiment was in ruins, and the native threat, far from being contained, was poised for a final irresistible attack. Her semi-jocose account of how she defended her political principles in an 1845 conversation with the English cleric and advocate of Catholic Emancipation, Sidney Smith, got to the nub of the matter. 'We poor Protestants', as she put it, didn't wish 'to be trampled upon' by the Catholic majority,

and to have our Church pulled down about our ears, and to have our clergy buried under the rubbish, and their church lands and our estates taken from us. He scoffed at such suppositions. But I appealed to his own knowledge of history regarding the encroaching and predominantly predatory nature and art of Catholics.

Her own knowledge of history had a more local focus, and the 'Catholic' threat to the family had taken many forms since 1641. Its purpose, however, was perceived to be always the same, the recovery of ancient rights to land appropriated through colonization. Her response to the Tithe War, in 1835, offers another instance of her awareness of this. Agreeing that the system was unjust and should be reformed, she felt that it was still wrong to penalize the present owners of tithes, 'because in former times injustice was done in which we had neither act nor part, but took our property as it came to us and made our contracts with tenants honestly'. Whatever its original injustices, the colonial settlement was so built into the fabric of Irish society that it must be accepted. Equally, however, the legacies of 'former times' must be made less abrasive. To the end of her life she continued to dislike Protestant extremism, and to believe that to be *'really liberal'* was to be *'properly* conservative',[84] but her earlier optimism that the ultimate security lay in her father's model and moral landlordism did not long survive his death.

This was the main reason, as Marilyn Butler argues, why she wrote no more Irish novels after *Ormond* in 1817. Her completion of her father's *Memoirs* had also involved summing up the principles which had informed them, and she was not capable of confronting the collapse of her hopes in a different kind of fiction whose theme would be conflict rather than consensus.[85] She did indeed write another important novel, *Helen* (1834), which, among other things, finally celebrated the rights of women to hold independent political opinions. It was ironic that when she felt most capable of expressing such views, she believed that circumstances prevented their being translated into fiction. Writing to her half-brother, Pakenham, who was a magistrate in India, she told him that *Helen* was finished, but warned him, there is no humour in it and no Irish character. It is impossible to draw Ireland as she now is in a book of fiction - realities are too strong, party passions too violent to bear to see, or care to look at their faces in the looking glass. The people would only break the glass, and curse the fool who held the mirror up to nature - distorted nature in a fever.[86]

Holding 'the mirror up to nature' was a classic statement of eighteenth-century views of fiction, but Edgeworth's novels had never been fully 'realistic', despite their reputation. Instead, elements of realism combined with a range of stereotypes to create 'moral' tales of caring landlords and a grateful deferential peasantry, in which the nature of peasant speech was a barometer of social interaction and morality. The underlying 'realities', especially the unresolved tensions arising from the colonial nature of Irish rural society, were submerged and are even now fully apparent only when the novels are seen in the context of her grandfather's 'Black Book' and her father's *Memoirs*.

NOTES

I am grateful to Clare O'Halloran, Fergus O'Ferrall, Jimmy Kelly, Kevin Whelan and Charlotte Holland for their help in the preparation of this paper, and to the Arts Faculty Fund of University College, Cork.

1. Maria Edgeworth to Fanny Robinson, 17/5/1831, in Michael Hurst, *Maria Edgeworth and the Public Scene: Intellect, Fine Feeling and Landlordism in the Age of Reform* (London 1969), p. 57.
2. E.g. W. A. Maguire, *The Downshire Estates in Ireland, 1801-1845* (Oxford 1972), and the series of articles on the Shelbourne estate by Gerard Lyne in *Journal of the Kerry Archaeological and Historical Society*, no. 12 (1979), *passim*. A large collection of estate papers of the type used by these historians also exists for the Edgeworth estate in this period, P.R.O.I., M 1482-1506, M 3422-3430, D 15899-16017, D 20445, C 3513-3528, T 5549-5560.
3. N.L.I., Ms 7361, ff. 1-2.
4. Maria Edgeworth, 'Appendix to the Black Book'. P.R.O.I., Ms 2320, f. 2.
5. *Memoirs of Richard Lovell Edgeworth: begun by himself and concluded by his daughter, Maria Edgeworth*, 2 vols (London 1820).
6. A fourth layer was added by Maria's stepmother - 'A memoir of Maria Edgeworth, with a selection from her letters, by the late Mrs Edgeworth. Edited by her children'. 3 vols. Not published. Printed in London, 1867.
7. Maria Edgeworth, 'Appendix to the Black Book'. P.R.O.I., Ms 2320, ff. 1-130.
8. W. J. Mc Cormack and Kim Walker (eds), Maria Edgeworth's *The Absentee* (Oxford 1988), pp. ix-xlii.
9. Marilyn Butler, *Maria Edgeworth: A Literary Biography* (Oxford 1972), pp. 16, 112.
10. N.L.I., Ms 7361, ff. 1-85.
11. H. J. Butler and H. E. Butler (eds), *The Black Book of Edgeworthstown and Other Edgeworth Memories, 1585-1817* (London 1927), pp. 12, 26-7. Mc Cormack and Walker, op. cit., pp. xxii-xxxii. See also W. J. Mc Cormack, *Ascendancy and Tradition* (Oxford 1985), pp. 139-47.
12. N.L.I., Ms 7361, f. 3.
13. Maria Edgeworth, *Castle Rackrent, An Hibernian Tale. Taken from facts, and from the*

manners of the Irish squires before the year 1782 (London 1800), pp. 28, 76. The edition used here is that edited by George Watson, Oxford University Press, 1980.

14. E.g. Ciaran Brady and Raymond Gillespie (eds), *Natives and Newcomers: The Making of Irish Colonial Society, 1534-1641* (Dublin 1986), especially Bernadette Cunningham, 'Native culture and political change in Ireland, 1580-1640'; Brian Mac Cuarta, 'Newcomers in the Irish Midlands, 1540-1641', M.A. thesis, U.C.G., 1980.

15. H. J. and H. E. Butler, op. cit., chapters 2-6; C. S. Edgeworth, *Memoirs of the Abbé Edgeworth* (1815).

16. W. L. Renwick (ed.), Edmund Spenser, *A View of the Present State of Ireland* (Oxford 1970). Cf. also N. Canny, 'Edmund Spenser and the development of an Anglo-Irish identity', in *The Yearbook of English Studies*, xiii (1983), pp. 1-19; C. Brady, 'Spenser's Irish crisis: humanism and experience in the 1590s', *Past and Present*, cxi (May 1986).

17. H. J. and H. E. Butler, op. cit., p. 91; Maria Edgeworth, *The Absentee* (vols v and vi of *Tales of Fashionable Life* [London 1812]), Garland facsimile edition (New York 1978), vol. vi, p. 4.

18. *Castle Rackrent*, pp. 7-8. Cf. Tom Dunne, 'Maria Edgeworth and the Colonial Mind', O'Donnell Lecture, National University of Ireland, 1984.

19. Maria Edgeworth, *Ennui* (vol. i of *Tales of Fashionable Life*, London 1812), Garland facsimile edition (New York 1978), pp. 39, 76, 86, 324.

20. Maria Edgeworth, *Ormond, A Tale* (London 1817), Irish University Press reprint (Shannon 1972), pp. 56, 78-9, 399.

21. *Castle Rackrent*, pp. 56-7; P. Dineen and T. O'Donoghue, *Dánta Aodhagáin Uí Rathaille* (1911), no. 21; Tom Dunne, 'The Gaelic response to conquest and colonisation: the evidence of the poetry', in *Studia Hibernica*, xx (1980), pp. 7-30.

22. *Castle Rackrent*, pp. 8-9.

23. *Ennui*, p. 27; *The Absentee*, v, pp. 210, 237, 375; *Ormond*, pp. 43, 64-72, 390.

24. *Ennui*, p. 400; *The Absentee*, vi, pp. 456-63; *Ormond*, p. 399.

25. Cf. Cóilín Owens, *Family Chronicles: Maria Edgeworth's Castle Rackrent* (1987) for a range of modern criticism; Marilyn Butler, op. cit., pp. 126, 174, 240-1.

26. *Castle Rackrent*, pp. 99-114; N.L.I., Edgeworth Ms, nos. 107,116; A. J. C. Hare (ed.), *The Life and Letters of Maria Edgeworth*, 2 vols (London 1894), i, pp. 154-5, 176-7, 231; cf. also the peasant speech in Richard Lovell Edgeworth and Maria Edgeworth, *Essay on Irish Bulls* (London 1802).

27. H. J. and H. E. Butler, op. cit., chapters 3 and 4; Edgeworth, *Memoirs*, ii, pp. 213-32.

28. *Ennui*, p. 304.

29. Cf. Tom Dunne, 'Fiction as "the best history of nations": Lady Morgan's Irish Novels', in Tom Dunne (ed.), *The Writer as Witness: Literature as Historical Evidence* (Cork 1987).

30. *Ennui*, pp. 369-71; cf. also *Ormond*, p. 110.

31. Edgeworth, *Memoirs*, i, p. 233.

32. H. J. and H. E. Butler, op. cit., p. 23n.

33. Ibid., ch. 4; Edgeworth, *Memoirs*, i, pp. 12, 9, 18. Cf. also *Castle Rackrent*, p. 78.

34. *Ennui*, p. 369; *Memoirs*, i, pp. 37-8.

35. *Memoirs*, i, pp. 234-5.

36. *The Absentee*, v, p. 376; *Memoirs*, i, pp. 359-60.

37. *Memoirs*, i, pp. 48, 63; ii, pp. 244, 291-2.

38. Cf. also her satire on the language of the landlord family, the Clonbronys, in *The Absentee*, v, pp. 201-392.

39. Marilyn Butler, op. cit., pp. 59ff; Hare, op. cit., ii, p. 153; N.L.I., Edgeworth Ms,

no. 109, Richard Lovell Edgeworth to Dr Beaufort, 2/3/94.

40. *Memoirs*, ii, pp. 375-6, 139-41; Marilyn Butler, op. cit., pp. 115-16.
41. N.L.I., Edgeworth Ms, no. 126, Maria Edgeworth to Mrs Ruxton, 20/4/95; *The Absentee*, vi, p. 154; *Memoirs*, ii, pp. 205-6.
42. For the influence of her father's politics, see Marilyn Butler, op. cit., p. 456.
43. *Memoirs*, ii, pp. 60-5; Marilyn Butler, op. cit., pp. 95-6.
44. *Memoirs*, ii, pp. 48-51.
45. Ibid., pp. 205-6; Thomas Bartlett, 'The end to moral economy: the Irish militia disturbances of 1793', in *Past and Present*, no. 99 (May 1983).
46. *Memoirs*, ii, p. 148.
47. Ibid., pp. 155-7; Hare, op. cit., i, pp. 41-2, 39; Marilyn Butler, op. cit., p. 119.
48. *Memoirs*, ii, pp. 119-202, 205-7; Hare, op. cit., i, pp. 53-5.
49. Ibid., pp. 209-10; Hare, op. cit., i, p. 56.
50. *Memoirs*, ii, pp. 213-32; Hare, op. cit., i, pp. 59-60.
51. Marilyn Butler, op. cit., p. 141.
52. *Memoirs*, ii, pp. 234-5; N.L.I., Edgeworth Ms, no. 200; Hare, op. cit., i, p. 61; Mc Cormack and Walker, 'Introduction' to *The Absentee*, p. xxxiv.
53. *Ennui*, pp. 222-8.
54. Ibid., p. 232; *Memoirs*, ii, p. 240.
55. *Ennui*, pp. 260, 265. In *The Absentee* the echoes of the rebellion are so faint that only Maria's family were likely to have been aware of the extent that the names of key characters are taken from local place-names, and 'relate closely to the geography of the Edgeworths' survival in 1798'; Mc Cormack and Walker, op. cit., p. 285.
56. *Memoirs*, ii, pp. 237, 246-51, 252-3; N.L.I., Edgeworth Ms, no. 241, 26/1/1800, to an unnamed peer.
57. *Castle Rackrent*, pp. 5, 96-7.
58. *The Absentee*, vi, pp. 1-29.
59. *Memoirs*, ii, pp. 30-1; *The Absentee*, vi, p. 2; *Ennui*, pp. 76-9.
60. *Memoirs*, ii, p. 2; 'A memoir of Maria Edgeworth', i, p. 13; Marilyn Butler, op. cit., p. 81.
61. *Ennui*, p. 85. Cf. also *Memoirs*, ii, p. 3; Marilyn Butler, op. cit., pp. 90-1.
62. *Castle Rackrent*, pp. 20-1, 15, 103-4, 108-9.
63. *Ennui*, pp. 103, 86, 76, 109-11.
64. *The Absentee*, vi, pp. 51-73.
65. Ibid., pp. 202, 219, 201, 227, 456-63.
66. *Ormond*, pp. 15, 22, 265-6, 35.
67. Ibid., pp. 275, 56, 78-9, 51, 399, 275-6, 300.
68. *Ennui*, pp. 103-13, 158-9.
69. Ibid., pp. 122-6.
70. Arthur Young, *A Tour in Ireland; with general observations on the present state of that kingdom, made in the years 1776, 1777, and 1778, and brought down to the end of 1879*, 2 vols (Dublin 1780). Daniel Augustus Beaufort's *Memoir of a Map of Ireland* (1792) is also recommended. See the argument of Mc Cormack and Walker (op. cit., p. 298) that 'the reading list is not so much a body of recommended material, but a chronological sequence indicating various successive policies towards Ireland ... Indeed, *The Absentee* itself might be read as the latest item in such a sequence.'
71. *The Absentee*, vi, pp. 71, 121-31, 133-4.
72. *Memoirs*, ii, pp. 1, 14-15.
73. Marilyn Butler, op. cit., p. 83.
74. *Memoirs*, ii, chapter 11, and p. 368.

75. The colonial theme also features in Young's 'Author's Preface', op. cit., vol. i.

76. *Memoirs*, ii, pp. 34, 331-2. The German traveller, Kohl, noted that Irish landlords often spoke of when their families 'first came over'. J. G. Kohl, *Travels in Ireland* (London 1844), p. 23.

77. *Memoirs*, ii, pp. 19, 3, 37-9, 31-2, 39, 26-30.

78. Ibid., pp. 246-8, 251, 308-13, 457, 460-72.

79. Ibid., p. 402; Hare, op. cit., i, pp. 269-70. Lockhart echoed this description, when staying in Edgeworths town with Scott in 1825. D. J. O'Donoghue, *Sir Walter Scott's Tour in Ireland in 1825* (Glasgow and Dublin 1905), p. 58; W. S. Scott (ed.), *Letters of Maria Edgeworth and Anne Letitia Barbauld* (London 1953), pp. 34-5.

80. Maria Edgeworth, 'Appendix to the Black Book'. Quotes from ff. 56-7, 62, 29, 53, 27, 77-8, 63-4, 113-15.

81. Marilyn Butler, op. cit., pp. 452ff; Hurst, op. cit.

82. Hurst, op. cit., pp. 42, 44, 49-50; Fergus O'Ferrall, 'The emergence of the political community in Longford, 1824-29', p. 123 below. It may be even more remarkable that the leading historian of the Catholic Emancipation movement today should be a Longford O'Ferrall!

83. Hurst, op. cit., pp. 73, 65-6, 77-87; Marilyn Butler, op. cit., p. 454.

84. Hurst, op. cit., pp. 128-31, 91, 86-7, 105.

85. Marilyn Butler, op. cit., pp. 452-5.

86. Hare, op. cit., ii, pp. 202-3, 19/2/34.

The Emergence of the Political Community in Longford, 1824–29

Between 1823 and 1829 the most prominent figure in Irish political life was Daniel O'Connell. The origins of his predominance can be traced to 1823 when he established the Catholic Association in Dublin. His purpose in setting up yet another Catholic organization was to mobilize Irish Catholics into exerting novel popular pressure on the government in order to achieve his objective of Catholic Emancipation. After decades of fruitless effort to win the admission of Catholics to parliament and equality with Protestants, in January 1824 O'Connell found the recipe for ultimate success. He proposed to collect a penny a month from all Catholics as a Catholic Rent. This remarkable device transformed the Catholic Association from a small, middle-class political club in Dublin into a mass movement which politicized the Irish countryside.

In 1825 the government, alarmed at the success of the Association, suppressed it with a law prohibiting permanent organizations. The Rent collection had also to cease. O'Connell, having failed to secure Emancipation by negotiation in London, used his legal ingenuity to revive the organization as the New Catholic Association in late 1825. With the unexpected triumph of Association-backed candidates in the 1826 general election a New Catholic Rent collection was launched to aid the freeholder voters who had dared to oppose their landlords.

From 1826 to 1828 the mass Catholic struggle ebbed and flowed until the final surge towards victory came with O'Connell's election as Member of Parliament for Clare in 1828 which made it impossible for the Wellington government in London to resist his popular organization. The danger that every county might replicate Clare and elect a popular Catholic candidate became a real possibility. Catholic Emancipation was passed in the spring of 1829.

In the national context Longford was not an important county in the campaign for Catholic Emancipation. The aims of this essay are to analyse the response in Longford to the Catholic struggle of the 1820s and to trace the emergence of an O'Connellite political community at local level. Such local communities were not only the basis of future O'Connellite popular politics in the 1830s and 1840s; they signified the birth of Irish democracy.[1]

I

The first response in County Longford to the Catholic Association's Rent plan came in September 1824, eight months after the adoption of the Catholic Rent. The Catholics of Longford town held a meeting at the chapel, in Chapel Lane, to organize the collection of the Rent. According to a hostile eye-witness this meeting 'was composed of all the huxtermen, publicans, and petty fellows of the town and country'.[2] However, it is clear that well-to-do urban Catholics were to the fore: the two who were in contact with the Catholic Association in Dublin in connection with the Rent were Richard Dempsey and Christopher Carbry. Dempsey lived on Bridge Street and in *Pigott's Directory, 1824* is named among the gentry living in the town. Carbry was a local businessman who was a grocer, spirit dealer and general merchant in Main Street. Like many of the shopkeepers in small towns, Carbry also farmed some land. His wealth and property are indicated by the fact that he was registered as a £20 freeholder in 1828 and a £50 freeholder in 1832. Dempsey was a £50 freeholder in Longford during the 1820s.[3]

In October 1824, Carbry made the first returns of Catholic Rent from Longford when he sent just over £11 from the parish of Ballymacormick. The total for the county as a whole for October was a little over £18.[4] By November the Rent collection had spread to other parishes in the county. George Dowdall chaired a Catholic Rent meeting in the parish of Shrule at Ballymahon where a committee of ten was appointed and the last Sunday in every month was fixed for the Rent collection. The Dowdalls were a well-off local family engaged in milling and farming at Terlicken and in the town of Ballymahon. There were four brothers, George, Luke, Henry and Francis, and all became involved in local political activity, especially George and Francis. Resolutions were passed at the Ballymahon meeting thanking the local landlord, John Brady Shuldham, for his £100 donation for repairs to the chapel, and the liberal Protestants of the town for their contributions. These resolutions are evidence of a certain amount of Protestant goodwill towards the Catholic population in an area of the country which had the largest number of Protestants and which was to suffer most from sectarianism during the 1820s, as discussed above by Liam Kennedy and Kerby Miller.[5]

The Rent from County Longford in 1824 was slightly over £50 or about 50p per thousand persons. The Catholic Rent for that first year from Ireland was just over £7500 or about £1.10 per thousand persons.[6] The money collected was of relative insignificance; what was of paramount importance was the organization of parishes under local lay leaders who were in correspondence with a national political organization.

During 1825 the Rent collection spread to at least half of the parishes in Longford. The areas involved included Abbeyshrule, Carrickedmond, Ardagh, Moydow, Granard, Killashee, Templemichael, Columbkille, Ruskey and Edgeworthstown.[7] Priests became active: for example Fr Farrell Sheridan, curate of Granard parish, sent in the sizeable sum of £32. Sheridan became a notable local political activist in the Granard area, where he was parish priest from 1825 to 1849.[8] Other priests who were prominent were Fr Richard O'Ferrall, parish priest of Killashee from 1823 to 1843, and Fr Philip O'Reilly of Columbkille. Both O'Ferrall and O'Reilly were held in special regard by the people, according to MacNamee's *History of the Diocese of Ardagh*. O'Ferrall was remembered 'as a thaumaturgus and a valiant defender of his people against their oppressors' and O'Reilly was 'venerated by the people as a saint before and after his death. They were wont to want to visit his grave for many years to commend themselves to his intercession.'[9]

The total Catholic Rent from County Longford from January 1825 to the dissolution of the Catholic Association in March 1825 was just over £118 which compares favourably with the £50 sent in between September and December 1824.[10] An embryonic framework now covered the county for the politicization of the people and it is important to ask why Longford Catholics, both lay and clerical, responded to the call of the Catholic Association in Dublin.

II

In March 1825 James Magauran, the Catholic Bishop of Ardagh, gave evidence to the Select Committee of the House of Commons on the State of Ireland. Magauran lived at Ballymahon where the largest Protestant population in Longford was concentrated. The bishop referred to the strong feeling on the subject of Catholic Emancipation which existed amongst the bulk of the peasantry:

I know if they were asked what emancipation means, they perhaps would not be able to define it; but they have a feeling that they are belonging to an excluded caste, and that they are not treated like other subjects; that there is something wrong with them, and they are very anxious to be relieved from this kind of slavery which they are not able to explain.[11]

The Catholic Association articulated for the people their sense of oppression and injustice. County Longford in the 1820s suffered from the familiar pattern of Irish agrarian unrest and violence. The county was also marked by a strong Orange presence and in 1824 Protestant fears were expressed about a possible Catholic rising.[12] Robert Sandys, an important landowner of Creevagh, near Ballymahon, wrote to Dublin Castle in February 1824 recommending the 'urgent necessity' of putting County Longford under the Constabulary Act as there were 'continued nightly meetings'.[13]

In December 1824, in the course of reporting a robbery of arms, Gustavus Brooke, Chief Constable, County Longford, stated how he found the October 1824 Rent Report of the Catholic Association on the person or in the cabin 'of almost everyone of the *lower* class and extensively circulated at the chaples [*sic*]...'. In the same months there were reports of an alleged meeting near Granard of

2000 men who were supposed to be plotting to extirpate Protestants.[14] The police reports for the county in 1825 reveal the same 'symptoms of Rockite insubordination', as Brooke termed them, as those of 1823 and 1824. By December 1825 reports indicated that in parts of County Longford the Ribbon or Rockite system was 'in full operation' and the police ascribed the disturbed state of the county to the want of a resident gentry.[15]

Longford was not, however, among the most troubled Irish counties and was not proclaimed (and thereby placed under legal restrictions) as many southern counties were, between 1822 and 1824.[16] It is clear, though, that agrarian grievance underlay the disturbances and now with the Catholic Association religious divisions exacerbated these economic disputes. Protestants represented the economically better off and, being less than one in ten of the population, they were bound to be fearful of the tendencies of resurgent Catholicism. Protestant reactions gave a political and religious interpretation to the disturbances.

Major O'Donoghue, a police inspector, reported after a close examination in County Longford that the combination which existed was confined 'to quite the lowest class and has nothing of a religious or political character in it'.[17] When Protestants found that the Catholic Association was achieving an impressive local response their anxiety about the disturbed rural scene was bound to be greatly increased and, with something of the siege mentality which Tom Dunne describes above, they feared a general uprising though in reality none was being planned.

Bishop Magauran was asked in March 1825 about relationships between Catholics and Protestants in the county and he replied that while there was 'no open hostility', there was 'something of a heat of mind or an irritation'. He attributed this enmity and distrust to

the party feeling of Orangemen and Ribbonmen, and the question of Catholic Emancipation, with the feelings of hope on one side, accompanied with some fear perhaps, and apprehension of the other side, altogether; there are two parties, and they are kept at that kind of distance, arising from a variety of causes, that I am not able to describe.

The grievances felt by Catholics at all levels generated 'the heat of mind' as Protestants feared Catholic incursions upon their status, property and religion. The administration of the law by the Protestant magistrates was an example of an area where Catholics felt they had suffered injustice: Bishop Magauran told the Select Committee that disrespect for the law arose in the people as they 'are of the opinion, that the laws were not made for their protection; they know no part of them, except the penal and the punishing parts'. Magauran maintained that amongst the upper classes there was: 'a strong feeling at the coming on of an assizes, that it was necessary to make examples', and that this was done without sufficient inquiry or regard for justice.[18] However, as Desmond McCabe's essay below shows, these grievances were more perceived than real. The historical consciousness of oppression was reinforced, according to Bishop Magauran, by the 'many traditionary stories regarding the sufferings of their ancestors' which were told 'in their little meetings on winter nights'.[19]

Catholics who had attained some wealth, either through farming or in the towns through business, were anxious to achieve equality with Protestants. Lord Forbes in his evidence to the Select Committee on the State of Ireland noted that the lower orders 'of later years' had taken more interest in Emancipation: 'I never saw it exist before to the same extent.' He believed this interest was founded 'upon a proper feeling of pride; a wish on their part to be placed on a level with their fellow subjects'. Forbes believed that there was a connection between the Catholic question and tranquillity as there was no possibility of peace without Emancipation: it was the only issue which could unite the 'whole mass of Catholics ... in pursuit of one common object ... to obtain an equality of civil privileges'.

Both Forbes and Magauran gave evidence of the participation of both the Catholic clergy and the magistrates in keeping the peace. Forbes noted that the bishops and priests had 'uniformly co-operated' with him and Magauran praised the magistrates in the county, especially Lord Forbes. It is revealing that both men thought the county tranquil while the police, who had a generally hostile relationship with the people, reported rural unrest. Given the state of many counties in Ireland there was what might be termed an 'acceptable level' of violence in County Longford.[20]

The latent conflict between the 'two parties' in the county identified by Magauran preceded the rise of the Catholic Association but the O'Connellites harnessed the feelings of the Catholic people to support the national campaign and so brought the conflict to the surface. In December 1824, for instance, there was widespread fear in the county's Protestant community that a general Catholic uprising was about to take place. The alarm was associated with the circulation of Pastorini's *Prophecies* which was held to predict 1825 as the year of Catholic triumph over Protestants. Magauran told of how many Protestants locked their houses and others quitted the county for Dublin – some had not returned by March 1825. According to the bishop, the fear was particularly strong amongst the Protestant and Orange Yeomanry who were in the habit of reading exclusively 'newspapers of a party spirit'. Forbes, said the bishop, 'would not have any hesitation or fear to leave his doors open' and this was true of other Protestants in the county also.

III

In August 1825 a group of lay Catholics in County Longford, responding to O'Connell's desire to renew the struggle after the suppression of the Catholic Association and the failure of Emancipation efforts in London, called the first county meeting. This group is listed in Appendix 1, insofar as they can be identified from diverse sources. They included those who signed the requisition for the meeting and those who participated at it - 20 out of a possible 22. Analysis of these indicates the relatively high social status of the O'Connellite nucleus in County Longford.

The meeting took place on Saturday 24 September in the Longford chapel:

A space near the Altar was appropriated for the accommodation of the Gentlemen who took an active part in the proceedings. The aisles and galleries of the Chapel, which is, we understand, capable of accommodating two thousand persons, were completely occupied by the crowds of peasantry who thronged in, as if to show that *they* felt deeply their degrading condition.[21]

This was the first major political mobilization of the people for a parliamentary objective: it was a very significant politico-religious occasion in the growth of local consciousness.

A member of the local gentry, John C. Nugent, took the chair at the meeting. Fr Felix Slevin was appointed secretary. Fr Slevin was ordained from Maynooth in 1821 and he was then a curate in Longford town and prison chaplain. Later parish priest for a short time in Edgeworthstown and then in Kiltoghert, County Leitrim from 1832 to 1847, he became a senior priest of the diocese as Vicar-General in 1834.[22] Slevin also emerged as an important political activist and later acted as the first secretary of the Liberal Club in the county; indeed he usually acted as secretary for the Catholics of the county during the Emancipation campaign.

J. C. Nugent told the meeting amidst cheers, 'Our Question was formerly called the Catholic Question, but it has become the National Question'; the struggle of the Catholic masses became closely identified with the growing feeling of national identity and this was important with respect to future popular nationalist response in the county. In the evening, after the county meeting, 'a select party, comprising the greater part of the gentlemen who had conducted the business of the Meeting, partook of an elegant dinner prepared for the occasion at Montfayon's Hotel'. Bishop Magauran, 'invited as a guest', replied to the toast to the Roman Catholic clergy of his diocese; he spoke, in particular, of their participation in politics, observing that he had

probably better opportunity of knowing each member of that respectable body ... than they had individually themselves. They had not been in the habit of coming together at public meetings, and he hoped that there would not, after the next session of Parliament, be any necessity for holding such a meeting as he had the satisfaction of being present at that day. Of the clergy under his control, he would say that the only reason for their keeping out of the political arena was because they acted entirely as they conceived it to be their duty, and took the tone of their conduct from the tenor of his own.

He went on to say that he had realized the necessity of clerical participation in politics when he had gone to London with the bishops who accompanied the Irish deputation from the Catholic Association. After this experience 'he was resolved to lend his assistance to the laity'.[23]

The county meeting was organized by the rural and urban middle and upper class lay Catholics of County Longford who were anxious to obtain the benefits of Emancipation. They used the framework of the Catholic Church but it is important to remember that the lay response was prior to and separate from that of the bishop and his priests, who from 1825 on took an increasingly important part in local politics. Maynooth and non–Maynooth priests were equally active in politics. Out of 27 priests in the county noted for political activity in newspapers between 1824 and 1829, 12 had attended Maynooth.[24]

IV

In the spring of 1826 the rural secret organization in County Longford was temporarily crushed.[25] In this Fr Slevin, as prison chaplain, played a crucial role by securing a pardon for a convicted man in return for information which broke up the rural conspiracy. This weakened the underground agrarian organization for precisely those years which were dominated by the Catholic struggle.

The 1826 general election marks a watershed in Irish constitutional development. A Catholic democratic organization emerged at local level with the potential to undermine Protestant control in Ireland. The Catholic Association provided, for the first time, a national framework for local popular electoral organizations.[26] County Longford, shared between a Forbes and a Fetherston for every election since 1806 without opposition (except for a minor challenge by Luke White in 1819), could hardly fail to be influenced by the Catholic voters' revolt in Cavan, Westmeath and Roscommon. No Association-backed candidate emerged in Longford so Forbes and Fetherston were returned unopposed. However, during the autumn of 1826, Catholic organization developed significantly in the county.

The initiative to collect the New Catholic Rent (to support the 40-shilling freeholders) came from the bishop and his priests. Bishop Magauran and 14 priests held a 'conference' in Longford to arrange the collection of the Rent in every parish in the diocese. Each of the priests at this meeting subscribed £1 towards the Rent and the bishop £5. The £19 sent in by Fr Slevin from this meeting was the first sum from the county towards the New Catholic Rent.

By the end of October a total of £28 was subscribed in County Longford with a further £37 sent in by the end of November. By the end of 1826 County Longford was credited with a total of £71.9s.9d. in the accounts of the New Catholic Association.[27] A second county meeting was held in October. In contrast to the requisition for the first one, the notice calling the 1826 meeting was signed by Bishop Magauran and his curate Fr Michael O'Beirne; it was also signed by two other priests, Fr James O'Donoghue of Edgeworthstown and Fr John Sheridan of Granard.

The same men who signed in 1825, with only one or two changes, signed the requisition in 1826. The 1826 meeting strongly recommended the 'immediate adoption of Parochial Meetings' to petition parliament for unqualified Emancipation and to collect the new Catholic Rent. The meeting was amongst the first post-general election county meetings and significantly a motion in praise of 'the patriotic ardour' of the 40-shilling freeholders at the contested elections was passed at Longford; their conduct demonstrated that the 'enthusiastic spirit of Civil and Religious Liberty' was 'widely diffused'. J. D. Brady, of Springtown, Granard, spoke of the 'great moral revolution' which had occurred at the general election: 'a great lesson has been taught to our rulers, and a practical answer has been given to the assertion that the peasantry care nothing about Emancipation'.[28]

Though the elections passed off without a contest in County Longford the implications of the other contests, including that of neighbouring Westmeath, were not lost on the local activists. A turning-point had been reached and from 1826 electoral politics was a main focus of popular political activity in the county even though the franchise remained limited between 1829 and 1832.

The New Catholic Rent served electoral politics in a direct way as it was collected to protect the voters who were punished for supporting Emancipationist candidates. This was significantly different from the more general purposes set out for the Old Catholic Rent before March 1825. The political role of the Catholic priesthood was also more obvious and important from 1826. Several resolutions in favour of the priesthood were passed at the 1826 meeting, including one of thanks to Bishop Magauran 'for that generous impulse of liberty which he had given the Catholics of this County'.[29] The meeting was marked by the notable part taken by some priests. Fr Slevin was again secretary and three other priests spoke at the meeting.

One of these was particularly important in the Catholic struggle: Fr Michael O'Beirne, curate to the bishop in Ballymahon, was a Maynooth priest, ordained in 1824, who became a noted speaker at Catholic meetings. At the 1826 meeting he spoke 'in a powerful and impressive strain' about the rank and character of the Catholics in the county, of their devotion to the British Constitution and of their rights: they were 'men who have a stake in the country' and who felt anxious about its welfare and prosperity. He praised the respectable Protestants who attended the meeting and concluded with a defence of the part taken by priests in politics at the recent elections. O'Beirne spoke 'at considerable length' and was apparently well received by the assembly.

J. D. Brady took up O'Beirne's theme, declaring that the Catholics came 'before Parliament to seek our rights - not to deprive our neighbours of theirs. We seek not for political ascendancy but political equality - not the possession of power, but eligibility to office.' It is clear that the well-to-do Catholics in Longford were motivated by their desire to partake in public life on equal terms with Protestants - they expressed their political aims in terms of the liberal Catholic ideology which dominated the political argument of O'Connell and the other leaders in the Catholic Association. About 50 of these Catholics attended a dinner after the meeting and the toasts and speeches at this smaller meeting illustrate the political sentiments of the Catholic political nucleus which had emerged in the county. The King was toasted with the sentiment that he might 'never forget his own declaration that he holds the Crown in trust for the good of the people'. W. C. Plunket, Lord Forbes and 'our Friends in the Lower House' were toasted to 'great applause'. Dr Tierney, a Protestant, returned thanks and remarked that 'any eulogium on the character of Lord Forbes would be superfluous in this County'; Forbes was declared by both Dr Tierney and Bishop Magauran to be 'a friend of universal Emancipation'; the bishop declared that the occasion was 'one of the happiest days of his life'. It was the second meeting he had attended and he considered moderation in politics to be a virtue necessary to men but 'essential to clergymen'; as soon as Emancipation was granted he would advise his priests to withdraw from politics but, at present, these meetings 'were useful to the cause of Catholicity'.[30]

The recommencement of the Rent collection in County Longford in the autumn of 1826 involved the organization of the parishes through parish meetings. The meeting at Mostrim parish chapel in Edgeworthstown on Sunday 12 November, 1826, is a typical example. Fr James O'Donoghue, who had been involved in the first phase of the Rent collection, was in the chair. The issues raised and discussed at this parish meeting are significant. One resolution expressed the 'warmest gratitude and respectful esteem' to the Catholic priests 'for their spirited and constitutional exertions during the late elections in promoting the cause of civil and religious liberty'. Another resolution deplored 'the support given to proselytising schools' but expressed thanks to 'our liberal Protestant friends', especially the local landlord, Richard Lovell Edgeworth, 'for his liberality in establishing and patronising a school in this town where children of all sects are educated at a moderate expense, without any improper interference with their religious principles'.[31]

Another typical meeting took place on Sunday 29 October, 1826, on the western side of the county in Tarmonbarry parish at the chapel in Ruskey. Fr James McNally, the parish priest, took the chair. Resolutions at this meeting attacked the violation of the Treaty of Limerick, which ended the Williamite war in 1691, and the enforced support for the Established Church, and several praised O'Connell. The account of the meeting notes that the people separated 'highly impressed with a just sense of their political rights'.

The Treaty of Limerick was important in the historical and political argument of Irish Catholics. At the meeting in Ruskey chapel it was seen as having been violated in an act of 'National Treachery', which was 'one of the most perfidious acts' as it had been supported 'with almost unprecedented national honour by our ancestors when they had it fully in their power to turn the tide of war in their own favour'. The perfidy was ascribed to 'the English of that day'. Like many Catholic parishes Tarmonbarry was having difficulty maintaining a chapel, and an important resolution which is worth quoting related to this:

That until we are fully Emancipated we shall consider ourselves unjustly and Tyranically [sic] treated by being obliged to build a Church and Steeple a few years ago when there was not one Protestant family in the Parish nor is there yet more than a few individuals including 6 of the Constabulary while we are in this inclement season obliged to worship our God in the open air our Parish Chapel having fallen to ruin and our finances quite inadequate to rebuild it.[32]

These two parish meetings illustrate how local grievances were highlighted in the Catholic struggle for Emancipation, and activists learned constitutional methods of publicizing them through the press and petitions to parliament.

    'Emancipation' involved the whole nexus of economic, political, social and religious grievances felt by Catholics. Church cess, tithes and education were key issues at parish level. A sharpening of the Catholic response may be traced from 1826 in the matter of the education societies which were held to be 'avowedly at variance with the tenets and discipline of our Holy Church', as Richard Dempsey put it at a county meeting; they existed 'for the unmasked purposes of proselytizing'.[33] Proselytism became a major issue in the Catholic struggle in County Longford and an account of this issue provides the essential background to the political agitation of the later 1820s.

V

A leading characteristic of Protestantism in the first half of the nineteenth century was the evangelical fervour which moved many to attempt the conversion of Catholics. A resurgent Catholicism, described above in James Kelly's essay, was unlikely to suffer lightly this missionary activity of revivalist Protestantism. The clash between the two exacerbated political relations in the 1820s.

    In September 1824, the Longford Bible Society, a branch of the Hibernian Bible Society, was 'revived' by the alliance of Tory landlords and Established Church clergy which was to form the basis of the Tory/Protestant party in county politics in the next decades. The meeting, held in the court-house, was chaired by Lord Lorton and attended by leading clergymen, such as the Archbishop of Tuam, and by notable county clergymen such as Revd George Crawford, of Newtownforbes, Revd Wm Digby and Revd W. C. Armstrong of Moydow. Bibles were to be distributed 'to rectify the ills of society'.[34]

    Thus, at the same time as the Catholic Rent took root in the county, the Protestant evangelicals were becoming organized. Shortly before the county meeting in 1825 the first anniversary meeting of the County Longford Bible Society was held with 'at least six hundred persons', including those 'of the first respectability in the Town and Country', present.[35] The start of what became known as the 'New Reformation' coincided with the years of heightened Catholic consciousness.

    In March 1825 Bishop Magauran gave evidence that there was less proselytism in Ardagh diocese 'than in many others'. There was some, but he did not believe that it was effective: 'the result was in the inverse ratio', as Protestants became Catholics because of the 'proselytising disposition that was all over the neighbourhood; it was quite disgusting'.[36] One indication of the increased efforts to win converts in the subsequent period is that at the second anniversary meeting of the Longford Bible Society in 1826 the sale of Bibles was reported to have increased five times over the previous year.[37]

In early 1827 a meeting of the Established clergy of the county took place: it was decided to deliver weekly lectures in the church at Longford town on the 'errors of the Church of Rome', the clergymen taking turns to speak. Lecturers and the Catholics of the town and neighbourhood were invited to attend and it was reported that many had 'declared their determination to do so'. Reports of conversions were noted from the county in the *Dublin Evening Post*: three persons were reported to have conformed to the Established Church at Killashee. In March further Catholics conformed. These conversions, while numerically not very significant, were spread over the whole county and with the activities of the Longford Bible Society and the lectures organized by the Protestant clergy there was certainly sufficient cause for the priests to be stimulated into counter-activity. The Longford Bible Society had spread to Granard with the formation there of the Granard Bible Society in 1827.[38]

Cases of conversions to Catholicism were also given publicity: two people 'conformed' to Catholicism in the parish of Cashel and these were noted in the *Midland Chronicle* which observed that it had 'never heard of a Catholic becoming a Protestant at the point of death'. The *Dublin Evening Post* under the heading 'Counter-Reformation at Longford' reported Fr Michael O'Beirne's activities in Ballymahon. O'Beirne was using his oratorical powers by preaching

two or three times a week to a vast assemblage of Protestants as well as Catholics, and the result is, that, within the last four days, four Protestants have embraced the Catholic faith in Ballymahon, and many applications have been made to the Right Rev. Dr. Magauran by Respectable Protestants who are wavering in their faith.

Eight converts to Catholicism were confirmed at Ballymahon by the bishop on Easter Monday, 1827, and others were confirmed elsewhere. In March 1827 applications were also reported as having been made to Fr Slevin in Longford. In the parish of Killashee, where the politically active priest Richard O'Ferrall presided,

upwards of ten Protestants have, since the commencement of this year, been converted to the Catholic Religion; and in the parish of Clonbroney, near Longford, upwards of forty Protestants were, within the last twenty months, received into the bosom of the Catholic Church.

In April 1827 the *Post* reported that a conversion to Catholicism had taken place at the parish chapel of Columbkille, County Longford. In June Bishop Magauran confirmed six former Protestants in a large ceremony in Granard.[39]

VI

It is in this context of increasing proselytism and sectarianism that the motivation of the two contending political forces in the county has to be viewed. The political response of the people and priests cannot be separated from this rapidly developing religious cleavage. The religious divide largely corresponded with the socio-economic divisions in the county and thus laid the foundations for the popular Catholic/Liberal party and the more narrowly based Protestant/Tory party which emerged as organized forces out of the Emancipation struggle in the 1820s. There was little room in the middle ground as is revealed by the shift to the right of the Edgeworth family in the face of O'Connellism; their pro-Emancipation feeling yielded gradually to a defence of British authority and of property rights. The victory of O'Connell in Clare in 1828 signalled that the Catholic masses had dispensed with liberal Protestant guidance and the Edge-worths had no sympathy with the rising Catholic democracy.

There was little political activity either nationally or locally by the Catholic Association in 1827. Very little Rent was collected in County Longford, most of it paid before March; Rent payments were always a critical indicator of local feeling.[40] In 1827 George Canning, who had long been an advocate of Emancipation, became prime minister and the Irish Catholic leaders adopted a moderate approach in the hope of government action in favour of Catholics. However, some events of that year in Longford were important in relation to the Catholic struggle. One of these was the demonstration at Lanesborough when Col. Henry White, MP for County Dublin, finally defeated the Tory attempt to oust him from his seat in early May 1827. The town of Lanesborough, which had a population of about 1500 and was on the estate of the Whites, was 'brilliantly illuminated to celebrate the overthrow of the Intolerants' and there was great 'joy' amongst the tenantry: 'What gave particular effect to the beauty of the scene was the magnificent appearance of the house of Rathcline hanging over the Shannon in a blaze of light ...'.[41] This political demonstration was the first of many great popular occasions in the county which were directly related to parliamentary elections. It was a foretaste of the popular demonstrations which accompanied the White challenge for the seats in County Longford in the 1830s.

Another important local political occasion in 1827 was the visit of O'Connell to Longford town in August to defend Fr Edward McGaver, PP, in a case over a disputed will.[42] This visit is important both because there was a popular demonstration in favour of O'Connell and because O'Connell came to Longford specially for Fr McGaver, who became an important local O'Connellite priest.

O'Connell's visit caused the usual crowd to collect: 'The people in the evening collected in great numbers, and having prepared a chair for the purpose, chaired the learned Gentleman from the Inn where he dined with the Bar, to his Lodgings.' O'Connell addressed the crowd 'in an energetic manner' on their duty to obey the law. C. S. Edgeworth spoke of O'Connell's 'furious speech' to the crowd but he also found him 'vain, entertaining and good-hearted' when he dined with him. Fetherston, the Tory MP, claimed that O'Connell was causing a riot in the town but Judge Moore refused to take any action, replying, 'Wherever Mr. O'Connell goes, my dear Sir, he is always chaired by the people and you cannot prevent it.'[43]

The McGaver family were well off, indeed rich, by contemporary farming standards. They were large farmers in the barony of Moydow. Joseph McGaver held 106 acres and Fr Edward McGaver over 200 acres, mainly in Taghshinny parish as a tenant of Henry White, the County Dublin MP. Edward was educated at Paris and ordained in 1822 or 1823, serving as parish priest at Cashel, County Longford, until 1835. In the year after the Whites gained supremacy in the county, 1838, Fr McGaver gave very important evidence of his local political involvement. Bishop MacNamee notes that

Father McGaver stood by his people against landlord oppression; but on one occasion, addressing a meeting at Doory gates, he made a reference to the Jessops of Doory Hall which was interpreted as libellous. Fearing the consequences of an unfavourable verdict, he was prepared to sell out his belongings and go abroad to escape a possible sentence of imprisonment. He was convicted and fined £3,000. Further evidence, however, was forthcoming and on a re-trial Father McGaver was acquitted.

Fr Thomas McGaver, Edward's brother, was parish priest in Scrabby and Columbkille East from 1833 to 1854 when he died aged fifty-six. He supported the O'Connellite local effort also but not as strongly as Edward, who was probably the single most important priest in local politics between 1826 and 1850 in County Longford.[44]

The most active year of the 1820s in Irish local politics was 1828 and County Longford was no exception. In this year permanent electoral organization took root and shape for the first time. A peak of political activity was reached at the time of the Clare election in July 1828 though a high level was maintained until the spring of 1829.

In January 1828 a number of Longford parishes held meetings on a Sunday nominated by the Catholic Association, as did other parishes throughout Ireland. The parish of Shrule met at Ballymahon chapel. This meeting was attended by the bishop, Dr Magauran, who proposed that his curate, Fr Michael O'Beirne, take the chair. O'Beirne gave a typical display of his oratorical skill in a long speech which was published in the *Dublin Evening Post*. He began by announcing that 'the trumpet of liberty has resounded from the Giant's Causeway to Cape Clear - from Newry to Galway'. He ridiculed the fears of local Protestants: 'I am told there are some saintly old ladies in this town, whose pious and Bible-unctioned imaginations are haunted by frightful apprehensions, that we are to rush on them from our meetings and massacre them in their church.' Such fears, he stated, were ludicrous: the Catholics assembled for 'the restoration of their rights'.

Nine of the 16 men who moved or seconded resolutions at the Shrule meeting can be identified from various sources and Appendix 2 gives an indication of the social composition of those who attended.[45] It is clear that the local activists were a mixture of urban and rural middle-class farmers, shopkeepers or professional men ranging from the relatively wealthy to quite small tenant farmers. After the meeting about 40 of the participants had dinner at McDermott's Hotel.

On the same day, Killashee, Clongesh, Ardagh and Moydow parishes also held meetings. The parish of Clongesh met in the chapel of Newtownforbes under the chairmanship of Fr James Keon, the parish priest. At the end of the meeting, James Farrell Esq. of Minard, a well-to-do landowner, took the chair. A resolution was passed at this meeting praising Forbes as MP and as a resident magistrate. The Ardagh and Moydow parish union had a meeting in the chapel of Ardagh under the chairmanship of Fr Thomas Farrelly, the parish priest. The Killashee meeting, held in the chapel of Clondra, was chaired by the activist priest Fr Richard O'Ferrall. At this meeting two collectors were appointed to return the Rent on a half-yearly basis and a resolution was passed condemning the Sub-letting Act of 1826 in accordance with Catholic Association policy.[46]

A notable feature of the political activity during 1828 was the more systematic collection of the Catholic Rent. In January the Catholic Association distributed a detailed report on the appointment and duties of Catholic churchwardens, of which there were to be two in each parish: the priest was to nominate one and the parishioners were to elect the second.

In January Simon Nichols, one of the leading local politicians in Longford, forwarded £1.5s.0d from the parishes of Templemichael and Ballymacormick. This small subscription included 17 named subscribers of one shilling each. Many of these subscribed £1 or 10 shillings in July 1828. A number were also active at a parish meeting to form a general committee and a managing committee in the parish for the County Longford Liberal Club which was established in November 1828.[47] Thus a reliable list of Longford town activists can be formed and 20 out of a possible 28 activists have been identified in Appendix 3.

As with the Shrule activists it is clear that most of the Longford town activists were well-established business, professional or farming people: four of the most important were £50 freeholders in the county. Longford was a prosperous trading and market town and the Catholic struggle received support from many of the important sections of the Longford business community. One-half of the grocers and spirit dealers were politically active and about the same proportion of the publicans. The categories which were not represented include the boot-and shoe-makers, of which there were 11 in the town, and others such as the tailors, saddlers and harness-makers, tanners and watchmakers; painters and glaziers and other miscellaneous artisans and traders did not become active either.[48]

Patrick Reilly, the churchwarden in Granard, sent in typical reports of progress in the Rent collection. There were 10 collectors appointed in the period and Reilly reported that there was no 'New Reformation' activity, there had been no expulsion of the peasantry and no persecution due to the educational activity of 'fanatics'. The Rent was collected with 'great alacrity' in the monthly collections and 'the very beggars' contributed to it. Reilly noted some converts to Catholicism. At the end of September he sent in 'the September gale' which had been collected in pence and halfpence to the amount of £3; the 'December gale' also came to £3.[49] The Granard activists were similar in their social composition to those in Longford, as Appendix 4 confirms. Granard had a 'very extensive market' in corn, linen, yarn and provisions, according to *Pigott's Directory, 1824*: it is significant that the activists were drawn from linen traders, grocers and publicans. Three of the 12 publicans were collectors as were three of eight linen and woollen drapers in the town; five of the collectors had both business and farming interests. Two of the 11 grocers in the town were collectors. The seven boot- and shoe-makers, six bakers, four ironmongers, two leather-sellers, three painters and glaziers and eight other artisans were not represented by a political activist though one of the four tailors in the town, John Glynn, was a collector.

Analysis of rural areas, when possible, indicates that collectors of the Rent and activists were fairly substantial tenant farmers. In Lanesborough, for example, seven out of eight collectors had holdings, ranging from 10 to over 60 acres; one, Patrick Costello, held over 100 acres. The eighth, Michael Mulvihill, almost certainly belonged to the family which had a public house in Lanesborough.[50]

VII

During 1828, and especially in the aftermath of O'Connell's election in Clare in July, the collection of the Catholic Rent in Longford parishes proceeded steadily. In July Bishop Magauran subscribed £5 towards O'Connell's election. Longford town subscribed £50 through Simon Nichols, who was described as 'Secretary for Longford'. About half of this was in small sums ranging from one penny to 7s. 6d. with the rest in sums of £1 or 10 shillings.[51]

Appendix 5 sets out the Catholic Rent contributions from County Longford between 1824 and 1829; the years 1828 and 1829 have been estimated as no published accounts appeared from the Catholic Association for those years. It is unlikely that the newspaper returns in the *Dublin Evening Post* missed any significant contributions from the county. County Longford in these years contributed just over £400 to the Catholic Association. This was less than half the national average per head of population and was a very small amount in comparison to the total Catholic Rent of over £50,000 subscribed in Ireland between 1824 and 1829.[52]

Much of the Catholic Rent collected in the county was in the form of personal subscriptions of £1 or 10 shillings and the 'penny a month' collections operated only for short periods and not in every parish. O'Connell's Catholic Rent scheme involved great numbers but not every area or social group responded to the same extent. From the analysis of the activists in County Longford it is clear that wealthier Catholics were most involved, whether those in the towns or the tenant farmers and small landowners. In 1828 regular small subscription, as in Killoe and Clonbroney, began to involve poorer people on a more continuous basis. However, it was the rural and urban middle class which provided the leaders at the local level and this class also supplied the priests. The 'poor man' was more of a spectator than a participant in the Catholic struggle, albeit an enthusiastic spectator.

As mentioned above, an analysis of the educational background of the clerical activists in the county makes it quite clear that a Maynooth education was not a prerequisite for political activity: less than half of the activist priests attended Maynooth. Out of six priests who were active in the first phase of the collection in 1824 and 1825 only one can be found in the Maynooth lists. Some Maynooth products, such as Felix Slevin and Michael O'Beirne, were much more involved than many other priests but this was hardly due to their education. Frs McGaver and Thomas Grey and others were equally keen local politicians, and they had not attended Maynooth. The two bishops in the O'Connellite period in the county, Magauran and Higgins, were not educated at Maynooth though Dr Higgins taught there between 1826 and 1829. Both supported the local political drive by the lay Catholic leaders.

After O'Connell's Clare victory the whole of Ireland was activated by the electoral situation and the prospects of Catholics sitting in parliament and of sweeping popular victories. In November 1828 a permanent electoral organiza-tion was established by the Longford Catholics, who called a meeting of the Friends of Civil and Religious Liberty, to petition parliament and to adopt 'such other Constitutional Measures as will be deemed expedient in the present state of Catholic affairs'.[53] This meeting revealed the first cracks in the alliance between the O'Connellite politicians in the county and Lord Forbes. It was supposed at first that Forbes would take the chair but before the meeting he let it be known that this 'might be incompatible with the public station' which he held. The real differences, however, arose over the resolutions to be proposed. Forbes did not attend the preparatory gathering to consider the resolutions submitted to him by a deputation from the organizing committee. He objected to the vote of thanks to O'Connell and suggested it might be included in a general vote of thanks to the other Liberal MPs. This was not accepted by the deputation. After Clare, O'Connellism had become too powerful, and the implications all too clear to the more moderate Protestants. A realignment began to occur: Forbes moved towards the Tory camp and in the early 1830s fought alongside the ultra-Protestant Lefroys against the O'Connellite candidates in the county.

In the event Richard More O'Ferrall, 'the heir to one of the most ancient properties' in the county, took the chair and Fr Slevin was appointed secretary. The *Dublin Evening Post* thought the meeting 'one of the most imposing and numerous ever convened in the Province of Leinster' while the *Evening Mail* called it 'a rabble meeting of Radicals and Papists' and the *Mail* hailed Forbes's action as 'a signal triumph'. The independent action of the local activists was, however, more significant as they had refused to defer to Forbes, their former 'friend' and the most prominent and powerful man in the county. When he met the deputation some were in favour of meeting his wishes but the majority would not sacrifice 'a public principle' to convenience. The *Post* stressed the confidence Catholics in Longford had in Forbes but it stated that County Longford 'could not manifestly adopt a course different from that pursued by the other Counties in Ireland'. It tried to paper over the cracks by saying that it only 'appeared' as if there had been 'a difference of opinion'.

At the meeting the most significant resolution was proposed by J. D. Brady and seconded by Val Dillon: 'That we earnestly recommend the formation of Liberal Clubs, formed on the principle of Civil and Religious Liberty in order to promote the Registry of Freeholds, and the better to preserve uncorrupted the exercise of the Elective Franchise.' The Liberal Club system had been developing on a national basis from 1826 and had received a great impetus after O'Connell's election success. The County Longford Liberal Club was set up in January 1829 as a result of this resolution. Another resolution was proposed by Fr O'Beirne and seconded by Fr McGaver in praise of the 40-shilling freeholders 'for the manly and uncompromising patriotism by which they wielded that mighty engine, the Elective Franchise'. Yet another urged greater efforts 'to purify the representation of Ireland'. This resolution was proposed by Vance Williams, a physician and surgeon who lived on Bridge Street, and seconded by Simon Nichols, and declared that candidates should 'afford evidence' of their sincerity by contributing to the success of Liberal candidates in all counties where they had property.[54] A petition was forwarded to parliament. Forbes, 'our long tried representative', and Henry Grattan, who had some property in the county, were asked to present it to the Commons and the Duke of Buckingham was asked to present it to the Lords.

The *Dublin Evening Post* carried a long report of this Longford meeting. The town was 'thronged with parties of men arriving from all parts of the county' long before the start of the meeting and it estimated that 30,000 people attended. This is probably an exaggeration. However, it was certainly a major mobilization of the people in the county. O'Ferrall in his address condemned the 'debasing effect' of the Penal Laws on the Catholics as shown by the way they had exercised the franchise in the past; this had resulted in the 'annual farce' of petitioning 'a hostile tribunal' which they themselves had helped to create. He stressed that Catholics must think and act for themselves and that the constitutional exercise of the franchise would 'tend to give the People a confidence in the laws which are sanctioned by their representatives'; thus Ireland could be governed 'by the influence of public opinion'. This speech set the tone of the meeting, which focused on the electoral aspect of the Emancipation struggle. Fr Slevin, in a strongly worded speech, did not agree with the 'cant of the present day' whereby the priest apologized for his political activity: he exulted in his political actions 'to throw the shield of his experience and learning between the people and their oppressors ...'.

J. D. Brady, in proposing the formation of a County Liberal Club, declared that its duty would be to attend to the registry of the freeholders so that 'at the next election, secure in the proper organisation of all the resources we possess, we may show our enemies our strength, and evince our gratitude to our friends (Hear Hear)'. He observed that all were convinced 'of the great, the all-prevailing consequence of a due attention to the registry ...' and stressed the benefit of similar clubs in other counties. Fetherston, who voted against Emancipation, ought not to be allowed, declared Brady, to continue beyond the next election. The Club would instruct the freeholders 'in the value of the power they possess of becoming their own liberators'. Brady's resolution was 'carried amid loud cheers'.

It is important to realize that in the wake of the Clare election the Protestants of Longford also formed local clubs such as the Ballymahon Brunswick Club and the Longford Brunswick Club. These clubs were representative of the local anti-Catholic feeling in the county; there were 100 subscribers to the Ballymahon Club and at least 2000 were reported to have attended the Longford meeting which set up the Club in the town.[55] The Established clergy and the landed proprietors who organized the clubs also had influence in the county much greater than these numbers would suggest.

Thus the ultra-Protestants in the county had an organization which the New Liberal Club was designed to oppose. At the November meeting Fr O'Beirne described Fetherston, the Protestant MP, as 'the long-winded orator of aye and no - the creature of Lady Rosse, the patroness of bigotry'.[56] O'Beirne went on to condemn the Longford Brunswickers who formed 'in little stagnant pools at Ballynakill, Killashee and Keenagh' which at length flowed to Longford 'composing there a muddy stream'. He also condemned their paper, the *Longford Journal*, and the way Orangemen at Ballymahon had terrorized the people when they fired into houses for several hours on the night of 17 November.[57]

This November meeting marks a significant point in the political development of the county; politics had sharpened considerably at the local level. By the time of Catholic Emancipation in 1829 County Longford was polarized between a Liberal/Catholic party and a Tory/Protestant party, both of which were the product of the Catholic struggle during the 1820s. These two parties engaged in frequent and fierce election battles during the years of the Tithe War in the next decade and in the process made County Longford one of the most hotly contested constituencies in Ireland whereas before it had been one of the most dormant. The county cleavage endured through the Repeal agitation of the 1840s.

The County Longford Liberal Club was formed in 1829 at a meeting called for Tuesday 13 January by the Friends of the Independence of County Longford.[58] Fr Slevin was secretary of the Friends and became secretary of the Liberal Club. A preliminary meeting was held at the residence of Mr R. Dempsey, who had been the first to respond to the Catholic Rent back in 1824. J. D. Brady chaired the meeting and Richard More O'Ferrall read the necessary series of resolutions setting up the Club; 80 members were enrolled and officers appointed. George Dowdall chaired the public meeting in the chapel which 'publicly sanctioned' the Club. All the new members met for dinner at the Forbes Arms where the usual speeches praising 'the majesty of the people' were made. Fr O'Beirne advised the Club to 'work' the power of the 40-shilling freeholders and Bennet, a liberal Protestant, declared that the people were the source of political power:

He hailed it as a proud and happy omen for the people of Longford, that a conductor of that power had been this day created ... by the formation of a Liberal Club to watch over the interests of the people and to direct their energies.

J. D. Brady and James Rock were appointed to accompany O'Connell to London. Lord Forbes was toasted at the dinner and the parish priest of Clongesh where Forbes lived, Fr Keon, 'was delighted to find gentlemen had in some measure changed their opinion of Lord Forbes since the last day of meeting in Longford, when his Lordship's health was omitted'. 'Pledges' were toasted, however, as 'the best security' for the constituents, though one priest, Fr Lyons, a nephew of Bishop Magauran, thought these were necessary only for unsatisfactory MPs.[59]

The first parochial branch of the Club was set up in Ballymacormick and Templemichael in February 1829 when a general committee was formed by those who subscribed £1 and seven were elected to a managing committee. The Club continued after Emancipation and, even when the franchise was limited between 1829 and 1832, played a key role in the politics of County Longford as it developed in subsequent decades.

VIII

The Catholic struggle in the 1820s had transformed modern Irish politics and O'Connell may be credited with the achievement of a democratic revolution at the local level through the gradual emergence of the county electoral organization and the orientation of the people towards parliament.

The Emancipation struggle began a novel and basic transformation in the political consciousness of the Irish people and this process can be explored only by the study of politics at the local level. The Catholic agitation, led by O'Connell, activated a local political leadership which in a matter of years developed durable machinery. In the Emancipation struggle, for the first time in modern Irish history, a large-scale popular orientation towards parliament may be discerned: the struggle to achieve political goals became focused on parliamentary politics. The Catholics of County Longford assumed for the first time a political role within a *national* organization under a great leader in a constitutional movement.

The long slow process, which familiarized the people with the methods of popular parliamentary politics, commenced in County Longford in the years after the 1826 general election. A local political organization emerged under the guidance of local political activists both lay and clerical. These local activists - the political nucleus which formed to collect the Rent in 1824 and subsequently - were to be at the centre of County Longford politics until the death of O'Connell in 1847 and even into the 1850s. The county political organization - the Liberal Club - was the progenitor of subsequent local popular parliamentary organizations in the county. The Catholic clergy from the 1820s played a new and vital role in local politics.

Before the Emancipation struggle elections in County Longford did not signify much to the general population: there was no contested general election between 1792 and 1831. County Longford was a classic case of a county controlled by a few landed families. The dramatic change wrought by the emergence of the O'Connellite political community in the county became apparent in the 1830s. There were five hotly contested elections between 1831 and 1837.[60] Men like Carbry and Nichols were key, but typical, O'Connellite products of the 1820s. Nichols acted as secretary of the Liberal Club in the 1830s, and he and Carbry were Repeal leaders and Town Commissioners in the 1840s. The leading local activists of the 1820s continued as O'Connellite activists in the 1830s and 1840s. The electoral 'revolts' of Waterford, Clare and other counties in the 1820s set the pattern for Longford's 'revolt' in the 1830s.

	Name and Activity	Social Position/ Occupation	Sources
1.	John C. Nugent Esq., Killessona, Granard, M. dau. of Richard O'Ferrall, Ballyna, Co. Kildare; Chairman of county meeting	Landowner and £50 freeholder in county, member of county gentry	*Pigott's Directory, 1824*; Walford's *County Families* (1871), p. 736; G.O. 444
2.	Richard Dempsey Esq., Longford Catholic Rent organizer; spoke at county meeting and signed requisition for meeting	£50 freeholder and member of gentry in county	*Pigott's Directory, 1824*; G.O. 444; T.A.B. 19/8
3.	George and Luke Dowdall, Ballymahon. Catholic Rent organizers; both spoke at county meetings and George signed requisition	George was £50 freeholder and Luke £20 freeholder; millers and large farmers	G.O. 444; T.A.B. 19/21; 19/16; 30/29; Griffith 1854; S.P.O., C.S.O. R.P.– (outrage)/1832/2267
4.	J. D. Brady Esq., Springtown, Granard, spoke at county meeting and signed requisition	£50 freeholder and owned estate of over 2000 acres; member of county gentry	G.O. 444; S.P.O. Official Papers (M.A.) 1832-82/109/2
5.	James Rock Esq., spoke at county meeting	£50 freeholder	G.O. 444
6.	Michael Kiernan, Granard, spoke at county meeting and signed requisition	£50 freeholder; medical doctor	G.O. 444
7.	Simon Nichols, Longford; spoke at meeting and became a leading activist; signed requisition	£50 freeholder, apothecary	G.O. 444; H.C. (643) xiii, Part II, 1837-8, Qs 10354-10785
8.	Christopher Reynolds Esq., Longford and Dublin; spoke at meeting	£50 freeholder; attorney, sub-sheriff	*Pigott's Directory, 1824*; G.O. 444; H.C. (319) x, 1837, 147
9.	Christopher Carbry, Longford; Catholic Rent organizer; signed requisition and became leading activist	£50 freeholder; prominent shopkeeper in Main St	*Pigott's Directory, 1824*; G.O. 444

10.	Ambrose O'Ferrall Esq., Co. Kildare and Co. Longford, signed requisition; his son, Richard More O'Ferrall, chaired 1828 county meeting and was MP for county 1851-2 and a prominent Whig politician 1835-9	£50 freeholder; member of county gentry	Burke's *Irish Family Records* (1976), pp. 907-10; G.O. 444
11.	Henry Mullaniff Esq., Augharea House; signed requisition and participated at meeting	£50 freeholder; became a magistrate in 1840	G.O. 444; *The Longford Journal*, 3 Oct. 1840, 4 Mar. 1843
12.	John Nanry Esq., spoke at county meeting and signed requisition	£20 freeholder substantial farmer	G.O. 444; T.A.B. 19/22; 19/17
13.	Gerald Tiernan, spoke at meeting	£20 freeholder	G.O. 444
14.	Edward Rooney, Ballymahon; signed requisition; important political activist in 1830s	Large tenant farmer on Shuldham estate	H.C. (643) xiii, Part II 1837-38, Qs 11413-11568
15.	Val Charles Dillon Esq., Tenelick, Ballymahon, signed requisition	Large farmer of about 200 acres	*The Westmeath Journal*, 1 May 1828; *The Longford Journal*, 3 Aug. 1844
16.	James Davis, Longford, participated at meeting	£20 freeholder	G.O. 444
17.	Myles O'Reilly Esq., signed requisition; spoken of as a candidate in May 1831 for parliament	Colonel; member of county gentry	D.E.P., 3 May 1831; *The Pilot*, 4 May 1831
18.	John McManus, Barry, Ballymahon, signed requisition	£20 freeholder; tenant of Lady Rosse	G.O. 444
19.	Thomas Farrell, spoke at meeting	£10 freeholder	G.O. 444

Appendix 2. Social Composition of Shrule Activists 1828

	Name*	Occupation	Sources
1.	George Dowdall	Large farmer: *c.* 200 acres; £50 freeholder	G.O. 444: Griffith 1854; T.A.B. 19/16; 19/21; 30/29
2.	George Corcoran	Doctor/apothecary	T.A.B. 19/21; S.P.O., C.S.O. - (outrage) /1832/1480
3.	Mr McDermott	Tenant farmer; hotel keeper; 13 acres	T.A.B. 19/21: *D.E.P.*, 19 Jan. 1828
4.	H. Tormy	Shopkeeper; small tenant farmer	S.P.O., C.S.O.-(outrage)/July 1832/1294; T.A.B. 19/21; 30/29
5.	M. Shanly	Spirit dealer	S.P.O., C.S.O. R.P.-(outrage) /July 1832/1294
6.	Thomas Bracken	Small landowner; land agent; house, office, Main St, Ballymahon†	H.C. (319) x, 1837, 162; T.A.B. 19/21; Griffith 1854
7.	F. Dowdall	Tenant farmer, 25 acres Noughaval, house in Ballymahon, see No. 1 above	Griffith 1854; S.P.O., C.S.O. (outrage)/1832/1480
8.	F. Dowdall	See no. 1 above; probably brother	see p. 124 above on Dowdalls
9.	P. Dungan	Lived in Ballymahon beside H. Tormy (no. 4 above) & shared 5 acres tenancy with him	T.A.B. 19/21

* Names as given in *D.E.P.*, 7 Feb. 1828
† Bracken also noted as apothecary, *The Longford Journal*, 29 June 1839

SOURCES: P.R.O.I., Tithe Applotment Books (T.A.B.), Genealogical Office, Dublin, Ms 444, Griffith, *Valuation* (1854).

Appendix 3. Social Composition of Longford Town Activists 1828

	Name	Occupation	Sources
1.	Simon Nichols	£50 freeholder; Main St; apothecary, surgeon	*Pigott's Directory, 1824;* T.A.B. 19/8; see Appendix 1 (1825)
2.	Richard Dempsey Esq.	£50 freeholder; gentry	*Pigott's Directory, 1824;* T.A.B. 19/8; see Appendix 1 (1825)
3.	Henry Mullaniff Esq.	£50 freeholder; Aughorea House	T.A.B. 19/8: see Appendix 1 (1825)
4.	Christopher Carbry	£50 freeholder; tallow chandler, leather seller, grocer, spirit dealer, Main St	T.A.B. 19/8: see Appendix 1 (1825)
5.	John Hare	Brewer, Water St	T.A.B. 19/8
6.	Patrick Keon	Grocer, spirit dealer, merchant	*Pigott's Directory, 1824;* T.A.B. 19/8
7.	Patrick O'Connor	Innkeeper, tallow chandler, baker, grocer, spirit dealer, Main St	*Pigott's Directory, 1824;* T.A.B. 19/8
8.	Mick Kenna	Shopkeeper, baker, publican, Main St	T.A.B. 19/8; *Pigott's Directory, 1824*
9.	Michael Maguire	Baker, publican, Water St	T.A.B. 19/8; *Pigott's Directory, 1824*
10.	Owen Farrelly	Shopkeeper, Main St	T.A.B. 19/8
11.	Ed. Flood	Baker, Main St	*Pigott's Directory, 1824*
12.	Patrick Phillips	Shopkeeper, cloth merchant, Main St	*The Longford Journal,* 15 July 1843: T.A.B. 19/8
13.	John Tuite	Ironmonger, grocer and spirit dealer, Main St	T.A.B. 19/8; *Pigott's Directory, 1824*
14.	Thomas Cahill	Publican, Main St and tenant farmer	T.A.B. 19/8; 19/14
15.	Edward Hare	Shopkeeper, linen and woollen draper, Main St	T.A.B. 19/8; *Pigott's Directory, 1824*
16.	J. Sheridan	Publican, Main St	T.A.B. 19/8
17.	Ed. Murray	Publican, Main St	T.A.B. 19/8
18.	P. Daly	Publican, Main St	*Pigott's Directory, 1824*
19.	T. Mc Goey	Tenant farmer (*c.* 50 acres)	T.A.B. 19/8
20.	G. Fitzgerald	Tenant farmer (*c.* 50 acres)	T.A.B. 19/14; 19/8

SOURCES: *Pigott's Directory, 1824,* P.R.O.I., Tithe Applotment Books (T.A.B.).

Appendix 4. Social Composition of Granard Activists 1828

	Name	Occupation	Sources
1.	Patrick Reilly Churchwarden	Linen and woollen draper; £10 freeholder Greville estate	*Pigott's Directory 1824*; G.O. 444
2.	Thomas Pettit Collector	£20 freeholder; publican, tenant farmer	S.P.O. O.P. (M.A.) 1832-82/18 Sept. 1833/58/17; G.O. 444; T.A.B. 19/6
3.	Joseph Reilly Collector	Baker, grocer, publican	T.A.B. 19/6; *Pigott's Directory, 1824*
4.	Michael Murtha Collector	Grocer, linen draper tenant farmer, £10 freeholder on Greville estate	*Pigott's Directory, 1824*; T.A.B. 19/6; G.O. 444
5.	Michael Phillips Collector	Linen and woollen draper, tenant farmer (*c.* 10 acres)	T.A.B. 19/6; *Pigott's Directory, 1824*
6.	John Glynn Collector	Tailor	*Pigott's Directory, 1824*
7.	Philip Reilly Collector	Publican	*Pigott's Directory, 1824*
8.	Owen Lynch Collector	Tenant farmer (*c.* 25 acres)	T.A.B. 19/6
9.	James Dalton Collector	Tenant farmer (*c.* 39 acres)	Griffith 1854; T.A.B. 19/5

SOURCES: *Pigott's Directory, 1824*; P.R.O.I., Tithe Applotment Books (T.A.B.), Genealogical Office, Dublin, Ms 444; Griffith's *Valuation* (1854).

Appendix 5. County Longford Catholic Rent 1824-29

Year/month	Amount			Sources
1824	£	s	d	
October	18	1	2$^1/_2$	
November	9	17	0	
December	22	5	4$^1/_2$	
Total 1824	50	3	7	*D.E.P.*, 17 Feb. 1825
1825				
January	87	1	0	*D.E.P.*, 3 Mar. 1825
February	21	12	0	*D.E.P.*, 15 Mar. 1825
March	9	10	6	*D.E.P.*, 27 April 1826
Total 1825	118	3	6	
Total 1824-5	168	7	1	*D.E.P.*, 27 April 1826
New Catholic Rent: 1826 Total September-December	71	9	9	*D.E.P.*, 29 March 1827
1827 Total January-December	10	12	4	*D.E.P.*, 28 Feb. 1828
1828 Total January-December	121	12	0 est.	*D.E.P.*, Jan.-Dec. 1828
1829 Total January-February	29	0	0 est.	*D.E.P.*, Jan.-Feb. 1829

SOURCE: *Dublin Evening Post.*

NOTES

1. A detailed treatment of the 1820s is given in Fergus O'Ferrall, *Catholic Emancipation: Daniel O'Connell and the Birth of Irish Democracy* (Dublin 1985).
2. *The Westmeath Journal*, 9 Sept. 1824.
3. *Pigott's Directory, 1824*, pp. 166-7; *A List of All the Freeholders ... County Longford to January 1830* and *A Return of All the Freeholders ... County Longford* (Mullingar 1833), Genealogical Office, Ms 444 (hereafter G.O. 444); for Carbry's land (approx. 10 acres) see Tithe Applotment Book, parish of Templemichael, P.R.O.I., 19/8 (hereafter T.A.B.); for further details on Dempsey, see S.P.O., Chief Secretary's Office, Registered Papers - (Outrage) /July 1829/H.50; for Longford's contacts with Catholic Association see *Dublin Evening Post* (hereafter *D.E.P.*), 7, 14 Sept. 1824.
4. *D.E.P.*, 9 Oct. 1824, 17 Feb. 1825.
5. *D.E.P.*, 2 Nov. 1824; G.O. 444; George had over 200 acres in various parishes, see P.R.O.I., T.A.B. 19/21; 19/16; 30/29; Henry and Francis had smaller farms, see P.R.O.I., T.A.B. 19/21 and R. Griffith's *Primary Valuation County Longford* (Dublin

1854); Luke rented mills at Abbeyshrule which were burned maliciously, see S.P.O, C.S.O. R.P. - (Outrage) 16 Dec.1829/H. 103; Luke was registered as a £20 freeholder in 1832, see *A Return of All the Freeholders Registered ... in County Longford*, G.O. 444; George and Francis Dowdall were active in the Tithe War, see S.P.O., C.S.O. R.P. - (Outrage)/1832/2267 and C.S.O. R.P. - (Outrage)/1832/1480; George had a milling business at Newcastle near Ballymahon and a large illegal meeting took place at the rear of Francis Dowdall's house in Ballymahon. The Dowdalls were a branch of an ancient and distinguished Catholic family who settled at Ballymahon in the late seventeenth century; I am grateful to Mr P. Whelan, Drinagh, Ballymahon (whose mother was a Dowdall) for information on the Dowdall family; see also J.P. Farrell, *Historical Notes and Stories of County Longford* (Dublin 1886), pp. 157-8.

6. *D.E.P.*, 17 Feb. 1825; O' Ferrall, op. cit., appendix 1, p. 317. The population figures are for 1821 and are given in W. E. Vaughan and A.J. Fitzpatrick (eds), *Irish Historical Statistics: Population, 1821-1871* (Dublin 1978), pp. 3, 6.

7. *D.E.P.*, 8, 13, 15, 22 Jan., 17 Feb., 3, 10, 15 Mar. 1825.

8. James J. MacNamee, *History of the Diocese of Ardagh* (Dublin 1954), pp. 425, 653, 656.

9. MacNamee, op. cit., pp. 416, 566-7, 616, 670-2, 687, 727.

10. The county contribution in January was £87.1s.0d; in February £21.12s.0d. and in March £9.10s.6d. *D.E.P.*, 3, 15 Mar. 1825; 27 Apr. 1826.

11. Magauran's political and ecclesiastical activities have been neglected but see O.F. Traynor, 'Dr James Magauran, Bishop of Ardagh (1815–29)', *Breifne*, iv, no. 15 (1972), pp. 336-44; Traynor considerably underestimates the part played by Magauran in politics. MacNamee notes of Magauran, 'Though this prelate died little more than one hundred years ago, practically nothing is known of his episcopate' (op. cit., p. 416). There are a few letters relating to Bishop Magauran at St Mel's College, Longford, but they add little to our knowledge; the main sources are newspapers and his evidence in the parliamentary papers which throw a good deal of light on his political attitudes and his involvement in the local Catholic struggle; *Second Report from the Select Committee on the State of Ireland*, H.C. (129) viii, 1825, 269-70, 279.

12. Police reports from the county are in the S.P.O., State of the Country Papers (hereafter S.C.P.); robbery of arms and 'Ribbon Legislators' were complained of, see for example S.P.O. S.C.P. 1824/823/2503/8/9/11/12/13 and 1824/2603/9/13/ 15/17/18/19; for Orangeism see report of 12 July Orange procession in *The Westmeath Journal*, 22 July 1824; folk memories of Orange excesses in 1798 were strong, see department of Irish Folklore, U.C.D., Ms 1430: ff. 82-6, 350-5; also Ms 1486: 319-27.

13. S.P.O., S.C.P. 1824/2603/9.

14. S.P.O., S.C.P. 1824/2603/19/20; Brooke enclosed a copy of the October Rent Report published by the Catholic Association; the Protestant population of the county was about 8 per cent of the total population, see *Public Instruction, Report*, H.C. 1835 xxxiii, 103-17.

15. Crimes of 'an atrocious character' were prevalent according to police reports, S. P.O., S.C.P. 1825/2721/44/45/47/48 and 1825/2731/5/7; County Longford's six baronies were policed by 96 men when fully staffed, 16 men to each barony, see S.P.O., C.S.O. R.P. - (Outrage)/ Oct. 1826/L.15.

16. See List of Places Proclaimed under 3 Geo. iv, c.1 and 4 Geo. iv, c.58, S.P.O., S.C.P., 2nd Series, Carton 48.

17. S.P.O., S.C.P., 2nd Series, Carton 49, 8 Jan. 1826.

18. H.C. (129) viii, 1825, 269-70; 272, 276; examples of public whippings and harsh sentences may be found in *D.E.P.*, 24 Mar. 1825, and *Midland Chronicle and West-meath Independent*, 18 Apr. 1827.

19. This popular consciousness may be traced in outline in the considerable body of folklore collected in County Longford and now in the department of Irish Folklore, U.C.D.

20. H.C. (129) viii, 1825, 269-70, 715-18; Forbes, the pro-Catholic MP in the county, resided at Castle Forbes, Newtownforbes, County Longford for most of the year, ibid. 714; he was an active magistrate until his illness and death in 1835 and 1836.

21. *D.E.P.*, 27 Sept. 1825.

22. MacNamee, op. cit., p. 425, 711-12, 734, 736; *Pigott's Directory, 1824*, pp. 166-7.

23. *D.E.P.*, 27 Sept. 1825.

24. I have examined the role of Catholic priests in the politics of the 1820s in F. O'Ferrall, 'The Only Lever ...? The Catholic Priest in Irish Politics, 1823-29', *Studies*, lxx, no. 280 (Winter 1981), pp. 308-24.

25. See F. O'Ferrall, 'The Links Between Agrarian Unrest and the Emancipation Campaign in County Longford, 1826-29', *Teathbha*, ii, no. 3 (forthcoming).

26. See O'Ferrall, *Catholic Emancipation*, chapter 4.

27. See letter of Fr Felix Slevin, read at Catholic Association, 7 Oct. 1826, S.P.O, Catholic Association papers; *D.E.P.*, 28 Oct., 25 Nov. 1826; 29 Mar. 1827.

28. *D.E.P.*, 17, 28, 31 Oct. 1826.

29. *D.E.P.*, 28 Oct. 1826.

30. *D.E.P.*, 31 Oct. 1826.

31. A manuscript account of this meeting which was sent to the Catholic Association for insertion in the newspapers survives in D.D.A., Catholic Proceedings; the motions were published in *D.E.P.*, 28 Nov. 1826.

32. A manuscript account of this meeting survives in D.D.A., Catholic Proceedings.

33. *Midland Chronicle and Westmeath Independent*, 14 Feb. 1827.

34. See report of meeting in *The Westmeath Journal*, 9 Sept. 1824; apparently there had been a defunct Bible Society before this 'revival'.

35. *D.E.P.*, 30 Aug. 1825; Alexander Kingston Esq. of Mosstown House, Keenagh presided.

36. H.C. (129) viii, 1825, 290.

37. *The Westmeath Journal*, 31 Aug. 1826; Lord Lorton presided at this meeting.

38. *D.E.P.*, 6 Feb., 6, 27, 29 Mar. 1827; one conversion was reported at Edgeworthstown, one at Templemichael and two at Newtownforbes; *The Midland Chronicle and Westmeath Independent*, 7 Mar. 1827, analysed the Ardagh Diocesan Protestant clergy to show their wealth and property; *The Westmeath Journal*, 6 Aug. 1829, reported the third annual meeting of the Granard Bible Society.

39. *Midland Chronicle and Westmeath Independent*, 14 Mar., 2 May, 13 June 1827; *D.E.P.*, 31 Mar., 14 Apr. 1827.

40. £9.12s.4d. was collected Jan. - Mar. 1827; the total for 1827 from the county was £10.12s.4d. *D.E.P.*, 12 Apr. 1827, 28 Feb. 1828.

41. *Midland Chronicle and Westmeath Independent*, 9 May 1827; Rathcline was the residence of Luke White Esq.; the only exception in the illumination was the parson's house and some of his windows were broken.

42. O'Connell was 'specially retained' by Fr McGaver in the case Robinson *v*. McGaver; O'Connell won the case. See O'Connell to John Primrose, Jr, 26 July 1827, in M. R. O'Connell (ed.), *The Correspondence of Daniel O'Connell*, iii (Dublin 1974), Letter 1403, p. 335.

43. *D.E.P.*, 4 Aug. 1827; *Midland Chronicle and Westmeath Independent,* 8 Aug. 1827; M. Hurst, *Maria Edgeworth and the Public Scene* (London 1969), pp. 45-6.

44. Fr Edward McGaver and Joseph McGaver were both £50 freeholders in 1820s , see *A List of All the Freeholders ... in County of Longford up to January 1830,* G.O. 444; by 1832 four McGavers, including two priests, were registered as £50 freeholders, see *A Return of All the Freeholders ... in the County of Longford up to January 1833,* G.O. 444; *Minutes of Evidence Taken Before the Committee on the Longford County Election Petitions,* H.C. (319) x, 1837, 303; *Committee on Longford Election 1833* (Haliday Pamphlet, Royal Irish Academy, vol. 1570, no. 9, p. 145); McGaver did not reside in Cashel parish of which he was parish priest; see also details in T.A.B. 19/20; after 1835 he was transferred to Taghshinny parish where he remained until 1850; he then became parish priest of Granard until 1877 where he died aged eighty-two, see MacNamee, op. cit., pp. 426, 477, 578, 654, 761 and 788; see *Third Report from the Select Committee on Fictitious Votes (Ireland) with the Minutes of Evidence,* H.C. (643) xiii, Part II, 1837-8, Qs 11775-12824.

45. *D.E.P.*, 19 Jan., 7 Feb. 1828.

46. *D.E.P.*, 19 Jan., 2, 5 Feb. 1828.

47. *D.E.P.*, 31 Jan., 19 July 1828; 12 Feb. 1829.

48. *Pigott's Directory, 1824,* pp. 166-7, makes it possible to estimate the sources of support as it lists all the shopkeepers, traders and artisans in the town.

49. *D.E.P.*, 6 Mar., 15 Mar. Suppl., 30 Sept. 1828, 10 Jan. 1829.

50. *D.E.P.*, 12 Feb. 1828; *Pigott's Directory, 1824,* p. 164; T.A.B. 19/18.

51. *D.E.P.*, 8, 19 July 1828.

52. See O'Ferrall, *Catholic Emancipation,* p. 317.

53. Account of this meeting is based upon *D.E.P.*, 13, 27, 29 Nov. 1828; the *Dublin Evening Post* carried reports from the *Evening Mail.*

54. Vance Williams can be identified in *Pigott's Directory, 1824.*

55. See *The Westmeath Journal,* 9 Oct., 6 Nov. 1828 for extensive reports on these local clubs and their formation; in January these clubs were put on the 'alert' and their petitions were imbued with the 'no surrender' ethos more typical of Ulster counties, see *The Westmeath Journal,* 15 Jan. 1829.

56. *D.E.P.*, 29 Nov. 1828; Lady Rosse's 'sound policy' of spreading 'a salutary sprinkling of staunch and loyal Protestant yeomen ...' was praised at the formation of the Ballymahon Brunswick Club, see *The Westmeath Journal,* 9 Oct. 1828.

57. This incident is referred to in the national press, see *D.E.P.*, 10 Jan. 1829, under the heading 'Longford Justice!!!' as the local magistrates refused to indict the Orangemen but after a government investigation five were charged; the *Post* declared that '... the excitement produced in the minds of the people of Longford will not subside for many a long day'.

58. See notice in *D.E.P.*, 3 Jan. 1829.

59. *D.E.P.* Suppl., 17 Jan. 1829; there was apparently a pro-Forbes element in the Club led by some priests and encouraged by the Bishop, who had had a 'difference of opinion' with some Club leaders in November, *D.E.P.*, 29 Nov. 1828.

60. The great electoral battles in the 1830s are examined in detail in R.F.B. O'Ferrall, 'The Growth of Political Consciousness in Ireland, 1823-1847: A Study of O'Connellite Politics and Political Education',Ph.D. thesis, T.C.D., 1978, ff. 555-678.

'That part that laws or kings can cause or cure':[1] Crown Prosecution and Jury Trial at Longford Assizes, 1830-45

DESMOND McCABE

Reacting to the indictment of a large number of persons suspected of 'agrarian' offences at the Longford assizes of March 1832, Justice William Johnson, with the gloom that was a weakness of his profession, 'felt justified' in concluding that 'opposition to the law ... of fearful extent' prevailed throughout the county.[2] It was to meet such difficulties that a custom had evolved over the previous half-century whereby the crown initiated the prosecution of 'insurrectionary crime'. From the 1820s this system was continuously extended so that by the late 1830s the crown was responsible for the prosecution of most offences at assizes and quarter sessions. It was argued that this practice would 'prevent the prosecution of persons wrongfully charged' by detaching the investigation of cases from party prejudice. However, the danger remained that any attempt by the crown to use the system for its own ends would accentuate a seeming estrangement from due process of law among the Catholic peasantry derived from over a century of sectional monopoly of the Irish legal administration. The reality of this feeling in Longford is described in Fergus O'Ferrall's essay above and was apparently demonstrated by the vulnerability of 191 Catholic men indicted for trial at the assizes for agrarian crimes during the so-called 'Ballinamuck Land War' of 1835-9.[3] In such conditions of sectarian and political tension, what sort of trial did persons indicted on agrarian and other serious charges receive?

The lack of research into the Irish legal system denies the historian any long-term perspective of its workings in the eighteenth and nineteenth centuries.[4] The 1830s saw significant changes in the administration of justice. Catholics were admitted for the first time into senior legal posts as the administration of Lord Lieutenant Mulgrave, between 1835 and 1839, aimed to show state goodwill and impartiality in court, as elsewhere. At the same time the effect of Sir Robert Peel's transformation of the statutory code in the 1820s and early 1830s was beginning to be felt.[5] Theoretically, courts of justice were organized so as to provide several mutually independent agents of decision, each acting as a check on the other. This was intended to preserve a standard of justice which transcended the subjectivities of the participants for the benefit of both prisoner and prosecutor. Analysis of the format of trial and crown prosecution and of how the various elements in the legal system - crown, judge, jury, grand jury, and sheriff - behaved may help decide whether jury trials in early-nineteenth-century Longford were blighted by, for instance, bigotry of any sort or unprincipled crown prosecution.

The disposition of the Catholic peasantry towards the courts of law and lawful authority is an issue inextricably linked with these questions.

I

The trial of Michael Kenny, 'cooper and local travelling musician', for the murder of Hugh Moorehead, a tenant on the estate of Viscount Lorton near Ballinamuck in north Longford, was one of the most dramatic conducted at the Longford assizes during the 1830s. His prosecution was seen nationally as a severe blow to the activities of secret societies in the county. Moorehead had obtained land close to Ballinamuck in 1836. In 1838 a gang of five or six men was organized by an individual who 'had been in America and had returned ... to get the land', and anticipated a lease from Lord Lorton 'if Moorehead was not in the way'.[6] Although Moorehead was one of the Protestant settlers in the district, his murder was by this account connected only indirectly to the series of ejections on the Lorton estate.

The men gathered on the evening of 14 March 1838 and collected pistols locally. Two stood guard while the others burst into Moorehead's house as he, his wife and child, two servant boys and a servant girl 'were eating their supper off a basket laid on a stool'. Striking Moorehead to the floor they ransacked the house stealing several objects, looking for a gun, then shot their victim in the arms of his wife. Michael Kenny was one of three later arrested but the only one tried. On the day of the trial Kenny pleaded not guilty 'in a firm tone of voice' and his attorney challenged 20 jurors. The Attorney-General prosecuting the case set no juror aside. Kenny was not defended by a barrister (an attorney not being allowed to plead before the assize) which seems unjust in view of the eminence of the prosecuting counsel. It may also indicate Kenny's abandonment by former friends. There were five prosecution witnesses. The widow, Eliza Moorehead, gave the above version of events, adding that she did not see who fired the shot but that Kenny was present. He had lit a candle, and had stood upon a creel to scan the house-loft for the gun. In Moorehead's dying declaration, Kenny was mentioned. Anne Murphy, the servant girl, kidnapped for a time by friends of those arrested, bore witness now to Kenny having been 'the busiest among them'. The two servant boys had crouched under the table and dresser and could not identify him. A surgeon validated the cause of death. None of these witnesses appears to have been cross-examined by the prisoner. Three men put together alibis for Kenny 'which palpably contradicted each other'. The jury found him guilty after retiring for fifteen minutes: Kenny 'said nothing but gave a ghastly smile'. Two days later, at his sentencing, 'the galleries and body of the court were crowded to excess' by curious observers who heard Kenny compare his innocence to that of 'the child who was born last night'. Baron Richard Pennefather pronounced sentence 'after a most feeling and pathetic admonition ... which drew tears' from many there. The unexpected crying of Moorehead's baby and the wild exclamation of Kenny 'that the soul won't be 48 hours out of

Table 1. The motivation of outrages: Longford 1838, 1846 (% of cases)

Subjects of dispute	1838 %	Jan–May 1846 %	Total %	Total No.
Occupation of land	18	11	16	46
Rent	3	3	3	8
Employment and wages	15	11	13	37
Conacre	1	8	3	9
Obtaining arms	10	17	12	35
Assisting prosecution etc.	13	6	11	34
Estate organization	3	1	2	7
Other	19	21	20	54
No cause assigned	18	22	19	52
Total %	100	100	100	
Total cases	(201)	(81)	(282)	282

SOURCE: S.P.O., Outrage Papers (1838) County Longford; Assaults, etc. (Ireland) H. C. 1846 (369) xxxv.

my body when I will be revenged of my judge and my prosecutors' chilled the morbid audience. John Barnes RM later claimed that Kenny confessed his guilt in jail the night before his death. The following morning:

At an early hour, crowds of spectators proceeded ... to secure a standing place in the view of the gallows. As soon as the culprit appeared he stood silent ... [then said] 'I hope the faithful will pray for me; I forgive the world as I expect God to forgive me.' He then drew back a pace, knelt down and seemed to pray ... [on rising] the rope being long hung over his chest ... [he again spoke] 'I am sorry for what I said in the court house: I forgive my prosecutors'... then ... in a most determined, emphatic and vindictive tone, 'Beware of the breed of Breslan' ... The executioner adjusted the knot and performed his duty.[7]

The notoriety of the crime, the tragedy of capital punishment and the political tension of the time and place make it difficult to view the conduct of the case with any objectivity but it is suggestive of attitudes to the working of the law. To confirm or refute the implications of the Kenny case it is necessary to examine a broader range of the cases which appeared before the assizes and the working of the institution itself. Only in this way is it possible to reach any conclusion about the impartiality of the workings of the law.

II

While early-nineteenth-century Longford was relatively tranquil there were periods of disturbance, especially in the late 1830s. After the upsurge of Emancipation politics in the county from late 1825 the Protestant minority gradually became more introverted and politically more right-wing. In the face of Catholic political progress it became policy on several estates to strengthen the number of Protestant freeholdings at the expense of the poorer Catholic tenantry.

Table 2. Reported crime in County Longford, 1838

	Total	Reported by Victim	Reported by relative, friend, neighbour	Detected by police	Reported by J.P., Doctor, Priest, landlord	Reported by Observer	Others unknown
Crimes agt person	42	5	16	3	6	3	9
Crimes agt property	16	5	5	2	1	-	3
Crimes agt pub.peace	155	64	23	9	12	2	45
Res. to legal process	7	1	-	5	1	-	-
Totals	220	75	44	19	20	5	57
Percentages	100	34.1	20	8.6	9	2.3	26

SOURCE: S.P.O., Outrage Papers (1838) County Longford.

The resulting tensions came to a head in Ballinamuck about 1835. Between then and 1839, five Protestant settlers were murdered - Peter Hart, John Brock, Arthur Cathcart, William Morrison and Hugh Moorehead. Protestants attributed this to a 'murderous Papish conspiracy that desolates this country', while Catholics of all classes were convinced that landed power was being used to dislodge Catholic tenantry for Protestant colonization.[8] While it is clear from the types of offences committed in the county at this time (Table 1) that the 'land war' was not the only direct cause of agrarian crime, these tensions coloured virtually all crime. Protestant farmers were disproportionately represented among the targets of agrarian crime: the victims of 20 per cent of offences reported in 1838 bore Protestant surnames. As class and sectarian ranks closed, overt or passive resistance to police or courts and intransigence among participants in the administration of justice, was likely to increase.[9]

From 1822 the constabulary had acted as 'most able assistants' in the detection of criminals and the prosecution of crime. In 1839 the Longford force was substantially reinforced to help subdue the outbreak of agrarian violence.[10] But commitment of numbers alone could do little: local support for the constabulary was essential, as seen in Tables 2 and 3 which illustrate the factors determining the police investigation of serious crime. Less than one-tenth of specially reported crime was first noted by the police - there was an overwhelming reliance on public willingness to notify the police that a crime had been committed. For the purposes of prosecution, however, notification was of little value without the aid of eye-witness evidence as to the identity of the culprits. In 77 per cent of agrarian crimes in Longford, victims or their associates were content to relate the incident without passing on any suspicion. Intimidation among victims and sympathy among neighbours silenced those with information. A number of approaches were adopted to extract the necessary evidence: for example, summoning witnesses to petty sessions to be examined on oath in the hope of eliciting information.[11] There was generally also a batch of 'notorious characters' liable to be arrested for questioning.[12] The scene of the crime was

Table 3. Discovery of Suspects, County Longford 1838

	Total	Reporter named suspect	Police detected	No suspect suggested	Suspect described not named
Crimes agt person	42	20	3	15	4
Crimes agt property	16	4	–	10	2
Crimes agt pub. peace	155	18	11	120	6
Res. to legal process	7	4	1	2	–
Totals	220	46	15	147	12
Percentages	100	21	7	67	5

SOURCE: S.P.O., Outrage Papers (1838) County Longford.

searched for clues – a banknote lost by a member of a party raiding for arms in 1838 was used to trace and arrest him.[13] In cases that got to trial the police built up the material and circumstantial evidence of crime, and gathered all relevant witnesses, including 'approvers' (or accomplices turned king's evidence) who confessed to the police.[14] Once testimony and affidavits were sworn before magistrates this work became part of the evidence deployed by the crown counsel at assizes. As shown in Table 3 there was a chance of apprehension and trial in, at most, 30 per cent of reported agrarian outrages. Yet police success outside the area of agrarian crime was not so poor as contemporary laments about Irish hostility to legal processes might lead us to suppose.[15]

The framework of the law within which the police operated was relatively simple. There were three levels of statutory justice: petty sessions, quarter sessions and assizes. Petty sessions, introduced to Longford in 1823, had a local focus and provided cheap summary jurisdiction in certain civil and criminal cases. Magistrates diligently attended the nine weekly and fortnightly sessions, and the scale of court case-work is evidence of peasant confidence in low-level litigation. Other than intoxication and nuisance prosecutions these cases concerned neighbourly squabbles among farmers and townspeople.[16] The litigious spirit of the 'poor man', deprecated by Maria Edgeworth in 1800, found an outlet here.[17] About 6.6 per cent of summarily triable cases at petty sessions (assaults, larcenies, rescues) were sent up for trial at quarter sessions or assizes.[18] Most serious cases at these higher courts were first reviewed, however, in camera. An alleged case of burglary, for instance, would be reported to the police, who would notify a magistrate and secure his attendance, while witnesses were gathered for his examination. It was the magistrate who decided whether or not to take information on oath, issue a warrant for the arrest of suspects, or bind over prosecution witnesses in recognizances of between £10 and £30 to testify. Bail was commonly available.

Difficulties encountered in the prosecution of agrarian crime often made it seem as if 'all real law is an object of hatred to the mass of the Irish people'. On a visit to Longford in 1834, Henry Inglis interpreted stories of concealed runaway criminals as evidence of 'a determination ... to regard all men as martyrs ... [if] brought ... within the operation of the law'.[19] Yet the peasant decision to prosecute ordinary violent and non-violent crime at petty and quarter sessions suggests a basic endorsement of the processes of justice. Sympathy for agrarian offenders cannot automatically be equated with sympathy for a legal framework alternative to that of the common law, despite Catholic peasant embitterment at the injustices, perceived or real, of colonial minority rule.[20]

The government's uncertainty as to the degree of peasant faith in the courts caused the gradual growth of interest in criminal cases at the assizes and quarter sessions from the 1790s onwards. Private prosecution had been superseded on occasions in the seventeenth and early eighteenth centuries, but the practice became more common during the severe agrarian and political disturbances of the 1780s and 1790s when it was seen as 'preferable to allowing the law to be tacitly repealed by the insurgents'.[21] By 1810 there were several crown solicitors on each circuit of assize; until the early 1820s the crown generally restricted itself to 'cases of an insurrectionary nature'.

In those years the crown began to undertake the prosecution of 'the worst descriptions of homicide' and other serious cases of violence.[22] Simultaneously a statutory scheme for the remuneration of prosecutors and prosecution witnesses was developed. In June 1815 an Act 'for the payment of costs and charges to prosecutors and witnesses in cases of felony in Ireland' guaranteed their 'reasonable expenses' out of county funds. In the case of the more serious misdemeanours triable at assizes, Robert Peel's Criminal Justice Act of 1826 made the same provision.[23] Although private prosecution was thus encouraged, state anxiety was not allayed. Shifts in policy with regard to crown prosecution tended to coincide with the tenure of different Attorneys-General and are, as yet, little studied. However, from about 1830 it became the practice to prosecute occasionally at quarter sessions, while by 1834 nearly all murders and manslaughters, all agrarian crimes, robberies with violence, and most rapes and abductions were prosecuted by the crown at assizes. In 1836, sessional crown solicitors were appointed in each county to prosecute 'all cases of assault riot and breaches of the peace' when directed; usually when factional violence was involved. In early 1837, the crown commenced prosecution of non-violent robberies, such as the theft of cattle, sheep and horses and 'stealing from shops or outhouses'. By 1839 only the simplest of larcenies and offences such as fraud or embezzlement, in which it was believed that large institutions capable of hiring counsel were involved, were left at assizes to private prosecution. Sessional solicitors were made salaried officials in January 1842 and required 'to prosecute in all criminal cases at sessions' though, until the later nineteenth century, a certain number of cases continued to be privately prosecuted there.[24]

In theory, cases for crown prosecution were chosen by the Attorney-General well before each assizes but this was often a matter of form. By the mid 1820s crown solicitors were bypassing clerks of the crown and applying directly to the, often dilatory, magistrates for criminal informations. In correspondence,

Table 4. Prisoners for Trial Longford Assizes 1823–45 (%s)

Year	Nos. cttd	% Acquitted on trial	% Convicted	% No bill found	% No prosecution	% Bailed not tried	Total nos. tried	% Convicted
1823	193	22	40	33	4	1	120	65
1830	158	35	43	11	9	2	125	56
1834	132	35	26.5	13	21	4.5	81	43
1835	132	26	26.5	17	23.5	7	69	50
1836	132	12	14	10.5	63.5	–	34	56
1837	43	60	38	–	2	–	42	40
1838	74	58	42	–	–	–	74	42
1839	159	26	31	11	29	3	90	53
1840	76	37	32	16	14	1	53	49
1841	81	28	36	20	16	–	51	57
1842	101	51.5	28	10	11	–	80	35
1843	81	32	25	16	27	–	46	43
1844	43	51	21	18	10	–	31	35
1845	67	18	38	25	19	–	37	67
1823–34	483	30	38	20	10	2	326	56
1835–9	540	36	30	8	24	2	308	48
1840–5	449	36	30	17.5	16	0.5	298	46

SOURCE: see note 27.

the crown solicitor suggested 'necessary enquiries' to rectify material omissions in evidence, and required the attendance of witnesses before each assizes for crown examination. Stipendiary magistrates, aided by the local chief constable, were expected to advise on the deficiencies of cases. When, for instance, Pat Tiernan swore informations against Lawrence McCowran for firing on him on 6 January 1844, Patrick Howley RM considered the case 'extremely doubtful' but was loath to vote against crown prosecution, 'having no means of testing the particulars'. Again, after a perplexing series of incendiary fires in 1844 on the McGreevy farm in Templemichael, two constables happened to catch two farm servants with lighted coals, in incriminating circumstances. Nevertheless, Edward Tierney, a crown solicitor, decided against prosecution after an exhaustive discussion of the stringency of the evidence. As the range of crown prosecutions increased, the likelihood of pre-trial preparation diminished except in the more serious crimes. Hurried consultations between crown counsels, their agents and prosecution witnesses outside the court-room before indictment or arraignment became the norm of ordinary assize practice. However, cases involving 'approvers' and protected witnesses were more elaborately researched.[25]

III

The workings of this legal system are examined here based on a selection of 49 cases (and three retrials) tried at Longford assizes between 1833 and 1845 (mostly between 1836 and 1839) which were treated in some detail by the national press.[26] All were prosecuted by the crown. Forty-one can be classified as being of agrarian or political significance. The evidence in this case-sample is supported by a statistical analysis of persons committed, tried and sentenced at Longford assizes between 1836 and 1845, and is conveniently summarized in Tables 4 and 5.[27]

County Longford was usually the first of the five counties on the north-west circuit to be visited by judges on commission. Several weeks before the Hilary and Trinity vacations each year the 12 judges of assize divided the Irish circuits among them, the more senior judges tending to monopolize favourite circuits. Baron Richard Pennefather and Justice Robert Torrens were the judges most often assigned to the north-west circuit, presiding together at six assizes and with other judges on eleven other occasions. Justices John Doherty and Arthur Moore were also regularly assigned to this circuit. The duration of each assize was estimated two weeks before the judges set out, but was extended if necessary. Justice Torrens added a day in March 1838 due to the heavy case-load on the Longford assize calendar that spring. A busy assize meant a bustling crowded town for the three or four days of the court sittings: 'a vast concourse of people' flooded Longford town in February 1833. By contrast in July 1840 a light calendar partly explained there being 'scarcely any person to be seen on the streets'.[28]

By the 1830s assize ceremonial had become more restrained and less martial than in earlier decades, though the high sheriff, local dignitaries, and mounted policemen continued to parade with the judges to court on the opening day. In the Irish context such ceremony was symbolic of more than the majesty of law, and as Lovell Edgeworth found when he, as high sheriff, dispensed with armed guards in 1819, demilitarization of the assize released some of the tension usually associated with such displays. Prior to the judges' arrival the grand jury was called on and sworn in by the high sheriff to study county presentments. This body of magistrates, 'gentlemen of the best figure in the county', usually numbered 23 but could not be fewer than 12.[29] The grand jury was a highly politicized body, liable to contribute resolutions or memorials on national topics of the day. Its composition could also be sensitive to the political popularity of the high sheriff: the summer assize of 1836 seems to have been avoided by many Tory magistrates on account of the strongly Whig leanings of the High Sheriff, Sir Percy Nugent.[30] But presentment business was not often deserted. During the period 1830 to 1845 the grand jury stalwarts were John Thompson (19 appearances) William Ledwith (17), James Richardson (15), and a solidly Tory contingent of 13 other magistrates averaging 11 to 13 appearances each. The only Catholic magistrate to approach this level was J.L. O'Farrell with 11 appearances. The four other

Table 5. Prisoners Returned for Trial, Longford Assizes, 1836–45

	Total number offenders	Convicted													Acquitted				
		Transportation					Imprisonment					Discharged on sureties	Sentence respited	Total convicted	Not guilty on trial	No bill found	No prosecution	Bailed and not tried	Total acquitted
		Death	Life	14 yrs	7 yrs	Other periods	Over 3 yrs	2-3 yrs	1-2 yrs	6 mths –1 yr	0-6 mths								
1836-9																			
Non-violent property offences	75	–	5	1	10	1	–	–	2	9	10	–	–	38	16	6	15	–	37
Violent property offences	53	3	3	–	–	–	–	–	–	–	9	–	–	15	13	6	19	–	38
Violence agt person	48	5	2	–	–	–	–	–	–	4	4	–	–	15	7	12	14	–	33
Agrarian offences	191	5	9	3	10	–	–	–	1	5	3	–	–	36	82	7	62	4	155
1840-5																			
Non-violent property offences	119	2	2	12	8	7	–	–	2	4	17	–	–	54	28	8	29	–	65
Violent property offences	44	–	2	4	–	–	–	–	–	1	1	–	–	8	32	1	3	–	36
Violence agt person	93	4	1	–	–	–	–	–	1	2	10	–	–	18	28	32	15	–	75
Agrarian offences	133	–	5	3	8	5	–	–	1	3	14	3	–	42	49	22	19	1	91

Note: Certain uncategoriable and officially uncategorized commitments for trial, viz. 56 'other felonies' and 28 'suspected other offences', have been excluded from the table.

SOURCE: see note 27.

Catholic magistrates on the county panel were named from once to four times each. There was virtually no Catholic presence on grand juries of the early 1830s although it was said that one or two Catholic gentlemen had regularly been accommodated up to the 1820s.

Crown court commenced on the afternoon of the first day of assizes, when the judge handed his commission to the clerk of the crown, who formally opened court by reading it aloud. Then the grand jury was resworn for criminal business. The delivery of a 'charge' or judicial speech of direction to the grand jury was often perfunctory and sometimes so low-key as to be inaudible. It had a certain stock content and various phrases and propositions recurred in the charges of different judges speaking even decades apart. The grand jury was graciously informed that it was too experienced for any lecture on its duties, but that if needs be the judge was willing to give help. Recent enactments were expounded.[31] While the more eccentric judges sometimes viewed small gaol calendars with a dismal suspicion of mass peasant conspiracy, judicial charges generally became impassioned only when calendars were full. In March 1839 (an unusually busy assize for agrarian crime) Baron Pennefather was accused of trying to convince his audience that 'half the devils in Pandemonium had been let loose' in Longford.[32]

The role of the grand jury was to evaluate the legitimacy of complaints of crime set out as bills of indictment. Having listened to the judicial charge the magistrates withdrew into a private room where prosecution witnesses were interviewed. The flimsier cases could be dismissed as unworthy of an assize trial by the vote of at least 12 grand jurors. True bills were to be found and sent for trial 'upon legal evidence, which, if uncontradicted or unaffected by evidence from the prisoner, would warrant a conviction before the petty jury'. With the onset of crown prosecution one might imagine that grand juries would have begun to defer to the decision of the crown solicitors to prosecute but the body retained its power of assessment. The Longford grand jury continued to reject between 15 and 20 per cent of bills at assizes until the 1860s, even though allegedly the evidence of witnesses was 'except in very peculiar cases ... not sifted very strictly'. It is significant that the number of bills let through for trial varied with the state of agrarian violence in the county. In the later 1830s, for instance, the grand jury approved proportionately more bills of all kinds for trial, in response to agrarian disturbance, than in the early 1830s or the 1840s (Table 5). The proportion of bills rejected dropped from one-fifth to one-tenth between 1836 and 1839. In 1837 and 1838 not one bill was dismissed.[33]

Though it was unlikely that grand jurors were directly swayed by the judicial orations of this period, these probably helped consolidate their own sense of crisis. A tone of urgency in court could well have affected the more impressionable *petit*, or petty, jurors, who would actually try the case. These were sworn in as the bills were discussed. The sub-sheriff was primarily responsible for the constitution of the jury panel, summoning freeholders, generally strong farmers and shopkeepers, from lists provided by the clerk of the peace. From 1833 the qualifications

Table 6. Longford County Officials, 1829–45

Year	High Sheriff	Sub-Sheriff	
1830	Sir H. Crofton	–	–
1831	Barry Fox	–	–
1833	Samuel Blackhall	Robert Wilson	*Clerk of the Crown*
1834	Sir G. R. Fetherston	–	A. H. C. Pollock
1835	Fred T. Jessop	–	(1829–45)
1836	Sir Percy Nugent	Robert Morrow	–
1837	Hugh M. Tuite	James Ternan	*Deputy Clerk of the Crown*
1838	John Fetherston	Hugh Morrow	Thomas Gibbs (1829–44)
1839	Richard Maxwell	Hugh Morrow	Edmund Geale (1845–)
1840	Samuel Galbraith	Hugh Morrow	
1841	Henry Mustens	Hugh Morrow	*Clerk of the Peace*
1842	Hon. L. H. K. Harman	Hugh Morrow	John Vershoyle Crawford
1843	William Shirley Ball	Hugh Morrow	(1829–45)
1844	Thomas Hussey	Hugh Morrow	
1845	George Lefroy	Hugh Morrow	

SOURCE: *Thom's Directory.*

to serve on such a jury were to be male, aged between twenty-one and sixty, and a freeholder to the value of £10 a year.[34] Accurate lists of suitable candidates were hard to come by, however, and manipulation of the composition of the assize panel was notoriously common. Although the county panel contained numbers of Catholic freeholders, it was not hard to divert them from jury service. The practice of discrimination was not as overt in Longford as in other parts of the north-west circuit, but the provocative loyalism of the sub-sheriff, Hugh Morrow, aroused fiery denunciation of fixed juries during the 1830s. The panel was said to have become more restrictive in the later 1830s than it had been before the granting of Catholic Emancipation.[35] To judge by surnames the panels were 68 per cent and 59 per cent Protestant in the assizes of spring 1835 and spring 1836 respectively. An outraged *Freeman's Journal* reported that over 80 per cent of the Longford panel in March 1838 was made up of 'decided and redoubted Hanoverians'. It forbore from further comment in announcing that a mere 5 per cent of the panel was Catholic in March 1839. This did not in fact appease conservative opinion. 'Hundreds of murderers' were said to 'stalk with impunity through the land' in the late 1830s due to a rash of corrupt jury acquittals and the timidity of Lord Lieutenant Mulgrave's administration.[36] The controversy centred on the crown's voluntary abdication of its right to order jurors to 'stand by'.[37]

True bills having been found, the accused was arraigned and asked to plead. On the good faith of the crown, plea bargaining was accepted in a small number of cases by the 1830s.[38] On a plea of 'not guilty' being entered the process of forming a *petit* jury began. Between 1832 and 1844 prisoners charged with capital felony in Ireland had the right to challenge peremptorily a maximum of 20 jurors.

By 'usage and by practice' crown solicitors had for many years exercised the right to postpone the swearing-in of an unlimited number of jurors of their choice in all prosecuted cases of felony and misdemeanour. Once a prisoner's challenge was exhausted the crown could literally handpick juries. There being little crown prosecution until the 1820s most prisoners had until then a more extensive and unmodified power of challenge. As crown prosecution extended, prisoners' rights were in effect curtailed, being most endangered by the habitual reliance placed by crown solicitors on the advice in court of the prosecutor and his agent. On the north-west circuit it had been a maxim from the early 1800s 'to have counsel to watch the counsel for the crown'. Despite the stated neutrality of Edward Tierney, a crown solicitor, crown principles were easily evaded in practice by manoeuvring sub-sheriffs. The principles themselves faltered: 13 Catholics were set aside before the trial at the Longford assizes in March 1833 of Thomas O'Reilly for conspiracy to prevent tithe payment. The completed jury contained four grand jurors and eight propertied Tory gentlemen.[39] Increasing crown embarrassment led in July 1835 to drastic qualification of the 'usage'. From then until early 1845 the crown assumed the right to turn aside only for legal cause. There was soon a conservative outcry against the Whig administration due to an allegedly pernicious level of jury disagreement. There were several much-debated acquittals and retrials in Longford in 1836 and 1837, although in none was judicial surprise or dismay recorded. Before John Rodahan was acquitted of the murder of John Brock by a denominationally balanced jury in March 1837, John Schoales KC acknowledged the 'wise and discriminating manner' in which he had challenged. There was much bitterness expressed about the conduct of the trial of John and Andrew Johnston for manslaughter in July 1838, in which Frs McGaver and Dawson 'on the part of the next of kin' had the ear of the crown solicitor when jurors were set aside for written cause. But while there is room for dispute on the reasons for the decline in convictions apparent in 1837 and 1838, loyalist grievances were exaggerated. Most juries were exclusively Protestant during those years.[40] Yet it was clearly to outnumber Catholic jurors that the panel was doubled, with extra Protestant freeholders, in 1838 and 1839. It was easy for local arrangements to neutralize crown initiatives.

The basic shape of assize trial had been set from the 1760s. Counsel for the prosecution examined witnesses. These were cross-examined by the counsel for the prisoner, or, if undefended, by the prisoner himself. The prisoner could not give testimony on oath on his own behalf. The judge and jury were free to question witnesses if necessary. Defence and character witnesses were examined and cross-examined. The judge teased out the evidence for the jury in a concluding charge and passed sentence if a 'guilty' verdict was given. There was some concern lest large-scale crown prosecution should violate the spirit of this well-established system. It was felt that crown prosecutions ought to be carried out 'in a becoming way' so that for the sake of legal justice and dignity no case 'should be unduly pressed'.[41] Naturally the reality could be more strained.

The crown solicitor oversaw the jury empanellment. Then the crown counsels (Protestant until 1829) took over. John Schoales prosecuted 16 of the cases sampled. Unlike English trials it was only in serious cases that counsel introduced the prosecution case to the jury: this occurred in 11 of the cases examined. Such speeches, often 'of decisive importance' to the direction which a case would take, were conventionally subdued and impartial, but the crown could apply moral pressure to a jury at this stage of a trial in pursuit of conviction. In March 1839, as the Mulgrave administration weathered conservative criticism, the Attorney-General, Maziere Brady, attended the Longford assizes and personally prosecuted in four notorious cases, in a display of 'determination [by] the executive government ... to grapple' with unrest there. His speech in the trial of Michael Kenny seemed to go beyond the usual statement of facts in dwelling on the troubled state of the country and the necessity to punish malefactors. The conviction rate rose substantially that year although Brady's individual success rate was moderate, two convictions and two jury disagreements. Opening speeches by John Schoales at trials of alleged Ribbonmen in the early 1840s also verged on the overbearing in 'appealing to the feelings' of the Longford juries.[42]

Of the 49 crown-managed prosecutions studied here, the principal witnesses in nine were Protestant. In 10 cases there was only one prosecution witness. In 27 cases, there were between two and four. Policemen testified on behalf of the prosecution in 16 cases. The crown secured convictions in 29 of the 49 cases. Typically, an agrarian prosecution was supported by the testimony of the male head of the household which had been attacked by the accused, that of his wife, often repeating her husband's story, and also by that of one of their children or servants. Prosecution credibility generally hinged on the exactness of the identification, the consistency of the evidence, and the apparent candour of the witness. The main crown worries were defaulting witnesses and witnesses with feeble or malicious evidence. Prosecution failures due to the non-appearance of witnesses cannot be exactly quantified. The fact that 24 per cent of those committed for trial were discharged for want of prosecution may indicate victims' reluctance to prosecute but may be equally indicative of the weakness of a case in crown eyes. Postponements accounted for a proportion too. Once a case was under way it soon became evident whether or not witnesses had been thoroughly vetted by the crown. About half the acquittals in the case-sample were due to clearly implausible testimony, sometimes by witnesses of unsavoury character. The case of John Hart, who prosecuted several men in March 1837 for breaking into his house two months earlier, robbing a pistol and bayonet and setting fire to his thatch, foundered on a medley of improbabilities. Although his wife's testimony 'was an echo of her husband's', Hart recognized two of the defendants only by their voices, saw the others dimly, claimed to have overheard his neighbour, in a cabin abutting his, loudly talk of the plot but could not explain why this neighbour should risk burning his own cabin along with Hart's. In cross-examination he admitted previous unsuccessful and widely distrusted prosecutions and 'evinced great hesitation in answering many questions'.[43]

Three-quarters of the prosecution witnesses in the sample received no more

than the statutory subsistence allowance for their pains. There were six cases in
which the main prosecution witness was an 'approver', or fellow culprit turned
king's evidence for payment and a pardon. A small, persistently controversial
number of Irish cases depended on the evidence of approvers and informers. Ten
such persons, including two in Longford, underpinned assize prosecutions in
November 1845 and February 1846. Use of such evidence was seen as a necessary
evil, and the crown tended to await their testimony with trepidation. Although
approvers helped to obtain convictions in the three major trials of members of
the secret society of Ribbonmen in 1840 and 1842, the crown was less fortunate
in the 1830s when two of three recorded cases failed. The untruthfulness of
Patrick Mulloy testifying against John Rodahan for the murder of John Brock
probably tipped the verdict to an acquittal in spring 1837, but the crown
persevered in using approvers in conjunction with other witnesses.[44]

Police testimony in aid of prosecution was not wholly governed by rules of
procedure in the 1830s, although judicial concern over cautioning prisoners on
arrest was mounting. The status of the reported confession varied so that it is
difficult to be sure what impact it had in court. During the prosecution of six men
in March 1838 for administering an unlawful oath to Catherine Keane, sub-
constable James Mills reported taking John Mountford into custody and being
'asked by him, was it for Keane's outrage I arrested him; I had not mentioned the
name of Keane before'. Mountford was convicted despite a later concession by
Mills that 'Keane's affair had made a great deal of noise in the country at the time'.
There are examples of both concerted testimony and extremely scrupulous
testimony by police witnesses.[45]

However refined in 'matters of right feeling' the crown representative, it was
the judge on the bench who bore responsibility for the integrity of the trial. The
judge monitored proceedings for transgression of rules of evidence, continually
assessed the sufficiency of prosecution testimony in the light of the indictment,
and instructed the jury in points of law and pitfalls in testimony during and at the
close of the trial. The duty demanded much mental acuity, and stubborn
insistence on completion of a circuit in ill health may have been unwise: Baron
Pennefather struggled through circuit in March 1838 suffering 'from a severe
attack of gout and a complaint of the eyes'. Although most judges frequenting
the circuit were in their sixties and seventies there is no evidence of lapses in
judicial concentration at the assizes examined. About half of the acquittals in the
case-sample were brought about by judicial direction. The judge either let
meagre evidence run its course and then spoke pointedly of the inadequacy of
the crown case, or impatiently butted in after the second or third prosecution
witness, to discount their testimony. In March 1838, in a trial for robbery of arms,
Justice Torrens heard Patrick Boylan relate how several men entered his house
at dusk in early January looking for a gun to shoot fowl, without bothering to
'melist a chick' there, and C.C. Walker describe how his patrol arrested these
men later on, carrying a gun but with the stated intention of shooting game; he
then interjected, 'I shall not trouble you longer, Mr Walker: there is no evidence

against the prisoners to convict them on such an indictment.'[46] On occasion the bench reprimanded the crown for letting weak cases go to trial (often thereby prolonging a committal to jail). The innocence until convicted of those tried was several times stressed in charges to the grand jury, and Chief Justice Doherty in July 1839 severely reproved John Barnes RM for detaining a dozen men without charge for several months, shocked that any such detentions should exceed eight days, 'such is the tenderness that the law has for the liberty of the subject'.[47] The instability of cases reliant on the uncorroborated evidence of informers or approvers was regularly emphasized.[48] Prejudice was not explicitly betrayed.[49] The bench was not, as a rule, biased towards the prosecution, though some leniency towards the crown among certain judges seems to show through in high-profile cases. One must guardedly accept a description of the Irish judiciary of the time as 'the same mixed bag of noble characters and exhibitionists, anxiously conscientious humanitarians and impatient bullies' present on most benches.[50]

The best precaution against falling prey to the judicial mood was for the prisoner to hire defence counsel. As the number of capital felonies decreased, court assignment of counsel to the defence of poor prisoners, never generous, became rare. But, if the sample is a fair guide, prisoners equipped themselves with counsel in an astonishing 86 per cent of serious cases at assize. Long-standing prohibitions on the inspection of the depositions of prosecution witnesses, and on addressing juries in defence of felonies, were repealed in 1836, which may have led to an upsurge in legal work.[51] Defence style had altered somewhat from the 1820s: wizardry in probing for technical defects in the prosecution case became less effective as the rules of evidence were simplified. As there were no defence witnesses in one-quarter of the cases sampled, and only loose alibis in many others, the often confused prisoner relied heavily on counsel.[52] One of the defence successes was in the trial in March 1839 of Thomas Tally and George Mullen for the wilful murder of PC Samuel Mahaffy. Armed only with imperfect alibi witnesses, defending counsel Messrs Chambers and Boyd persuaded the bench and the Attorney-General that 'as the police had no warrant for arresting the prisoner ... the offence at most was nothing but manslaughter'.[53]

Jury verdict followed on a judicial charge summarizing the evidence. These charges were for the most part bland and careful. That of Justice Arthur Moore after the trial in July 1836 of Patrick Brannan for the murder of John Brock seems a model of evenhandedness – imploring the jury 'to cast from their minds every prejudice' in the midst of fevered party expectations. Jury deliberations were swift – this was a contemporary norm, probably related to the speed of trial (on average ninety minutes to each serious case). It is likely that close on half of the verdicts were immediate. Even at its peak the rate of conviction did not rise above two-thirds of those tried, and it more often levelled out at less than half. In the period from 1836 to 1845 just over one-third of those tried in Longford for agrarian crimes were convicted. Between 1836 and 1839 the proportion convicted was slightly lower than this average, despite the exceptional year of

1839. At no stage were the cases at the assize merely a succession of show trials, whether juries were dominated by the judge or left to their own devices (this despite the frequently sectarian bias in the composition of the jury). Intimidation may have been a factor, though this was not reportedly a common Irish problem and no offence of this type occurs in the outrage papers examined. The mutual acquaintance of prisoners and jurors - attested to several times when jurors offered evidence of good character for the defence - is an overlapping consideration. But the absence of judicial condemnation of verdicts seems to speak for the relative honour of juries.[54]

All things considered, the chances of conviction were not high for the totality of crimes. About two-thirds of those committed for trial reached court and half of those again were convicted. In cases of agrarian crime the odds were slightly shorter: one-quarter of those committed were not prosecuted, no bills were found against one-eighth, and just under a quarter were convicted. The majority of assize prosecutors were Catholic farmers and small peasantry testifying voluntarily for the crown counsel (unless binding over on recognizance be seen as compulsion); prosecutions engineered on the basis of paid approvers were few and not certain of success. Intriguingly, the widespread provision of prosecution counsel by the crown did not raise the conviction rate - which at least suggests the lack of direct collusion between judge, sheriff and crown solicitor. Even the transparent contrivance of local authorities did not guarantee convictions. There can be no easy dismissal of the prevailing unease among Catholics in court - the denominational bias in the institutions of state at all levels was too clear, if its effects could be subtle. The Irish legal system was of colonial origin; there were differences in statute law between England and Ireland which have yet to be investigated and, at least in the 1820s, an apparent inequality in the severity of sentences imposed for comparable offences.

This study can throw light on only one aspect of the legal system. It is clear that the workings of that system varied considerably according to both the type of court involved in the legal process and the social context of the crime. Social relationships within other parts of the north-west circuit, such as Fermanagh, were certainly different from those of Longford and the circumstances of the assizes differed accordingly. Within Longford itself problems taken to law received different treatment before different courts. This essay has examined only the assizes but the workings of other courts, such as the petty sessions, deserve the sort of detailed study which has been attempted here. Such studies would do much to reveal a series of different perspectives on Longford life at different points in time.

NOTES

I am grateful to Colm Tierney B.L. for his advice and generous assistance during the preparation of this article.

1. 'How small of all that human hearts endure
   that part that laws or kings can cause or cure!'
   from Oliver Goldsmith, 'The Traveller', in Desmond Egan (ed.), *The Deserted Village*, by Oliver Goldsmith (The Curragh 1978), p. 9.
2. *Freeman's Journal*, 2 Mar. 1832.
3. *Sixteenth report of the commissioners appointed to inquire into the duties, salaries and emoluments of the officers, clerks and ministers of justice ... in Ireland: Crown office*, H.C. 1826-7 (341) xi, 148; R. Barry O'Brien, *Dublin Castle and the Irish people* (London 1912), pp. 134-5; Fergus O'Ferrall, 'The Ballinamuck "Land War" of 1835-39', in *Teathbha*, ii, no. 2 (1983), pp. 104-9; see Table 6.
4. Modern published work includes: John F. McEldowney, 'The case of the Queen *v.* McKenna (1869) and jury-packing in Ireland' in *Irish Jurist*, new series, xii, no. 2 (1977), pp. 339-53; J. P. Casey, *The Office of the Attorney-General in Ireland* (Dublin 1980); D. S. Johnson, 'The trials of Sam Gray: Monaghan politics and nineteenth century Irish criminal procedure' in *The Irish Jurist*, new series, xx (1985), pp. 109-134; S. J. Connolly, 'Law, order and popular protest in early eighteenth century Ireland: the case of the Houghers', in Patrick J. Corish (ed.), *Radicals, Rebels and Establishments, Historical Studies*, xv (Belfast 1985), pp. 51-68; Daire Hogan, *The Legal Profession in Ireland, 1789-1922* (Dublin 1986); S. J. Connolly, ' Albion's Fatal Twigs: Justice and Law in the Eighteenth Century' in Peter Roebuck and Rosalind Mitchison (eds), *Economy and Society in Scotland and Ireland, 1500-1939* (Edinburgh 1988), pp. 117-25.
5. M.A. G. O'Tuathaigh, *Thomas Drummond and the Government of Ireland, 1835-41* (Dublin 1977), pp. 7-18; Leon Radzinowicz, *A History of English Criminal Law and its Administration from 1750, vol. 4: Grappling for Control* (London 1968), pp. 303-53.
6. Fergus O'Ferrall, 'The Ballinamuck "Land War"'.
7. *Report on the State of Ireland since 1835*, H.C. 1839 (486) xii, p. 922 (John Barnes); *Freeman's Journal*, 1, 6, 25 Mar. 1839.
8. Threshers were active in 1806 and 1816 (William Ridgeway, *A report of the proceedings under a special commission of Oyer and Terminer and Gaol Delivery for the counties of Sligo, Mayo, Leitrim, Longford and Cavan in the month of December 1806* [Dublin 1807]; *A statement of the nature and extent of ... disturbances ... Ireland*, H.C. 1816 [479] ix, 17). By early 1836 it was said of Longford,'There is more combination openly exhibited in this small county than in any other in the province' (S.P.O. Official Papers [unreg.] 1836/116); Fergus O'Ferrall, *Catholic Emancipation: Daniel O'Connell and the Birth of Irish Democracy* (Dublin 1985), pp. 69-71, 106-7; Fergus O'Ferrall, 'The Ballinamuck "Land War"'; *Devon Commission Evidence*, pt ii, H.C. 1845 (616) xx, pp. 284, 287, 291-3; editorial of *Dublin Evening Mail*, 15 July 1838; see also, A Resident of Longford, 'Insurrectionary state of the county Longford' in *Dublin University Magazine*, xi, Jan. 1838, pp. 121-3.
9. Names such as Gouldsberry, Moorcroft, Gregg, Evers, Diamond, etc.; there were 8 Orange Lodges in Longford County (*Appendix to first report... into the nature, character, extent and tendency of Orange Lodges*, H.C. 1835 [377] xv, pp. 42). For Ribbonism, see *State of Ireland since 1835 in respect to crime and outrage*, H.C. 1839 (486)

xii, 925 and reports on Longford Assizes, *Freeman's Journal,* 15 July 1840, 28 Feb. 1842, 11 July 1842.

10. *Report on the Public Prosecutors Bill,* H.C. 1854-5 (481) xii, 150; *Devon Commission,* pt iv, H.C. 1845 (672) xxii, appendices pp. 79-83.

11. S.P.O., Outrage Papers (1838) 19/43, 120, 125, 137.

12. S.P.O., Outrage Papers (1838), 19/12, 58, 114.

13. S.P.O., Outrage Papers (1838) 19/86.

14. Police credulity and overenthusiasm in such cases often led to hard knocks due to the fickleness or falsity of informers, cf. S.P.O. Outrage Papers (1838) 19/21.

15. Between 1835 and 1839, of 1737 persons indicted for trial at Tipperary Assizes, the police managed to make 78 per cent amenable (*Report on the State of Ireland since 1835,* H.C. 1839 (486) xii, pp. 891-4.

16. For a general discussion of petty sessions courts see Desmond McCabe, 'Magistrates, peasants and the petty sessions courts, Mayo 1823-50', in *Cathair na Mart,* v (1985), pp. 45-53; S.P.O. Reg. papers 1825/12, 288; *A return of the courts of petty sessions in the several counties of Ireland etc.,* H.C. 1836 (415) xlii, pp. 140-3.

17. Maria Edgeworth, *Castle Rackrent* (Dublin 1800), glossary pp. 108-9; the staunchly Tory magistrate Sir George Ralph Fetherston, though involved in politically motivated evictions, commanded a patriarchal respect that enabled him, acting singly at Ardagh petty sessions, 'in nineteen cases out of twenty... to settle the disputes without reference to law, and generally to the satisfaction of both parties'. In wages cases he appears to have leaned towards the claimant (*Poor Inquiry Ireland,* supplement II to appendix [D] [E] [F], H.C. 1836 [39] xxxiii, p. 16).

18. P.R.O., Home Office papers, series 100, Jan.-Dec. 1839.

19. Nassau senior, *Journals, Conversations and Essays relating to Ireland,* 2 vols (London 1868), I, 40; H. D. Inglis, *Ireland in 1834: A Journey throughout Ireland during the Spring, Summer and Autumn of 1834* (London 1836), pp. 345-6.

20. 'I think it is always much easier to get evidence where the outrage was of a private than where of a public nature ... in a common murder of a private nature the people wish to have the case prosecuted; but any case connected with the government they do not like to see prosecuted' (George Cornewall Lewis, *Local Disturbances in Ireland* [London 1836], evidence of Mathew Barrington, crown solicitor Munster circuit 1825, p. 207).

21. Ibid., p. 219.

22. *Report on the State of Ireland since 1835,* H.C. 1839 (486) xii, pp. 581, 1003 (evidence of Thomas Drummond and Mathew Barrington); *Report on the office of the clerk of the crown,* H.C. 1826-7 (341) xl, p. 64.

23. 55 George III c. 91; David Phillips, *Crime and Authority in Victorian England* (London 1977), p. 113.

24. *Report on the State of Ireland since 1835,* H.C. 1839 (486) xii, pp. 538-9 (William Kemmis), 604 (Edward Tierney), 703 (Maxwell Hamilton), 827-8 (John Cahill); *Report on the Public Prosecutors Bill,* H.C. 1854-5 (481) xii, pp. 143, 153-4; *Circular to Sessional Crown Solicitors,* 24 Dec. 1841, *Ballina Advertiser,* 31 Dec. 1841.

25. J. P. Casey, op. cit., pp. 23-5; *Report on the office of the clerk of the crown,* H.C. 1826-7 (341) xi, pp. 65-6 (Walter Bourne), 101, 117, 121-2 (Benjamin Riley and George Gibbs), 148 (Mathew Barrington); S.P.O. Outrage Papers (1845) 19/3011, 6395.

26. Unless given specific reference, the relevant issues were, *Freeman's Journal,* 2, 11 Mar. 1830; 24 July 1830; 2, 7 Mar. 1832; 27, 28 Feb., 1, 2, 5, 11 Mar. 1833; 11, 13 July 1833; 4 Mar. 1835; 18 July 1835; 26 Feb., 2 Mar. 1836; 6, 9, 11, 12, 13 July 1836; 2, 3, 4, 8 Mar. 1837; 10, 24, July 1837; 28 Feb., 1, 2, 3, 6, 7, 8 Mar. 1838; 11, 14

July 1838; 1, 2, 5, 6, 7, 25 Mar. 1839; 11, 13, 16 July 1839; 27 Feb. 1840; 3, 11, 15 July 1840; 1, 2 Mar., 24 Feb. 1841; 27 May, 6, 11 July 1842; 5 July 1844; 26 Feb. 1845; 9 July 1845. *Dublin Evening Mail*, 11, 13, 15 July 1838; 4, 14, 23, 28 Feb. 1842; 7 July 1843. References are to extracts from the local press describing Longford assizes.

27. The statistical tables are based on the following Parliamentary Papers: *Reports of the Inspectors-General on the State of Prisons in Ireland*, H.C. 1836 (523) xxxv; H.C. 1837 (123) xxxi; H.C. 1837-8 (186) xxix; H.C. 1839 (91) xx; H.C. 1840 (240) xxvi; H.C. 1841 (299) xi; H.C. 1842 (377) xxii; H.C. 1843 (462) xxvii; H.C. 1844 (535) xxviii; H.C. 1845 (620) xxv; *Tables of the number of criminal offenders committed for trial, or bailed for appearance at the Assizes and sessions in each county, 1845, and the result of the proceedings*, H.C. 1846 (696) xxxv. The figures recorded in Tables 4 and 5 relate to persons committed or bailed for offences triable only at assizes. Certain assault and larceny cases continued to end up in this court, so these figures differ slightly from the actual numbers tried at assizes.

28. *Freeman's Journal*, 28 Feb. 1833; 11 July 1840.

29. Fergus O'Ferrall, 'Maria Edgeworth and the local scene: a review' in *Teathbha*, ii, no. 1 (1980), p. 57; Edmund Hayes, *Crimes and Punishments or a Digest of the Criminal Statute Law of Ireland*, 2 vols (Dublin 1842), p. 361.

30. Other excuses were offered: *Freeman's Journal*, 2 Mar., 12 July 1836.

31. For various charges see, *Freeman's Journal*, 2 Mar. 1832; 27 Feb. 1833; 11 July 1833; 1 Mar. 1838; 1 Mar. 1839; 11 July 1839; *Dublin Evening Mail*, 28 Feb. 1842.

32. See charge given by Baron W. C. Smith at Louth assizes, *Freeman's Journal*, 7 Mar. 1833; editorial in *Freeman's Journal*, 7 Mar. 1839.

33. Edmund Hayes, op. cit., p. 363; *Report on the Public Prosecutors Bill*, H.C. 1854-5 (481) xi, p. 153.

34. *Report on the Office of Sheriff*, H.C. 1826 (310) xvii, pp. 191, 196; 3 and 4 Wm IV, c. 91.

35. For conduct at assizes on the N.W. circuit in general see, *First Report on Orange Lodges*, H.C. 1835 (377) xv, pp. 68-98 (evidence of Randall Kernan, barrister); *Report on the Courts of Quarter Sessions*, H.C. 1828 (144) xii, p. 47; *Report on the Office of Sheriff*, H.C. 1826 (310) xvii, p. 130. Christopher Reynolds, attorney and Sub-Sheriff in the early 1820s, was, unusually, a Catholic. He later became involved in Emancipation politics (Fergus O'Ferrall, *Catholic Emancipation*, p. 107.)

36. *Return of Criminal Proceedings* (H.C. order 16 Mar. 1837) from clerks of petty sessions 1835-7 (S.P.O.), viic-8-17; *Freeman's Journal*, 2, 8 Mar. 1838; 5 Mar. 1839; A Resident of Longford, 'Insurrectionary state ...', in *Dublin University Magazine*, vol. xi, Jan. 1838, p. 122.

37. For lengthy consideration of this issue, see D. S. Johnson, 'The trials of Sam Gray'.

38. See Rex *v*. Christopher Carbry, *Freeman's Journal*, 13 July 1833.

39. *Report on the State of Ireland since 1835*, H.C. 1839 (486) xii, pp. 611-13 (Edward Tierney), 1055-8 (Louis Perrin), 1160-1 (Michael O'Loghlen); *Freeman's Journal*, 1 Mar. 1833.

40. *Freeman's Journal*, 4 Mar. 1837; *Dublin Evening Mail*, 15 July 1838; *Report on the State of Ireland since 1835*, H.C. 1839 (486) xii, pp. 797-8 (Edward Tierney), 1151-5 (Arthur Auchmuty Griffiths); Kerby Miller, 'The Ballymahon riot of 1837: a study of sectarian conflict in county Longford', unpub. paper, U.C.D., 1987; Regina *v*. Patrick Magee, *Freeman's Journal*, 3 Mar. 1838; Regina *v*. Anne Quinn, *Freeman's Journal*, 6 Mar. 1838.

41. Sir James Stephens, *A History of the Criminal Law of England*, 2 vols (London 1883),

i, pp. 428-56; *Report on the Public Prosecutors Bill*, H.C. 1854-5 (481) xii, p. 143; in 1825 Daniel O'Connell spoke favourably of the conduct of crown prosecutions (*Report and Minutes of Evidence on the State of Ireland*, H.C. 1825 [181] ix, p. 126).

42. Thomas Lefroy, *Memoir of Chief Justice Lefroy* (Dublin 1871), p. 52; Sir James Stephens, op. cit., i, pp. 428-9; J. P. Casey, op. cit., p. 25; Regina *v.* William Magrath, James Cowan, etc., *Freeman's Journal*, 11 July 1840; Regina *v.* Andrew Gill, *Dublin Evening Mail*, 28 Feb. 1842; Regina *v.* Francis McKenna, *Freeman's Journal*, 11 July 1842.

43. Rex *v.* John Hart, *Freeman's Journal*, 3 Mar. 1837.

44. Rewards offered to witnesses (Ireland), S.P.O., Official Papers (Unreg.) 1846/157; Rex *v.* John Rodahan, *Freeman's Journal*, 4 Mar. 1837; see also Regina *v.* William Eccles, John Stevin, etc., *Freeman's Journal*, 5 Mar. 1839; and Rex *v.* Hugh O'Neil, Peter Tierney, Daniel Quin, etc., *Freeman's Journal*, 13 July 1836.

45. Sir James Stephens, op. cit., i, pp. 440-1; Regina *v.* Bernard Flynn, John Mountford, etc., *Freeman's Journal*, 3 Mar. 1838; see Rex *v.* Thomas O'Reilly, *Freeman's Journal*, 1 Mar. 1833; Rex *v.* Revd Edward McCann, James Knight, etc., *Freeman's Journal*, 2 Mar. 1833; Regina *v.* Peter Prunty, *Freeman's Journal*, 6 Mar. 1837.

46. *Report on the Public Prosecutors Bill*, H.C. 1854-5 (481) xii, p. 143; *Freeman's Journal*, 30 Jan. 1838; at fifty, in 1835, Chief Justice John Doherty was the youngest man on the bench (F. E. Ball, *The Judges in Ireland, 1221-1921*, 2 vols [London 1926]).

47. Rex *v.* William Devany, *Freeman's Journal*, 11 July 1836; it turned out not to have been his fault (*Freeman's Journal*, 11, 16 July 1839).

48. See Rex *v.* Hugh O'Neil, Peter Tierney, etc., *Freeman's Journal*, 13 July 1836; *Freeman's Journal*, 1 Mar. 1838; 23 Feb. 1842.

49. Of course virtually every judge was, in this period, a Tory nominee.

50. See Rex *v.* Thomas O'Reilly, *Freeman's Journal*, 1 Mar. 1833; Regina *v.* Andrew Gill, *Dublin Evening Mail*, 28 Feb. 1842. John O'Donovan, 'The Irish judiciary in the 18th and 19th centuries (Part II)', in *Eire/Ireland*, iv, no. 4 (Winter 1971), p. 19.

51. *Report on the Public Prosecutors Bill*, H.C. 1854-5 (481) xii, p. 147; Prisoner's Counsel Act, 6 and 7 Wm IV, c. 114.

52. Daniel O'Connell had been an exceptional exponent (Sean O'Faolain, *King of the Beggars: A Life of Daniel O'Connell* [Dublin 1938], pp. 115-17); Sir James Stephens, op. cit., i, pp. 280-93.

53. Regina *v.* Thomas Tally and George Mullen, *Freeman's Journal*, 5 Mar., 13 July 1839.

54. Rex *v.* Patrick Brannan, *Freeman's Journal*, 11 July 1836; Cornewall Lewis, op. cit., p. 222; Regina *v.* James Scanlan, Francis Doherty, *Freeman's Journal*, 6 Mar. 1838; Regina *v.* Robert Betagh, *Freeman's Journal*, 2 Mar. 1838.

Politics and Electioneering in County Longford, 1868–80

GERARD MORAN

Historians have for a long time been interested in the workings and structures of politics and electioneering within Ireland and no period has been examined and analysed more intently than that between 1868 and 1880. Its fascination for students of both history and politics lies in the fact that it heralds the demise of the old political and electioneering system and marks the emergence of the modern political order from 1880 with the growing strength of Parnellism. The introduction of the Secret Ballot Act of 1872 and the arrival of a third political force, the nationalist movement, after the 1874 general election contributed to this dramatic change.

While a number of important studies at national level have been carried out, there has been little examination of contemporary trends at a local level. Yet local factors and influences played a major role in moulding nationalist politics to regional concerns and were of particular importance in the period up to 1874. Even within constituencies variations are to be found which at certain periods exercise a major influence on the internal politics of an area. At the same time the influence of national issues and how they are viewed at local level must not be overlooked. Nowhere is this more evident than in County Longford which might at first examination appear to have been uneventful and docile in electioneering affairs.

In examining the political and electioneering situation in Longford three points can be noted which make the county unique within the national experience. Firstly, Longford was the only county in the country where the Conservative party was unable to secure even one of the two county seats. Not since the election of two local landowners, Viscount Forbes and Anthony Lefroy in 1835, had Longford returned a Conservative to Westminster. Failing to secure even one of the seats in the 1860s, the Conservatives attracted only 561 voters, or 19.6 per cent of the electorate.[1] Their only chance of sharing the representation was a coalition with the Whigs but this was frustrated by the links between the Whigs and the Catholic clergy, which had existed since 1827. Between 1835 and 1874 the county's representatives came from the Liberal party, except for a brief period in the 1850s when the Independent Irish party secured both seats.

Longford also deviated from the national norm in the electoral power of the Roman Catholic clergy, which was much greater than in most other constituencies. As Fergus O'Ferrall's essay above has shown, the electoral strength of the clergy grew dramatically from the late 1820s and continued to increase right up to the 1870s, being at its height in 1874. In the country as a whole between 1857 and 1868 it was the clergy alone who were responsible for the selection and nomination of the parliamentary candidates. In most constituencies, the electors were given an opportunity of endorsing the candidates at a public meeting, although this was merely a rubber-stamping exercise. Within Longford, however, there is no evidence to indicate that the electors were given an opportunity to approve clerical nominees, even on election day, and the Conservatives' failure to propose candidates at election time meant that there were no contests. Only one election in the 1860s was contested, a by-election in 1862.

Longford was probably the best-organized county in the country in terms of clerical influence. The clergy could enforce the selection of its favoured candidates without the onus of having to account for their decisions to a meeting of electors. Their task was simplified in that most of the county fell within the single diocese of Ardagh and there was no need for a consensus amongst several bishops, as there was in counties like Galway and Mayo.[2]

Thirdly, the electorate in the 1850s and 1860s tended to be a politically moderate one, especially over issues such as Catholic education and other middle-class preoccupations. This was a result of the co-operation between the clergy and the Whigs in political leadership. The importance of the clergy can be seen in their selection of Major Myles O'Reilly in 1862, even though the candidate's connections were with County Louth rather than Longford. Although O'Reilly advocated the principles of the Independent Irish party of the 1850s, his significance lay in his involvement as leader of the Irish battalion of the Papal Brigade in Italy in 1860.[3] His selection was due to services to the Catholic Church rather than to the nation.

Up to 1868, all Longford contests during the 1860s were characterized by the predominance of local issues over national grievances, and the parochial nature of parliamentary politics was evident even during the general election of that year. In the rest of the country political feeling was running high because the election centred on Gladstone's policy of justice for Ireland; however, the demonstrations in support of Gladstone which marked the election in most constituencies did not occur in Longford. Much of Longford's apparent parochialism was due to the pervasive influence of the clergy and the Whigs, helped in no small way by the weakness of a nationalist movement in the county. Nationalism was already taking root in the rest of the country in the wake of the 1867 Fenian events. Yet only two candidates, Colonel F. S. Greville-Nugent and Major O'Reilly, were nominated in Longford and while they spoke in favour of the principal issues of the day - church disestablishment, land reform and Catholic education - the generally subdued tone of the election was obvious.[4] The demand for an amnesty for Fenian prisoners played a significant role in most constituencies in the three southern provinces in the 1868 election, but it did not figure in any way in the Longford contest. The clergy's success in refusing to allow it to become part of the Longford election meant that neither candidate was pressurized to make it part of his election manifesto.

The 1868 election confirmed the clergy as the principal power grouping in Longford politics, but before long it became clear that this authority was coming under threat. Elsewhere, the amnesty demonstrations in late 1869, the election of the imprisoned Fenian leader, Jeremiah O'Donovan Rossa, as MP for Tipperary and the amnesty petition drawn up by Dean O'Brien of Limerick all combined to give fresh impetus to the nationalist movement. In December 1869 the new-found nationalist fervour in Longford made the by-election between John Martin and Reginald Greville-Nugent one of the bitterest and most controversial contests ever to take place in Ireland. For this reason it is of interest to examine the contest in some detail.

I

The elevation of the sitting Longford MP, Colonel Greville-Nugent, to a peerage at the end of 1869 created a vacancy in the county. Even before the public was informed of the resignation, Lord Greville decided to seek the clergy's support for his son, Reginald, to succeed him. A meeting in St Mel's College, Longford on 28 November was organized by Fr James Reynolds, president of St Mel's, Fr Edward McGaver, parish priest of Granard and the most prominent cleric to engage himself in the political affairs in the county since the 1820s, as discussed above in Fergus O'Ferrall's essay, and Fr Peter Dawson, Dean of Ardagh; and Reginald Greville-Nugent was selected as the clergy's nominee.[5] The main reason for this prompt action was anxiety amongst the senior clergy after O'Donovan Rossa's electoral victory in Tipperary a few weeks earlier. However, the haste in adopting a new candidate was to lead to problems later as this meeting was representative not of the clergy as a body, but rather of the more influential few. The importance attached to this clerical backing is demonstrated by Greville-Nugent's failure to issue an electoral address until mid-December. At the time of seeking this support it would appear that he had not formulated his position with regard to education, agrarian reform and amnesty, which would have been the touchstones for popular support.

Such a situation was not exclusive to Longford, but in the absence of any other major political brokers, such as landlords, who were active in nearly every other county, the role of the priests was rendered more significant. Through the parish system, the individual cleric could organize electors and non-electors and provide very strong support for their particular nominee from the pulpit. It was an advantage which most of their opponents envied and which could be decisive.[6]

The essence of the priests' political power was their unity. From the mid 1860s the Catholic clergy had presented a unified front at election time. The clerical conventions in Longford prior to the nomination were at the behest of the Bishop of Ardagh and Clonmacnois, John Kilduff, who attempted to avoid the divisions that had occurred within the ranks in 1857.[7] In most constituencies the real decision was made not at the polling station but at such conventions, held prior to election day. While a division might occur at the selection meeting, once a candidate was chosen it was considered proper that all the clergy give him their full support, thereby making him almost impossible to defeat. No division was entertained within the clerical ranks and those priests who were not totally in support of the agreed candidate, such as Fr James Lee of Killashee at the 1869 by-election, soon found themselves removed to remote parishes.[8] Clearly the more senior clerics, such as Fr James Reynolds, laid it on the line to their junior colleagues that no dissension would be tolerated. This occurred even when the meeting nominating Greville-Nugent caught most priests by surprise.

While there is little doubt of the strong clerical unity within Longford for the 1869 by-election, the events of that year indicated that there was a breakdown in the political cohesion of the clergy in other parts of the country. It was this situation which prompted the Irish bishops in Rome to bring about the condemnation of the Fenians by name. For the first time the growing political problems confronting the Irish hierarchy came to prominence. Clerics with nationalist sympathies were now expressing their feelings in public and a large number of clerics from outside Longford made known their support for John Martin, the nationalist candidate in County Longford. They included Frs Lavelle of Cong in Mayo, Quaid of O'Callaghan's Mills in Clare and Mullen of Westmeath.[9]

Clerical involvement in Longford was most overt during the 1869 by-election itself. While no actual committee was established for Greville-Nugent, the task of electioneering was taken on by all the Catholic clergy in the county, with Fr Reynolds, Fr Michael O'Reilly, parish priest of Taghshinny, and John Maxwell acting as an unofficial inner committee. Reynolds's role in the proceedings can be judged by the fact that he was directly responsible for expending £3007 of the Greville-Nugent expenses and the clergy's overall involvement is clear from the £15 and £20 with which he provided each parish priest for electoral purposes.[10] At a practical level the priests indicated their support through their appearance on the platforms at the Greville demonstrations in the county: 12 were present at a public meeting in Ballymahon, 10 in Longford town and eight in Granard. The priest also used all his influence to ensure that the opposition candidates were ostracized. Fr McGivney, parish priest of Rathcline, excommunicated a Martin supporter, James Skilly, and instructed the people to shun him. Fr Duffy of Drumlish incited his congregation to attack the opposition candidate's supporters.[11] Such practices resulted in priests being called before the parliamentary petition inquiry which examined the case.

Despite the fact that it was a landlord who was contesting the election the landowners played little part in securing his victory. It was the priests who organized the electors, canvassed the meetings and scrutinized the electoral lists, thus consolidating their position as political power brokers within the county. One of the motives for their involvement was the belief that their support for Greville-Nugent was a means of indicating their support for Gladstone and his policy of redressing Irish grievances.

The challenge to the clergy's political dominance in the 1869 by-election came from the nationalists who were riding on the crest of a wave after the electoral success of O'Donovan Rossa in Tipperary. On 1 December, shortly after it was disclosed that the Longford clergy had nominated Greville-Nugent, a group of local nationalists, led by James B. Murtagh, a Ballymahon businessman, and Patrick Egan, a Ballymahon Fenian, put forward the name of John Martin. The idea of proposing a well-known Fenian, such as Thomas Luby Clarke, had been dropped since he would have been identified purely as a Fenian candidate and there was no Fenian power-base in Longford as had existed in Tipperary. By selecting a person on the basis of their sympathy with national issues and an amnesty for Fenians, support from all nationalist groups would be forthcoming. While prominent constitutional nationalists such as A. M. Sullivan and Isaac Butt had not openly supported O'Donovan Rossa in Tipperary, it was easier for them to espouse a constitutional nationalist like John Martin.[12]

Martin proved the ideal rallying-point for drawing together both constitutional and militant nationalists. In 1848 he had been a Young Irelander and in 1862 had established the National League, which opposed Fenianism. In 1868 he had been arrested on a charge of being a Fenian sympathizer.[13] Along with Isaac Butt he was probably the only person who could unite the two nationalist strands. Indeed whilst a constitutional nationalist he had professed a disdain for the 'hateful' House of Commons, especially the way in which Irish representatives were chosen.[14] Although in America on holidays when nominated for Longford, it was known he would accept the nomination providing it was on his terms.[15] He represented the growing nationalist identity that was emerging in Ireland during the closing months of 1869.

While the Grevilles had been regarded as enlightened landlords who were good to their tenants, Reginald Greville-Nugent was still branded by *The Nation* as:

a brainless boy, a beardless diminutive creature, who would be more at home in the play-ground spinning tops or playing marbles, than in a political assembly where important subjects are debated and the affairs of nations are at stake.[16]

The nationalist rejection of Greville-Nugent as a nominee suggests that during periods of extreme fervour the tendency existed to turn against candidates who would at other times have been acceptable. The polarized state of the country meant that all landlords were regarded as evicting peers, place-hunting English lords and traitors. In the elections of 1852 and 1868 it had been easy to classify candidates as either tenant or landlord supporters, but when the national question dominated an election, it became more difficult to classify people into distinct groupings. While Greville-Nugent, was acceptable to certain groups in Longford, as witnessed by his clerical support, in the Ireland of 1869 with its strong nationalist fervour, such candidates had great difficulties in securing popular support. The Longford by-election of 1869 highlighted the battle between localism, as represented by Greville-Nugent, and nationalism, as put forward by Martin. The situation was best summed up by George Henry Moore, MP for Mayo and a leading nationalist, in a public letter to the people of Longford:

The question you have to decide is whether your county shall be handed over periodically from father to son, as a family chattel; or whether the honour of representing you is to be made the reward of service, sacrifice, ability and experience.[17]

Perhaps the most important feature of both the Tipperary and Longford by-elections of 1869 was the emergence of a core of politically active nationalists who were independent of the clergy and prepared to challenge their electoral dominance when the opportunity presented itself. They were to become the third force in Irish politics during the 1870s and their roots were independent of the existing broker system of priests and landlords. However, at this point their efforts were unsustainable, depending on a continuous line of successes, demonstrations and electoral victories to maintain momentum. Already there were indications in the country that the land question was beginning to replace the national question as the all-important issue of the day. The Martin camp in 1869 was a temporary coalition of different interest groups: Fenians and constitutional nationalists, who in reality had little in common.

It must be stressed that by-elections were more advantageous than general elections in promoting the nationalist cause. In a by-election situation the advanced nationalists were able to put all their resources, both financial and personal, into the one contest. It was easy to attract national figures to counties like Longford for public meetings in order to give open support to a candidate. However, in a general election such resources were more stretched. Even the concentration on a few regions would not have had the same beneficial effects because exposure, in particular from newspapers, would have been swamped in the overall election coverage.

While the initiative for Martin's selection had come from inside Longford there was no internal political leadership to underpin this selection and this had to be provided from outside. In the months immediately following the passing of Gladstone's Disestablishment Act in 1869, the nationalists were dependent on outside help to promote their case and to highlight Martin's patriotic zeal to the Longford electors. Stephen Joseph Meaney, a Fenian, Edmond O'Donovan, and Denis R. Sullivan of *The Nation* were the main outside speakers at the Martin meetings. These meetings were characterized by overt displays of nationalist fervour with green badges and emblems being worn by most members of the crowd. The wearing of sashes was a Fenian custom and served to heighten the fear and suspicions of the authorities.[18]

The 1869 Longford by-election has been cited as a major reason for the growth of the Home Rule movement.[19] What it certainly did was draw men of diverse political backgrounds together, furnishing them with a basis on which to build. It provides an indicator of the type of person who was drawn to the Home Government Association when it was established in May 1870. Individuals like Isaac Butt, A. M. and T. D. Sullivan, Fr Patrick Lavelle and W. H. O'Sullivan at a national level, and James R. Murtagh and Patrick Egan in Longford, gave Martin either active or moral support during the contest. These were the men who would later become leading members of the new movement. The contest introduced Fenians like Egan to electioneering and no doubt contributed towards their drift to the constitutional movement. At the same time Conservative landowners like Captain E. R. King-Harman were prompted to move towards Home Rule.

Divisions emerged between the national and local bodies of Martin's supporting committees because of the unilateral decision by James B. Murtagh to withdraw Martin's candidature on 10 December 1869, following strong clerical pressure. This resulted in much confusion as the nationalist group, led by A. M. Sullivan, immediately re-entered Martin in the contest.[20] The move and counter-move spurred on the nationalists into a more concerted campaign which manifested itself in the dramatic increase in the number of Martin meetings over the following few weeks, starting off with a large demonstration in Longford town on 11 December.

The contest's national importance can be gauged by the involvement of people from neighbouring counties, especially Westmeath, Cavan and Leitrim, attributable to the influence of *The Nation*, which called on these counties to protect Martin's supporters from clerical intimidation.[21] The extent of these people's support for Martin becomes more apparent when the regional variations within Longford are examined. For electoral and poor law purposes the county was divided into three regions based on the three main towns: Longford for the west of the county, Granard for the north and Ballymahon for the south. With the county divided in such a manner it was inevitable that events in neighbouring counties would have major effects on those areas. The main areas of Martin's support were Granard and Ballymahon, which were close to Westmeath and Cavan. Granard proved to be the most volatile district in the county with disturbances taking place at each of the four Martin meetings. The culprits were found to be from Leitrim and Cavan.[22] On polling day, 31 December, the greatest disturbances in both Ballymahon and Granard were perpetrated by non-electors from the neighbouring counties.

External involvement in the election highlights the problem of electoral violence and the role of non-electors in elections before 1872. It must be noted, however, that there had been riots at election contests in Longford in 1852 and 1862. The involvement of the non-electors in Longford was greatest when the clergy were actively involved in the electioneering process and the non-electors were paid for their services. Yet in many instances the clergy regarded it as the only means of counteracting the opposition that came from outside the county.

Three main trends are evident in electoral violence in Longford, and in Ireland generally. In the first instance there was the open confrontation that occurred on market-day in the various towns of the county. While clergy used the altar and landlords threatened evictions, the nationalists took advantage of the market-place to publicize their message. The large crowds congregating in the towns on business created convenient assembly points at which to address both electors and non-electors. As churches and their grounds were out of bounds to the nationalists, the market provided their only opportunity of this type. The new procedure brought a response from the clergy, who organized counter-demonstrations on market-day rather than relying exclusively on the pulpit.

However, as the market-place brought people of every political persuasion together, opponents were very easily found to disrupt a meeting, as at Granard and Ballymahon on 15 and 17 December,[23] and it was difficult for the constabulary to provide adequate protection. In order to prevent trouble large numbers of police and military had to be stationed in the county, but even this did not ensure that peace would prevail.[24] Having to resort to fixing bayonets and loading rifles, as at Granard, led to potentially explosive situations.

The second aspect of electoral violence took the form of nocturnal visits by non-electors to electors in the days before the election in order to persuade them to vote in a certain way. During the 1852 contest there had been 52 night visits to Longford electors in support of the popular candidates, and the same method was to be used by Martin's supporters.[25]

A third type of electoral violence was seen on election day in 1869, 31 December, when large crowds from each side gathered in an attempt to intimidate their opponents. Once again rioting was at its most intense in Ballymahon and Granard, with extremely violent scenes occurring at the bridge leading into Ballymahon as a mob from Westmeath attempted to enter the town. The only way in which the voters could safely go to the polls was in large numbers under the escort of police and priests. Consequently, in Longford town nearly 70 per cent and in Ballymahon 93 per cent of Greville-Nugent's supporters had voted en bloc by midday.[26] The irony was that the army was engaged in protecting voters supported by the clergy and not, as on previous occasions, in protecting voters from supporters of the clerically backed candidate. While the Galway and Kerry by-elections of 1872 were the last occasions where the army had to be used for the collection of voters by the landlords, the Longford contest was certainly the last, and possibly the first, where they had to defend the clergy's voters.

Clearly intimidation influenced the voters. Although the clergy had worked at full stretch for the 1869 contest, the turnout (67 per cent) was lower than at the election three months later (77 per cent) or the 1874 general election. Many voters remained at home, fearing attacks by the Martin supporters from neighbouring counties. However, the turnout exceeded that in the election of O'Donovan Rossa when only 23 per cent cast their votes.[27] The higher turnout must be attributed to the greater co-ordination in mustering the voters to the polls, along with the fact that the priests had deduced from the Tipperary experience that a low turnout would be to the advantage of the nationalists.

The Longford contest highlighted the inadequacies in the Irish electoral system aggravated by the lack of a sufficient number of local polling stations. Electoral violence before 1850 was aided by the fact that each constituency had only one station. In 1868 there were 155 polling stations in the country although after the Secret Ballot Act of 1872 this was increased to 640.[28] At the time of the 1869 Longford contest there were only three polling stations in the county: at Longford, Granard and Ballymahon. This was subsequently increased to 12, which was a major factor in curbing electoral violence. The new stations were at Ballinalee, Ballinamuck, Carrickboy, Cattragh Beg, Drumlish, Edgesworthstown, Keenagh, Lanesborough and Newtownforbes.[29] Prior to 1874 opposing groups could concentrate on those few areas where the polling was being conducted, but now it became more difficult. However, the proliferation of polling stations also created problems for the constabulary, who now had to police a large number of venues. The new situation brought about more contested elections. In the 1874 general election only 17 seats in 10 constituencies were uncontested and this had the advantage of opening up the constituencies to the nationalists.

While the 1869 Longford by-election marked the pinnacle of electoral violence in the county, the constabulary took no chances at the election of May 1870 and large numbers of police were drafted in from Sligo, Leitrim and Roscommon. However, the contest was relatively peaceful, providing further proof that interference from adjoining counties had contributed greatly to the lawless state of the county in 1869.

At the parliamentary petition which sought to have the election of 1869 declared void the nationalists tried to apportion blame for the electoral violence to the clergy, but the presiding judge, Justice Fitzgerald, placed much of the blame for the disorder on the nationalists.[30] While the clergy emerged from the charge largely unscathed, 10 were found guilty of treating and corrupt practices. The experience made them adopt a much more cautious approach regarding their future electioneering and political activities.[31]

II

The attitude of the clergy towards political developments was well illustrated in the 1869 by-election. They were not averse to nationalism or nationalist candidates themselves as can be seen from the private sentiments expressed by many clerics concerning Martin's suitability; he was hailed as having some excellent qualities compared to Greville-Nugent, who was considered contemptible.[32] One of the most notable admirers was George Conroy, Bishop of Ardagh and Clonmacnois from 1871. As it was, both candidates were in agreement on the popular issues of tenant right and Catholic university education. What militated against Martin was that the priests were not prepared to accept a candidate who was selected by and answerable to the laity. While the clergy opposed Martin and the local landlord and Home Ruler, Captain E. R. King-Harman, in the 1870 by-election, they were still prepared to offer petitions of support, as when King-Harman was elected MP for Sligo.

One of the major fears of the Longford clergy was not the idea of nationalism but the form it took: Fenianism. In the 1860s the county had been little influenced by this movement, Ballymahon being the only area where it had any discernible impact. It was constantly observed that the county was one of the most loyal and peaceful in the county and that the government could rely on it. This was borne out by the low ratio of police to population compared to adjoining counties. In the early 1870s it stood at 1:411 in Longford, while in Westmeath it was 1:266; Leitrim 1:350, and Roscommon 1:369.[33] Longford lacked a strong labouring and artisan class and the Fenians failed here, as in Connacht, to make any noticeable impression. Nevertheless the Bishop of Ardagh, Dr Kilduff, still felt it necessary to warn his flock against secret societies in 1865, at a time when the Fenian movement was at its height nationally.[34] It was the events of the late 1860s which brought about sympathy with Fenianism and provided it with a base in the region. As in Connacht the inroads which Fenianism made prior to 1867 were with railway porters and teachers such as John Casey Keegan of Ballymahon. In the late 1860s and 1870s the Fenian commitment to the abolition of landlordism, as advocated by the local leaders, helped in the assimilation of the Ribbon lodges in places such as Longford. These lodges had their origins as far back as the 1830s when a high level of agrarian crime was evident throughout the county, and at least six murders were attributed to them between 1836 and 1839.[35] Their success with the lodges in Connacht and Longford made these the areas where the greatest strides for the Fenian organization occurred in the 1870s.[36]

It was not until the amnesty meeting on 12 September 1869 at Longford that the county seemed to come into line with national trends. Over 30,000 people and 15 priests attended the Longford demonstration. Unlike the meetings in the west of Ireland and south Ulster, Longford failed to incorporate the tenant right issue in the amnesty debate, suggesting that humanitarian rather than nationalist motives prompted the convening of the meeting. While the demonstration did not help in promoting a redress of Irish grievances it certainly went a long way towards advancing the Fenian movement in the county, a point which was constantly noted by clergy and constabulary alike.[37]

The clergy's objections to Martin's candidature were based on greatly exaggerated claims of a large Fenian presence in his camp. Much of the general lawlessness in Ireland in the late 1860s and 1870s tended to be attributed to the Fenians, just as any rise in agrarianism in the county was considered the work of Ribbonmen. Such simplistic responses certainly benefited the government in bringing the moderate and more law-abiding citizens closer to the authorities, and they used the emotive terms Fenianism and Ribbonism to denote crimes they could not solve or to categorize criminals that could not be brought to justice.[38] Any rumour concerning Fenian activities in Longford were magnified out of all proportion.[39] During the 1869 by-election the Martin committee was classified as a Fenian body. Bishop McCabe wrote from Rome:

Fenianism is now manifested as the enemy of religion, as well as the enemy of the tenantry, an enemy of our creed and our country ... be prepared to defeat Fenianism in what ever form it may manifest itself - either in violence or secret machinations. Rally together the people under the leadership of the priests.[40]

Any individual known to have even slight associations with the Fenians, such as James B. Murtagh, was kept under close scrutiny. There is no evidence to suggest that Murtagh was anything but an advanced nationalist, being a member of the Home Government Association from August 1870. However, his close connections with the Fenian group during the 1869 by-election resulted in the police keeping him under surveillance.[41] This highlights the failure of police and clergy to differentiate between the extremes that existed within the nationalist movement. Consequently individuals like Martin and Murtagh were tarred with the Fenian brush, despite their former opposition to the movement. The advanced nationalists who came together in public houses or other social gatherings, as in Newtownforbes in 1871, were regarded by the authorities as posing a social threat by becoming openly assertive.

In order to stamp out this Fenian threat during the 1869 by-election, the Longford clergy resorted to denunciations from the altar and other means at their disposal. Their tactics had many similarities with those of their Mayo counterparts during the 1857 general election, when a number of Mayo priests were sent forward for trial for their over-zealous activities.[42] The difference was that the Longford clergy felt their involvement was to save religion, while the Mayo priests acted for overt political reasons. Nevertheless such scenes caused much adverse publicity for Ireland and Longford was one of the nine constituencies between 1853 and 1892 where the MPs were unseated on the grounds of clerical misconduct during the election.[43]

The Longford clergy's retention of their political power must be attributed to the changing developments in Ireland in 1870. The political emphasis altered from nationalism to agrarianism with the introduction of Gladstone's first land bill in February 1870; this helped unite all groups within the country, initially as to the type of legislation required and subsequently to protest at what was given.

III

The 1869 by-election also provides insights into the financial aspects of electioneering in this period, not alone for Longford but for the country in general. Greville had £4825 at his disposal, of which over £4000 was expended. This contrasts with £932 for Martin, most of which was collected at Fenian events in London and Dublin.[44] Such expense was no doubt responsible for the low numbers of constituencies contested between 1852 and 1868 and illustrates the problem faced by Irish nationalist parties up to 1880.[45]

Electoral contests were major windfalls for publicans and people with lodging-houses, as large sums of money were spent on buying whiskey and treating electors. Fr Reynolds was the paymaster for the Grevilles during the election and issued money in amounts ranging from a few pounds to £200. With so much money involved it proved very difficult to keep detailed accounts of how it was spent. Under such circumstances it was inevitable that some form of impropriety would occur. After the Electoral Act of 1868 it was increasingly difficult to expend large sums of money for electioneering purposes as all groups scrutinized their opponents' expenditure with particular reference to treating. It was this issue of treating which was primarily responsible for the unseating of Greville-Nugent at the subsequent petition hearing.

The 1869 by-election indicates the financial difficulties which the newly emerging Home Rule movement had to contend with in its early years. Former practices were waning, otherwise there is little doubt that the new political movement would have found it difficult to compete with the existing political groupings. The introduction of the Secret Ballot Act and the virtual ending of the 'treating' system at election time allowed the Home Rule party to compete on a more equitable footing with its more affluent opponents. However, by 1880 it still cost an average of £414 to contest an election, [46] and this did not take into account the expenditure of electioneering agents and transport costs. It was a factor which no doubt restricted the advancement of the radical Home Rule grouping in the 1880 election.

IV

The clergy were severally reprimanded for their conduct in the 1869 by-election which resulted in the unseating of Greville-Nugent and the issuing of a new election writ. It undoubtedly cost Fr Reynolds the position of bishop of Ardagh when it became vacant in 1871. Nowhere was the criticism as strong as from Cardinal Paul Cullen, Archbishop of Dublin, who condemned the priests' activities during the election. [47] Consequently, clerical power was not as ostentatious in the 1870s as it had been in the previous decade. Their approach, particularly in the selection of parliamentary candidates, was more cautious and the laity was given a greater say in the political process. In the 1870 election, this was evident at the meeting in April at Longford court-house to select the clerical/Liberal candidate. On this occasion the clergy did not convene privately and unilaterally decide who their candidate was going to be. While providing the lead, through Fr Edward McGaver, in initiating the convention of clergy and laity to select a replacement for Reginald Greville-Nugent (15 attending) they did not dominate the proceedings as they had done in the past. Indeed it was two laymen, John Maxwell, chairman of Longford town commissioners, and Thomas Gregory, a small Ballymahon landlord, who nominated the replacement, George Greville-Nugent.[48] Similar discretion was noticeable when the result was declared on 16 May.

Despite their low profile in the period 1870-79 the clergy's power remained strong. The selection of George Greville-Nugent in 1870 indicated the degree to which the clergy were unwilling to abandon their former path of total commitment to the support of the Gladstone cause. It certainly made it appear that the seat was the preserve of the Greville-Nugent family. Even Captain E.R. King-Harman, whose family were the largest landowners in Longford with 28,779 acres,[49] failed in his attempt to gain the nomination at the Longford meeting because of clerical hostility and he contested the seat as the nationalist candidate.

In both 1874 and 1879 elections the influence of the clergy remained supreme. In 1874 the Longford clergy decided at their private meeting on 29 January who to support on nomination day. Again in 1879 it was the meeting with the clergy which was the important factor in securing the nomination and seat for Justin McCarthy,[50] at a time when the rest of the country was assuming a more advanced nationalist stand. McCarthy was guaranteed the seat only after he had been interviewed by the clergy at St Mel's College on 31 March and when they were sure that his views on education, land and grand jury reform accorded with theirs. Only then was he allowed to continue his tour of the county with their sanction. This indicates a tacit approval by McCarthy of the clergy's political role in the county as he was not prepared to begin his campaign of the county without their agreement. Once the priests had given their support the other candidates who had expressed an interest in contesting the seat withdrew, being well aware of the hopelessness of their cause. However, at this stage the clergy's attitude to their electoral importance had mellowed. In their circular to the electors they stated:

While we heartily recognise the absolute right of the electors of the county freely to choose their representatives for parliament, we deem it our duty as trusted friends and advisers of the people to put clearly before them the principles that we think the members of their choice ought to hold and profess.[51]

By 1879 it was also noticeable that the clergy were moving slowly towards an acceptance of a more advanced settlement of the national question. There were 14 clergy present at the Longford electors' meeting on 31 March and some of them, such as Fr Reynolds of St Mel's and Canon John Skelly of Taghshinny and Carrickedmond, had been vehemently opposed to Martin's candidature.

In examining the influence of the Longford clergy in electoral affairs one must take into account the position in neighbouring counties. In Meath the clerical presence was minimal, as in 1871 when the electors cast their votes as they wished and returned John Martin to parliament. In Roscommon in 1874 clerical power was strong enough to ensure that an electoral contest was avoided. In Tipperary between 1850 and 1891 56 per cent of the priests were actively involved in the electoral campaign. The figure was probably higher in Longford.[52] What becomes apparent is that it was the attitude of the bishops and the senior clergy which was most important. As it transpired, the elections of 1869, 1870, 1874 and 1879 were all conducted without the guidance of the bishop of

Ardagh, the see being vacant or the incumbent being abroad, and the lead was taken by the senior clergy of the diocese.

V

The May 1870 election saw a further alignment of those forces in the county which were to constitute the Home Government Association founded later that month. This new coalition can be discerned from the widespread support for the nationalist candidate, Captain Edward R. King-Harman of Creevaghmore. He was proposed on the nomination day, 10 May, by Major Dopping Hepenstal, a small landowner from Granard and a Conservative, and seconded by the nationalist James B. Murtagh. Amongst his supporters was the repealer P.J. Smyth. King-Harman's drift towards the nationalist camp had been evident from the previous by-election when he had contributed to Martin's election fund and made his support publicly known. He advocated the release of political prisoners, the repeal of the union and the introduction of a good land bill.[53] The fact that he was resident in the county was an added advantage.

The events of the late 1860s and early 1870s highlighted the changing political structures and the difficulties inherent in labelling politicians with contemporary tags. It was difficult for nationalists to come to terms with someone like King-Harman, his Conservative past giving the impression that his new outlook was just a means being used by the Conservatives to capture a seat in parliament.[54] At no time did the opposition make any attempt to see what underlying factors had brought this into being. It was not realized that both nationalists and Irish unionists had been brought together because for the former Gladstone's Irish legislation had not gone far enough, while for the latter it had gone too far.

While King-Harman's defeat was inevitable, a closer examination of the result, 1217 votes to 923, throws up a number of interesting points. The increased level of support for King-Harman compared to John Martin indicates that many Conservatives and Protestants who voted for him had not participated in the previous by-election. Secondly, there were those who transferred their support to King-Harman from Reginald Greville-Nugent, evidently having been worried by the Fenian element in Martin's committee. Thirdly, the regional variations were more pronounced than in previous elections, with Ballymahon voting strongly for the local man, King-Harman, and the other two areas being solidly behind the clerical nominee. Considering it was the Home Rule movement's first contest in an Irish county the result was a most creditable one, with King-Harman taking 43 per cent of the vote.

When the Home Government Association published its list of members in 1870 only three Longford people had joined the movement - Hon. Laurence King-Harman, Captain E.R. King-Harman and James B. Murtagh, each of whom had been actively involved with the nationalist side during the two by-elections. This indicates the difficulties which the Home Rule movement encountered within Longford; as long as the clergy remained the dominant political force in the county and supported the Gladstone government, the new movement would make little progress.

The break which the new movement needed occurred in March 1873 with the defeat of Gladstone's university bill, a major disappointment to the Catholic bishops. Consequently there was a gradual alignment between the Home Rule movement and the Catholic clergy, most noticeable in the electoral struggle of 1874.

While the Home Rule League was caught unawares by the sudden calling of a general election for April, it was a situation which should have been foreseen. After Gladstone's defeat in March 1873, a general election was inevitable, many believing it would occur in the autumn of that year. The Home Rule League delayed calling a convention to prepare for an election until November 1873, at the Rotunda in Dublin, seven months after the government had been defeated. This was no doubt done to allow wavering Liberal MPs and the bishops to make up their minds on whether to support the new movement.

By far the greatest problem which the Home Rule movement faced was its failure to establish any local organizations. Between 1870 and 1874 the movement was in the main a Dublin-based one and there was little attempt made to broaden its geographical base. Isaac Butt realized the importance of holding meetings throughout the country to generate support for the cause but in late 1873 there was little time to ensure that a wider public support was forthcoming because of the haste in which the general election was called.[55] The first indication of the spread of the Home Rule movement came in November 1873, when a demonstration was held in Ballinamore, County Leitrim, at which a large number of Longford people were present.[56] Once the 1874 election had passed, the urgency to organize local branches in Longford dissipated.

The central Home Rule authority left the onus on the local constituencies for the selection of candidates. As no criteria were provided, there were major regional variations in the nomination and selection of candidates. Where local farmers' clubs were in existence, as in the south of Ireland, the tenants were anxious to return representatives who were strong advocates of land reform.[57] The number of farmers' clubs rose in the 1870s and they began to play an increasingly important role in political affairs, in many instances becoming the local branch of the Home Rule movement.[58] However, the absence of any such clubs in Longford before December 1879, when the first Land League demonstration in Longford was held, deprived the Home Rule movement of any form of independent body within the county and resulted in continuing reliance on the clergy in electoral affairs.[59]

In those areas where the Catholic Church remained the only effective organization, as in Longford, the clergy were able to nominate candidates who felt more strongly about Catholic grievances than Home Rule principles. Both Myles O'Reilly and his new partner for Longford, George Errington, a small Tipperary landowner and honorary secretary of the Catholic Union, owed their success to their strong involvement with Catholic issues rather than to their former deeds for Ireland. Their manifesto in 1874 dwelt strongly on the temporal problems of the pope, an indication that they came from the Catholic–Whig section of the Home Rule party. However, their election was never threatened by the lack of support from the Liberal/Conservative groups. Instead of the Catholic/Liberal party dominating the county there was now a Catholic/Home Rule group. At the 1874 election George Slator provided the only opposition to the clergy-nominated candidates, and he finished a poor third with only 432 votes.

The difficulties encountered by the Home Rule movement regarding candidates are exemplified in the case of George Errington, who did not become a member of the party until two weeks after being elected an MP, even then justifying his membership purely on the grounds of Gladstone's failure to settle the university question.[60] It was unlikely, if not impossible, that the movement would ever be an effective and united parliamentary force because its priorities were as diverse as the groupings themselves. An example is the case of Major Myles O'Reilly, a typical Liberal politician of the 1860s and 1870s. Like so many of his peers he greatly feared for his political life because of the changing political direction in Ireland arising from Gladstone's failure to deliver adequately on the agrarian and Catholic university questions. Consequently he was one of the 18 Liberal MPs who jumped on the Home Rule bandwagon at the 1874 general election, having been fortunate enough to have attended the Home Rule conference in November 1873.

While it has been maintained that the 1874 general election saw the demise of the Liberal party in Ireland this does not take into account the manner in which the party clung on to power within the country. While many MPs, such as O'Reilly and Errington, were returned as Home Rulers they were in essence Liberals and their parliamentary activities between 1874 and 1880 bear this out. The Liberal party may have suffered a humiliating defeat numerically at the 1874 election but it continued to have a strong influence within the representation. However, the election denoted for the Irish Liberal party the potential which the Home Rule movement had for displacing them totally within the country in the near future.

From an early stage it was clear that O'Reilly's commitment to Home Rule was shallow. His election address to his constituents in 1874, the only one of his parliamentary career, indicated his peripheral sympathy with the movement. He deliberated much on the achievements of Gladstone's administration and little on the prospects of Home Rule.[61] It was clearly the address of a Liberal who had changed course in order to secure his seat. From an early stage O'Reilly was severely criticized for his absences from Westminster and for his voting pattern when present. This was especially so when issues such as the 1876 Butt land bill and the release of the political prisoners were being discussed.[62] O'Reilly's true sentiments concerning Home Rule can be gleaned from his not unexpected departure from politics in 1879. Like many of his Liberal contemporaries who had sought political refuge in the Home Rule League in 1873, O'Reilly realized that the advanced section of the party was becoming more powerful. Consequently he sought and attained, like many others, a position in the Intermediate Board of Education which had come into being in 1878.[63]

While Errington was criticized as vehemently as O'Reilly he survived the 1880 general election, partly because in 1879 he had espoused the concept of peasant proprietorship and provided his tenants in Tipperary with rent abatements. However, the main reason he retained his seat was Parnell's inability to secure a suitable replacement for him. In the early 1880s he moved well away from the mainstream of the party.[64]

The election of Justin McCarthy for Longford in 1879 was the first occasion that a non-landowning MP was returned for the county. It indicates the continuance of the process that first became apparent in 1874 when representatives with no landed connections, such as John O'Connor Power in Mayo and Joseph Biggar in Cavan, were returned to parliament. The political power of the landlords was eventually ended with the Land League's successful support of Parnell in the 1880 election, during a period which also witnessed the demise of their social position. The 1881 Land Act was to place the landlord in the position of rent collector with the land courts now fixing the rents. At the same time his local political prestige was under threat as the tenants began to win power in the poor law boards of guardians. One can thus understand why McCarthy's success in Longford was greeted so enthusiastically. On previous occasions the clergy had supported the landlord–Liberal element in Longford, but on this occasion the Liberals were subdued by the clergy and Lord Granard, the principal Catholic landowner in the county.[65] The main factor which seems to have been responsible for this was the growing nationalism within the country as expressed by the parliamentary obstruction of Parnell and Biggar. In this, Longford, by 1880, had joined the mainstream of political activity in Ireland.

VI

By 1880 Irish politics had become centralized, with power now emanating from the central executive of the Irish Parliamentary Party, rather than from within the individual constituencies. This was reflected not alone in Longford but in every county outside of Ulster between 1880 and 1885. While power had been transferred from the local scene onto the national plain, it must be emphasized that the county structure had played an important role in these developments in the preceding decades. In the absence of any centralized structure in the 1860s and 1870s for the advancement of popular politics, it was imperative that some form of leadership was available within the individual constituencies to ensure that certain grievances, such as Catholic university education and agrarian reform, remained at the top of the agenda at Westminster. In Longford, it was the Catholic clergy who provided this leadership. With the evolution of centralized politics and the extension of the franchise in 1884, which increased the Longford electorate from 2626 in 1880 to 8140 in 1885, it was inevitable that such power could no longer remain the preserve of one particular group. Between 1885 and 1917 this political dominance was divided between the clergy and the people. While the county was separated into two constituencies after 1885, reflecting the north–south geographical divide, this power was never in danger, coming under threat only from within the nationalist ranks themselves, as in 1892 when the Irish Parliamentary Party split over the O'Shea divorce case. When opposition to the existing order came in 1917, the change was once more to come from outside the county, in the form of Sinn Féin.

NOTES

I wish to thank the following for their help with this article: Raymond Gillespie, Fergus O'Ferrall, Emmet Larkin, Clodagh Moran and Martin O'Hare.

1. See *Freeman's Journal*, 3 Jan. 1870, p. 3; N.L.I., Thomas Larcom Papers, Ms 7762.
2. D. Thornley, *Isaac Butt and Home Rule* (London 1964), p. 44. Thornley deals with their importance in the 1868 election throughout the whole country, pp. 37–45.
3. For an account of O'Reilly's career see P. MacSuibhne, *Paul Cullen and his Contemporaries*, ii (Naas 1962), pp. 83–4; J. H. Whyte, *The Independent Irish Party, 1850-1859* (Oxford 1958), p. 165.
4. *The Irish Times*, 20 Nov. 1868, p. 3; 25 Nov. 1868, p. 3.
5. *Freeman's Journal*, 16 Dec. 1869, p. 3; N.L.I., Larcom Papers, Ms 7762. It afterwards transpired that a more representative clerical assembly of 40 clerics did convene at St Mel's in early December but it was pressure from the public, enraged at the clergy's earlier action, which brought this about. *Judgement delivered by Mr Justice Fitzgerald and minutes of the Evidence taken at the trial of the Longford Election Petition (1870)* (henceforth cited as *Longford Election Petition*), H.C. 1870 (178) lvi, pp. 28, 140.
6. A case in point is Henry Hughes who, though a Catholic, was forced to retire from the 1857 contest by the priests because he had brought his daughter up as a Protestant, K. Theodore Hoppen, 'National politics and local realities in mid-nineteenth-century Ireland' in A. Cosgrave and D. McCartney (eds), *Studies in Irish History* (Dublin 1979), p. 210.
7. *Longford Election Petition*, p. 31; on this point of unity see E. Larkin, *The Consolidation of the Roman Catholic Church in Ireland, 1860-1870* (Dublin and Chapel Hill 1987), pp. 346–7; Whyte, op. cit., p. 171.
8. *Longford Election Petition*, p. 106.
9. *Irishman*, 11 Dec. 1869, p. 3; *The Irish Times*, 11 Dec. 1869; *Longford Election Petition*, p. 138; it was reported that large numbers of the Meath clergy were speaking most violently against McCabe and the Ardagh priests, Ardagh Diocesan Archives, Longford, Conroy Papers 1868-70, Cullen to Conroy, 23 Mar. 1870.
10. *Longford Election Petition*, p. 144.
11. Ibid., pp. 69, 46; *Nation*, 2 Apr. 1870, p. 525.
12. A. M. Sullivan, *New Ireland*, ii (London 1877), p. 282; P. A. Sallard, *The Life and Letters of John Martin* (Dublin 1893), p. 226; *Freeman's Journal*, 4 Dec. 1869.
13. E.R. Norman, *The Catholic Church and Ireland in the Age of Rebellion, 1859-1873* (London 1965), p. 157; T. D. Sullivan, *Recollections of Troubled Times in Ireland* (Dublin 1905), p. 161. Martin was a firm supporter of the release of the political

prisoners, regarding their conviction as unconstitutional and tyrannical, N.L.I., Ms 8047 (2), W. J. O'Neill Daunt Papers, Martin to Daunt, 23 Jan. 1869.

14. N.L.I., Ms 8047 (2), W. J. O'Neill Daunt Papers, Martin to Daunt, 21 June 1867.

15. Martin always maintained he would enter parliament provided a constituency would accept and pay his election costs, Sallard, op. cit., p. 193; Thornley, op. cit., p. 58; O'Neill Daunt Papers, N.L.I., Ms 8047 (2), Martin to Daunt, 19 June 1868.

16. *Nation*, 25 Dec. 1869, p. 297.

17. Ibid., 18 Dec. 1869, p. 284; *Irishman*, 18 Dec. 1869, p. 408.

18. *Nation*, 1 Dec. 1869; *Longford Election Petition*, p. 11; B. Griffen, 'Social aspects of Fenianism, 1858-70', in *Eire-Ireland*, xxi, no. 1 (Spring 1986), p. 21.

19. T. D. Sullivan, op. cit., p. 158; the contest has also been described as one of the most memorable electoral contests in Irish history, T. P. O'Connor, *The Parnell Movement* (London 1886), p. 207.

20. *The Irish Times*, 11 Dec. 1869, p. 3.

21. *The Nation*, 1 Jan. 1870, p. 313.

22. *Longford Election Petition*, pp. 136-7; N.L.I., Ms 7762, Larcom Papers.

23. David N. Haire, 'In aid of the civil power, 1868-90' in F.S.L. Lyons and R.A. Hawkins (eds), *Ireland under the Union; Varieties of Tension* (Oxford 1980), p. 125; *The Irish Times*, 16 Dec. 1869; *Nation*, 18 Dec. 1869, 1 Jan. 1870, p. 317; *Freeman's Journal*, 1 Jan. 1870; *Irishman*, Jan. 1870, p. 449.

24. There were 1189 police stationed in the county for the 1862 by-election, *Number of cavalry, artillery and infantry ordered to or stationed in the Co. Longford for the late election*, H.C. 1862 (239) xliv.

25. K. Theodore Hoppen, 'Landlords, society and electoral politics in mid-nineteenth-century Ireland' in C.H.E. Philpin (ed.), *Nationalism and Popular Protest in Ireland* (Cambridge 1987), p. 315.

26. See *Irishman*, 8 Jan. 1870, p. 451.

27. M. Hurst, 'Ireland and the Ballot Act of 1872', in A. O'Day (ed.), *Reactions to Irish Nationalism, 1865-1914* (Dublin 1987), pp. 41-2.

28. K. Theodore Hoppen, *Elections, Politics and Society in Ireland, 1832-1885* (Oxford 1984), p. 417.

29. *Thom's Directory*, 1874, p. 1255.

30. See *Nation*, 16 Apr. 1870, p. 548.

31. Treating was regarded as the provision of free food, entertainment and especially alcoholic drinks in order to entice an elector to vote for a certain candidate. See Gerard Moran, ' "The advance on the North" : The difficulties of the Home Rule movement in south-east Ulster, 1870-1882' in R. Gillespie and H. O'Sullivan (eds), *The Borderlands: Essays on the History of the Ulster-Leinster Border* (Belfast 1989), p. 142; Hoppen, *Elections, Politics and Society*, pp. 429-32.

32. Dublin Diocesan Archives (hereafter D.D.A.), Cullen Papers, 1869 (Bishops), 16 and 20 Dec. 1869, Conroy to Cullen.

33. *Returns of the number of police allotted to each county in Ireland at the last allocation, the number of vacancies, and the extra force in each county, and the amount charged on the rates of the county;* H.C. 1872 (146) 1; *Thom's Directory*, 1874.

34. Dean Monahan (ed.), *Records relating to the Diocese of Ardagh and Clonmacnois* (Dublin 1886), pp. 43-4; James J. MacNamee, *History of the Diocese of Ardagh* (Dublin 1954), pp. 470-1.

35. *Report from the Select Committee of the House of Lords on the State of Ireland*, 1839, pt ii, pp. 919-25. These murders occurred because of people being evicted from their holdings, E.D. Steele, *Irish Land and British Politics: Tenant-Right and Nationality*,

1865-1870 (Cambridge 1974), pp. 12-13.

36. See S.P.O., Fenian Papers, F. Files, 1867-71 (7697R), 15 Sept. 1871; R.V. Comerford, *The Fenians in Context,1848-1882* (Dublin and New Jersey 1985), pp. 212-14; G. Moran, 'The changing course of Mayo politics, 1867-1874' in R. Gillespie and G. Moran (eds), *'A Various Country': Essays in Mayo History, 1500-1900* (Westport 1987), pp. 151-2.

37. S.P.O., Fenian Papers, F. Files, 1867-71 (5102R), 28 Nov. 1869. At Abbeylara a notice was posted up outside the church calling for prayers for the Manchester Martyrs. See also (5121R) dated 1 Dec. 1869. This was also the view of Fr James Reynolds, see *Longford Election Petition*, pp. 147, 151.

38. A.C.M. Murray, 'Agrarian violence and nationalism in nineteenth-century Ireland: The myth of Ribbonism' in *Irish Economic and Social History*, xiii (1986), p. 71; regarding rumours of Fenianism and Ribbonism in Longford see S.P.O., Fenian Papers, F. Files 1867-71 (7328R), 3 Mar. 1871.

39. D.D.A., Cullen Papers, 1871 (Bishops), Conroy to Cullen, undated.

40. *Freeman's Journal*, 13 Dec. 1869, p. 3: N.L.I., Ms 7762, Larcom Papers. For similar letters from clergy see *Freeman's Journal*, 8 and 17 Dec. 1869.

41. S.P.O., Fenian Papers, F. Files, 1867-71 (7690R), 18 Sept. 1871. The police kept his canal boats under close scrutiny fearing that suspicious goods were being unloaded in Longford.

42. See J. H. Whyte, op. cit., pp. 138-9; J. Waldron, 'Mayo and the 1857 general election' in B. O'Hara (ed.), *Mayo* (Galway 1982), pp. 102-121.

43. S. Connolly, *Religion and Society in Nineteenth Century Ireland* (Dundalk 1985), p. 37. In most instances the causes of the unseating were spiritual intimidation and physical violence.

44. *Longford Election Petition*, p. 133; Ms 10, 415 (11), Isaac Butt Papers, Longford election expenses.

45. In this period only 38 per cent of all Irish elections were contested, see Hoppen, 'Landlords, society and electoral politics', p. 291. For an account of the financial difficulties facing parliamentary candidates in the 1850s and 1860s see Whyte, op. cit., pp. 47-9; S.P.O., Fenian Papers, F. Files, 1867-71 (5086R).

46. C.C. O'Brien, *Parnell and his Party, 1880-1890* (Oxford 1957), p. 41.

47. D.D.A., Cullen Papers, 1870 (Bishops), Cullen to McCabe, 14 Jan. 1870.

48. *Freeman's Journal*, 13 Apr. 1870, p. 3; *Nation*, 16 Apr. 1870, p. 548.

49. *Return of owners of land of one acre and upwards in the several counties, cities and towns of Ireland*, H.C. 1876 lxxx, p. 53.

50. *Irishman*, 5 Apr. 1879, p. 638.

51. *Nation*, 5 Apr. 1879, p. 8.

52. See D.D.A., Cullen Papers, 1874 (Bishops), Bishop Gillhooly to Cullen, 24 and 25 Jan.,1874: J. O'Shea, *Politics and Society in Post-Famine Ireland: A Study of County Tipperary, 1850-1891* (Dublin and New Jersey 1983), p. 44.

53. See *Freeman's Journal*, 14 Apr., 6, 10, 12 May 1870.

54. *The Irish Times*, 3 Jan. 1870, p. 5; 14 Apr. 1870, p. 5; *Nation*, 23 Apr. 1870, p. 564. King-Harman said: 'I am not a Tory, and above all I am not a Whig. I am not a Gladstone man; I am not a Disraeli man, but I am a supporter of every measure calculated to improve my country. I will pledge myself to no party.'

55. N.L.I., Ms 830, Isaac Butt Papers, Butt circular of 27 Dec. 1873.

56. Ibid., Ms 8695 (32), William Crozier to Butt, Nov. 1873.

57. Lawrence J. McCaffrey, 'Home Rule and the general election of 1874 in Ireland' in *Irish Historical Studies*, ix, no. 34 (1954), p. 193.

58. See S. Clark, *The Social Origins of the Irish Land War* (Princeton 1979), pp. 198-9, 218-19.

59. This contrasts with the argument of McCaffrey, op. cit., p. 203, for he fails to take into account the regional variations in Ireland. He states the priest could no longer unilaterally select the nominees without consultation with the electors.

60. *Freeman's Journal*, 21 Feb. 1874; Thornley, op. cit., p. 210n.

61. Thornley, op. cit., pp. 163, 188; *Irishman*, 31 Jan. 1874, p. 496.

62. *Nation*, 12 Apr. 1879, p. 10, 25 Jul. 1874, p. 10; G. Moran. 'Land agitation in Connacht: The writings of James Daly, 1876-1879' in *Retrospect* (1980), p. 33.

63. *Irishman*, 29 Mar. 1879, p. 624; For an account of the MPs' scramble to secure posts in the new Intermediate Education Board, see Thornley, op. cit., pp. 349-59.

64. In the early 1880s Errington's politics continued to be exclusively Catholic and Liberal in direction. See Emmet Larkin, *The Roman Catholic Church and the Creation of the Modern Irish State, 1878-1886* (Philadelphia 1975), pp. 59-67, 135-44; A. Macauly, *Patrick Dorrian, Bishop of Down and Connor*, 1865-1885 (Dublin 1987), pp. 335-8.

65. See T. M. Healy, *Letters and Leaders of My Day* (London 1928), i, p. 68. A special relationship existed between Lord Granard and the Longford clergy.

IV
AFTERWORD

Into the Twentieth Century

RAYMOND GILLESPIE AND GERARD MORAN

The history of the twentieth century provides unique problems and opportunities for the local historian. Source material of unequalled diversity reveals fuller details of the workings of local society; diaries and correspondence become plentiful and there is an abundance of other ephemera, though much of this is still in private hands. Photographs and maps are also more common, enabling a closer reconstruction of the topography of the locality. There are also new types of evidence for the local historian, notably the reminiscences of those who can still remember the details of everyday life in the first quarter of the century.

Yet despite this abundance of material local historians in Ireland have shown a reluctance to become involved with the history of the twentieth century. Part of the reason for this is that the events of the last ninety years appear familiar and not worth examining. Yet the years after the 1914–18 war saw a sharper break with traditional ways of life than occurred at any other time in the county's history. Rural electrification, for example, brought dramatic changes not only in social life but in agricultural routine, with the introduction of farm machinery. Similarly the arrival of radio, cinema and television had a powerful effect in changing outlooks.

Another cause of this reluctance is the problem of how to dissect, analyse and interpret afresh events and memories which still have a powerful emotive influence in many communities. Many of these memories are bound up with the events of the years 1916 to 1923 and their local consequences and it is often more convenient to let sleeping dogs lie. The importance of the purely military aspects of these years in national history has admittedly led some local historians to deal with these in great factual detail; however, this has often been to the exclusion of the social context and other themes. One of the results of this distortion is that we lack even a framework to help us build the history of County Longford communities in the twentieth century.

If consideration were to be given only to the military aspect of 1916 to 1923 any commentary on Longford would be a slim one. Throughout these turbulent years Longford was strangely quiescent. With the exception of General Sean MacEoin's actions around Ballinalee and Cloonfin in north Longford there was little local violence. This is perhaps not so surprising, for Longford had in the previous generation been a tranquil county. An examination of the Land War of the late nineteenth century shows similarly little activity in the county; no

Longford estate, for example, became involved in the Plan of Campaign.[1] The electoral history of the late nineteenth century also shows relative peace. Between 1885 and 1917 the Longford electorate went to the polls only once: in 1892 James MacKay Wilson of Currygrane, the brother of Field Marshal Henry Wilson who was to be assassinated by the IRA in Dublin in 1922, stood as a unionist candidate for north Longford and lost to the nationalist MP Justin McCarthy by over 2500 votes. The Liberal unionist in south Longford, George Miller, fared no better in that election.[2] In all the other elections nationalist candidates were returned unopposed.

Fergus O'Ferrall's essay should be a warning to us that even when there are no spectacular political events to focus on in a county, profound changes may nonetheless be taking place. It can be argued that political sentiment in the county was becoming progressively more radical in the early twentieth century. In 1919, for example, Longford had a higher proportion of Sinn Féin members than any other county in the country.[3] The strength of this support was demonstrated in the 1917 by-election, when Sinn Féin ran the former Irish Republican Brotherhood member Joseph McGuinness against the nationalist Patrick McKenna. McGuinness's slogan was dramatic: 'Put him in to get him out.' He won by only 22 votes, but in the general election of 1918 enlarged his majority to almost 7000. The 1917 by-election had helped to forge an alliance between militant and constitutional nationalists which was important in spreading the influence of Sinn Féin throughout the country before 1922.[4]

The causes and the timing of this 'silent revolution' whereby Longford moved from being a conservative to a more radical region have yet to be examined by local historians. A useful guide here is David Fitzpatrick's study of County Clare in the early twentieth century[5] in which he identifies factors other than the purely political that shaped the political topography of the county. Emigration, family wealth and individual inheritance prospects were major factors in determining a man's political outlook. The role of newspapers and the rise of quasi-political organizations, such as the GAA, were also important in shaping local opinion. It is significant that James P. Farrell, MP for the county and a key nationalist until 1918, was both chairman of the GAA county board and editor of the *Longford Leader* (established in 1898). In Longford the northern part of the county was markedly more radical than the southern part: most of the limited military action during the War of Independence took place there. Similarly the dramatic increase in Joseph McGuinness's majority between 1917 and 1918 may be explained by the fact that in 1917 he stood for south Longford while by 1918 the constituency had been remodelled to take in the whole county. Even after Independence this divide between north and south appears to have continued. Four decades later in the 1957 election, north Longford provided a strong base for Ruaraidh Ó Brádaigh's victory for Sinn Féin in the constituency. An examination of this north-south divide and its influence is made more difficult by the fact that since Independence Longford has not formed a constituency by itself but has been merged with its neighbours, at present with

County Westmeath, and further study is required to separate the political history of the county from those of its neighbours, which have often tended to overshadow it.

This division between north and south in the county is also apparent in economic terms, the north a region of small farms, the south dominated by much larger farmers who have, it seems, been more conservative in their outlook. It may be no coincidence that at the beginning of the twentieth century the Longford branch representative on the Irish Unionist Alliance was Michael McCann, a large farmer from Newtownforbes and a Catholic. McCann was prominent in escorting parties of British electors around the county, showing them the merits of maintaining the Union. He was boycotted locally for his pains.[6]

One of the peculiarities of the agricultural economy of early-twentieth-century Longford was that it remained relatively unchanged from the pre-Famine period. Farming remained mixed, with both grain being grown commercially and livestock kept, despite the fact that poor soil in the county meant that grain yields of 19.5 cwts per acre were below the national average of 20.4 cwts per acre in 1933. In 1950 the area under grain, mainly oats, was almost the same as it had been in 1901. This, of course, fluctuated over the course of the century in response to demand and during the Second World War there was a dramatic increase in grain cultivation in Longford, with more than three times the acreage under grain in 1944 as in 1933. The detail of these variations and their causes need to be studied before we can appreciate the local impact of such events as the economic war of the 1930s and the Second World War.

There was some regional differentiation in agriculture. The rural districts of Granard and Longford in the north and west of the county had the highest proportion of farms below 30 acres in 1901 - almost 80 per cent , as opposed to 70 per cent in the southern rural district of Ballymahon. The agriculture of the north and west of the county was typical of small farms. In 1933 Longford and Granard rural districts had almost 80 per cent of the poultry production of the county and 85 per cent of the pig production. Ballymahon, by contrast, specialized in sheep with almost half the county's sheep flock in that area. The difference between the two regions is reflected in the valuation of the land around Ballymahon at £0.56 an acre in 1933 while at Longford rural district it was £0.42 an acre.[7]

In the area of marketing agricultural and other produce, there was relatively little change in the county before the 1970s, apart from the decline of fairs and the rise of marts. It is true that the co-operative movement did make some impact from the 1890s, but in the retail sector there was little development. The 1933 census of distribution shows 479 shops in the county, of which about 58 per cent were either grocery shops or public houses. In 1956 that percentage remained the same, although the number of shops had fallen slightly to 472. This number continued to fall and by 1971 there were only 379 in the county, the percentage of grocery shops and public houses remaining constant. There were some significant differences between 1933 and 1971. The number of butchers rose from 17 to 21, reflecting a greater demand for meat as a result of growing affluence; the increased role of the motor car is indicated by a rise in the number of garages from 12 to 28. The number of chemists had almost doubled from 7 to 13, because of improved medical provision. The distribution of shops points to another change in the economy: in 1933 only about 26 per cent of shops were in Longford town, by 1971 that had risen to over 31 per cent.[8] This reflects both increasing urbanization - Longford town had increased its population from 3685 in 1926 to 4791 in 1971 - and the town's enhanced importance within the county. In 1926 it contained about 10 per cent of the county's population; this had risen to almost 17 per cent by 1971.[9]

One dimension of increased urbanization was the trend away from land both as a source of wealth and as a source of employment and towards a growing reliance on industry. Longford had little tradition of industry with the exception of the domestic linen manufacture in the north of the county which had already collapsed before the Famine. The consequent reliance on agriculture was reinforced after the Famine and continued into the twentieth century. The Census of Industrial Production for 1926 and 1929 identified only milling, baking and building work as industries in County Longford; baking and milling employing 38 people in eight establishments and building employing 57 people at four establishments. In the course of the century this was to change, particularly in the 1960s. The setting up of the turf-burning electricity-generating station at Lanesborough and the bog development by Bord na Móna in south Longford from the 1950s both contributed significantly to the diversification of employment opportunities in the county. The Census of Industrial Production for 1979 showed 51 industrial establishments in County Longford employing over 1700 workers.[10]

Much of this diversification of the Longford economy came late in the twentieth century. Before the 1960s agriculture remained the staple. In the main, this did not grow quickly enough to absorb the rising young population of the county. In 1911, for example, almost 45 per cent of the population was under twenty-five and opportunities within the county for these people were limited. There was a reduction in the number of farms in the county - from 9301 in 1901 to 7075 in 1960. Worst affected were the farms of under 30 acres which fell from over 7000 in 1901 to about 4500 in 1960.[11] The collapse of the small family farm is not peculiar to Longford; emigration has remained the necessary corollary of this and the trends in emigration are linked to farm contraction. In the years 1946-51, for example, net emigration from the county was almost twice the national average at 16. 8 persons per thousand population, a figure exceeded only by Leitrim and Kerry.[12] It was emigration which accounted almost entirely for the fall in the county's population from 39,847 in 1926 to 32,969 in 1956 and to 28,250 in 1971.[13] The impact of such a movement on local communities was traumatic but such trauma rarely leaves any trace in the written records. Here oral history must play an important part in understanding the real significance of this migration for the county. Any understanding must include not only those who left but also those who returned, either permanently or on a temporary basis, bringing with them ideas from outside the community. It is important that such material relating to emigration should be preserved both in the form of autobiographies by those who lived through the periods of worst emigration and by local historians collecting material on these periods.[14]

The fall in population through emigration which has characterized the history of Longford in the twentieth century did not affect all the communities of the county equally. The fall in the Protestant population was more dramatic than that in the Catholic community. Between 1901 and 1926 the Protestant population fell by 36 per cent and between 1926 and 1971 by 56 per cent.[15] In the case of the Church of Ireland the number of rectors serving the diocese had fallen from 18 in 1936 to five by 1986 while the number of churches fell from 33 to 25 over the same period. Some of the reasons for this dramatic fall have been examined by Liam Kennedy and Kerby Miller above. Many, such as James MacKay Wilson of Currygrane, left because of political disillusionment with the granting of independence. Wilson was High Sheriff of Longford in 1887 and contested the constituency for the unionists in 1885 and 1892 but died in England in 1933, a bitter critic of self-government for Ireland. Others left for social and economic reasons. However, we know little about the Protestant communities which remained and the changes in denominational relationships after 1922. One useful approach to such a study may be to investigate the sociology of the various sporting organizations in the county such as the GAA, the Longford Harriers, the rugby clubs and the golf clubs. Since these bodies tended to be associated with particular religious groupings their history may well provide useful insights into relations between the various communities in the county.

In 1926 94 per cent of Longford's population was Catholic. This had risen to over 95 per cent by 1971. The organizational framework of the Catholic Church, which was in place by the 1870s, changed relatively little during the twentieth century. The parish structure of the diocese of Ardagh, for example, was not modified at all with the 41 parishes in use in 1875 still operating in 1975.[16] There was, however, a slight increase in the number of churches in the diocese from 72 in 1875 to 79 by 1950. Within that parish structure the number of clergy serving increased from 94 in 1900 to a peak of 115 in 1960 with a slight fall to 105 in 1970. Given that the population of the diocese was falling, this represents a significant improvement in the ratio of clergy to people, and it is the task of the local historian to understand how the elements within that community worked and to discern their relationship with the wider world.

The place of religious orders in the community is rarely studied by local historians yet it is an area which touches on many aspects of local society and reflects changes there. In 1900 St Joseph's Convent of Our Lady of Mercy in Longford (established in 1861) operated a 'poor school' which had 400 pupils, as well as 'a training school where young girls of the middle class are prepared to be teachers, governesses, etc., also a shirt and hosiery factory, where a number of poor girls are profitably employed'. They also had charge of the workhouse hospital. By 1925 the function of the Longford Convent of Mercy had changed somewhat. The 'poor school' was now a national school with some 300 pupils, where the nuns prepared pupils 'for scholarships, intermediate Dublin, local and civil service exams, Irish society of musicians, Leinster college of music'. Their shirt and hosiery factory had apparently ceased operations. The workhouse had been replaced by the county home hospital. By 1970 the school was still functioning but the number of nuns in the community had been reduced to half the 1925 level. Thus by studying the activities of only one convent - and there were also convents at Ballymahon, Newtownforbes and Granard - the local historian is forced to deal with not only religious change but also medical and educational provision in the area. These types of services should be of consider- able interest to the historian of Longford since emigration removed from the county much of the younger working population. The result was a family structure which in many cases could not provide for itself and was heavily dependent on local social services. Between 1926 and 1971 those under fourteen and over sixty-five rarely constituted less than 40 per cent of the population.[17] The role of enterprises such as the Longford shirt and hosiery factory in the local economy would also merit further investigation. The history of the convents also raises more indirect questions such as the role of women in an area.

This afterword has done no more than to point out some of the subjects requiring examination in the recent history of Longford and to suggest some of the approaches which might be adopted. Above all it is vital that it should not be reduced to a bare account of the national history learnt in school related in terms of the events which touched the county or in the form of pious biographies of local men who played a part in national events. The history of Longford in the twentieth century is no less complex and unique than that of any other region at any other time. The local historian of the twentieth century has the advantage of being able to consult those still alive who experienced many of the momentous changes in land, politics and religion of the last ninety years. There is a unique opportunity to recapture the past which must be availed of now.

NOTES

1. L. M. Geary, *The Plan of Campaign* (Cork 1986), appendices 2, 3.
2. B. M. Walker (ed.), *Parliamentary Election Results in Ireland, 1801-1922* (Dublin 1978), pp. 147-8.
3. David Fitzpatrick, 'The geography of Irish nationalism, 1910-21' in *Past and Present*, lxxvii (1978), map 1.
4. Charles Townsend, *Political Violence in Ireland* (Oxford 1983), pp. 314-15.
5. David Fitzpatrick, *Politics and Irish Life: The Provincial Experience of War and Revolution* (Dublin 1977).
6. Patrick Buckland, *Irish Unionism: 1. The Anglo-Irish and the New Ireland, 1885-1922* (Dublin 1972), p. 23.
7. *Agricultural statistics of Ireland with a detailed report for the year 1901*, H. C. 1902 cxvi,

pt 1, pp. 20-6; *Agricultural Statistics, 1927-1933* (Dublin, Stationery Office 1935); *Agricultural Statistics, 1944-1953* (Dublin, Stationery Office 1955).

8. *Census of Distribution, 1933* (Dublin, Stationery Office 1936); *Census of Distribution, 1956-1959* (Dublin, Stationery Office 1962); *Census of Distribution, 1971. Vol. 1: Retail Trade* (Dublin, Stationery Office 1977).

9. For population trends see W. E. Vaughan, A. J. Fitzpatrick (eds), *Irish Historical Statistics: Population, 1821-1971* (Dublin 1978), p. 31.

10. *Census of Industrial Production, 1926 and 1929* (Dublin, Stationery Office 1933); *Census of Industrial Production, 1938* (Dublin, Stationery Office 1940); *Census of Industrial Production, 1979* (Dublin, Stationery Office 1984).

11. Sources as note 7.

12. *Irish Catholic Directory* (Dublin 1955), p. 703.

13. Vaughan, Fitzpatrick, op. cit., p. 31.

14. For example George O'Brien, *The Village of Longing* (Gigginstown 1987), pp. 52-9.

15. *Census of Population of Ireland, 1981, vol. 5* (Dublin, Stationery Office 1987), p. 4.

16. Much of what follows on religion is drawn from issues of the *Irish Catholic Directory*, published annually from 1836, and is a useful beginning for the history of religious change in any area.

17. Vaughan and Fitzpatrick, op. cit., pp. 164, 208.

V
DOCUMENTS ON LONGFORD HISTORY

a. Description of the County of Longford
by N[icholas] Dowdall Esqr., 1682

In 1682 William Molyneux, then secretary of the Dublin Philosophical Society, undertook to compile an Irish section for the New English Atlas then being assembled by the London bookseller Moses Pitt. He circulated a set of printed queries to a number of gentry throughout the country. He received twenty-two replies, including one from Longford written by Nicholas Dowdall. The publishing project proved abortive but the replies, preserved in Trinity College Dublin Ms 883, provide a fine picture of at least some areas of Ireland in the late seventeenth century.

We know almost nothing of Nicholas Dowdall. His name suggests an Old English origin and the family may have come to Longford during the early seventeenth century. Although apparently not himself a landowner, his enthusiastic description of the great houses of the county suggests that he was at least an interested observer of gentry society. His interests in topography, place-names and local history typified the enquiring mind of the period.

Description of the County of Longford, by N[icholas] Dowdall Esqr., 1682. Trinity College Dublin Ms 883/ii, ff. 258–61.

This county is reputed to be or near the Centre of Ireland and in the Province of Leinster, but antiently it was of the Province of Conaught. The Air serene and wholsome the soil Fertile and profitable it is in Length 24 miles and in breadth fourteen. It is bounded on the Northwest and west by the River Shannon. This River taketh its rise from a mountain called Sleivenjerin or the Iron mountain and runneth between the Counties of Leitrim and Roscomon and so beginneth to Divide this County from Roscommon at a place called [blank] then runneth for about a quarter of a mile and spreadeth for the breadth of a mile and a half and is there called Lough boderge signifying the Lough of a Red Cow then runneth southward having much Red bog on both sides, then runneth with an Indifferent Current till it come to Rathleen which signifies a Private place then it Expatiates into a great Lough called Lough Ree or the Kings Lough which continues for seven miles being in breadth two miles the Channell running just in the middle. This Lough Ree hath many Islands in it, of which Islands there belong to this County in number 8 in which there are many old churches and Chappells. Some of these Islands contain 100 acres very profitable both for tillage and Pasture, the largest island is called Insula Sanctorum or ye Island of Saints wherein is a very great old Ruined Monastery and is the Chief of the Augustinian Order or the Canons Regulars of St Augustins Order and governed by a Pryor. This river Runneth to Athlone and is there very Rapid. It is well replenished with Fish, vizt. Pike, Salmon, Trout, Eel, Bream, Roach and the Pikes are of an incredible bigness being some above four ft in Length. It is navigable for Boats of about 10 or 12 Tun, but the vessells most made use of for fishing, Portage of Goods Timber &c, are made of one Tree like a Trough flat botomed and some of them so large that they will carry 60 or 80 men and are called Cotts, they usually carry horses and other

Cattle in them besides they make great use of them for carrying of Timber from the adjacent woods, and by laying of long Poles over across the said Cott and fastening great beams of Timber with wyths to the said Poles they will carry twenty tun of Timber or more.

There are many pleasant Seats on this River and first near the Entrance of the said River in this County is Castle Forbes about half a quarter of a mile from the main river but a branch of it coming near ye house, an antient Seat and is now ye Estate and habitation of the right Honble Arthur Forbes, Lord Viscount Granard who hath improved it to a very great Degree by reducing much the Red bog into firm and good Land and planting Orchards, Groves, Hopyards &c and hath by much Industry managed the soile that it beareth all sorts of Plants and Flowers that are Set or Sowed. There is now growing there in great Order Large Groves of Fir of all sorts with Pine, Juniper, Cedar, Lime trees, Beech, Elm, Oak, Ash, Asp and the Famous platanous Tree I suppose not growing any where besides in this Kingdom. He hath build a fair and specious house with Lovely Gardens of Pleasure inclosed by high stone Walls against which great plenty of Fruit of all sorts grows, and in the said gardens are all kinds of Flowers and Flower Trees that grow in this Kingdome, as the Lelaps Liburnum and many more, with Philarea Hedges, Lawrel, &c, and the Tubirose beareth here which is not to be raised but with ye assistance of Glasses. The said Lord hath built about half a quarter of a mile from his house a handsome Town wherein are now fine stone houses and more a building and hath built a fair and Large Church Sumptuously adorned within and hath Impaled a Large Parke that is well stored with Deers.

The next place of note in the River is now called Lanesborough, anciently called Belaleige, signifying a broad stone. In this place there was built in the year 1667 a fair stone bridge over the River Shannon where the said River runneth with a very rapid Current. This bridge was built by the Contribution of several of the Adjacent Counties and is in length and breadth at this day the largest in this Kingdome. This Lanesborough is the estate of the Right Honble George Lane, Lord Viscount Lanesborough so created in the year [blank]. Here he hath built fine stonehouses and very fair Church stately beautified within and with a Tall Steeple and Church Yard walled about. In this place is an antient Fort built 8 Square is Garrisened and is the King's. This town was named Lanesborough and made a Corporation in the year 1665 governed by a Sovereigne, two Bayliffs and 12 burgesses and is a Market Town; within a small mile of this Town is the Said Lord' house on the River, a very noble and spacious house called Rachcline of which I spoke before the seat being very pleasant and well Improved with Orchards, Gardens, Fishponds and a Deer Park, the next place is within a mile of this near the river and is called fformoyle, which place is now the state of Sir John Parker, Knt. where his father John, Lord ArchB of Dublin, built a fair house with stables and all necessary houses and planted a pleasure Garden and Orchards. This place is of great note in Irish History it being the dwelling place of the Famous Giant Henry Macoole and his Offspring and is called in Irish writings fformalenetiene which signifies the Chief place of the Giants; here was a very large round Rampier which men commonly called [blank] Fort, where the said Giants lived there was likewise under it. This County is Bounded on the East and South East by the River Eyney called by reason that the King of [blank] Daughter was drowned in it at Tineleck so called be cause they which took her up kindled a fire of sticks on a broad stone and called the place Tinyleek which signifies a fire on a Slate. I have seen a pair of horns which were found in this River in shape of a Buckshorn the Beam whereof is as thick as a man's arm, there was joined to these horns one joynt of the Neck bone and the hole of the Pith of it will receive a Hen's Egg by which we may Gather that there was in this County which was very woody, beasts and Dears of Strange bigness. These horns are yet to be seen this day at Tineleek so called from Lough Eny out of which it comes, some says by reason of a King's Daughter was drowned there whose name was [blank]. And dischargeth itself into the said Loughree it divideth it from the County of Westmeath on the East side and on the South it runneth thro this County for a space of five miles where it ends it is a very Rapid River well replenshed with Fish vizt Pike, Salmon, Trout and Eel and here is in great plenty a large Fish and in shape like a Trout tho not very good and is called by the Inhabitants Brodanroe which Englished is a Red Salmon. This river hath three stone bridges over it and three wooden ones. The first of these stone Bridges is called Belanalack signifying a slate from broad thin stones that are in the River, the next Bridge is Balnacarrow so called from a fishing near the River. The next Bridge is lately built by Robert Chawpen Esqr at a place called Abby Shrewell, here is the Ruines of a great Abby and is not built altogether after the Forme of other Abbeyes but like a Colledge where tis said the Famousest College in this Kingdome was once. It is situate close on the River, and was called Monaster Fluminis Dei. It was of St Bernard's Order governed by an Abbot. It is planted in the most Fertile Land of this County about a quarter of a mile from hence, on the North Side of this river is Tineleeke, Englished the House of Broad Stone where was formerly an old castle, it is now the Estate of Mr John Sankey, whose father Henry Sankey Esqr did much improve & built a large house on it. About a mile from it on the Southside the river is Newcastle, the antient Estate of the Earl of Kildare now the Estate & habitation of Robert Choppin Esqr where he hath lately built a fair house and a wooden bridge over the said River. Within a quarter of a mile from this is Ballinyboy on the North side of the River a very pleasant Seat and is now the Estate of Mr Daniel Molyneux within half a quarter of a mile is a market town called Ballymaghan where there is a wooden bridge over the river.

This County is bounded on the north and North East by the Counties of Cavan & Westmeath and did formerly belong to the Sept of the fferalls a very antient people deriving their Pedigrees as far as Adam. Lineally they are a sprightly active Couragious and ingenious people much praising their honour and Gentility and given to hospitality they were allways very numerous tho much division as I understand hath been amongst them which occasioned their separating into Clans. The First Difference was between two families known and distinguished by O'fferoll Boy signifying Yellow and O'fferall Bane signifying white which should have the preheminence. I find there was an accommodation and it passed on O'fferoll Boys Side Altho to this day the Line of O'fferall Bane do not admitt it. This jarring caused much fighting between them which occasioned their dividing their Countrey into Territories and other small divisions as the strength of each man's interest could uphold and called such their Division of ye Countrey by the names of their Fathers' Clan. Signifying children they called one part of the Countrey Clan Hugh another Clanshane, another Clanconner, Clanawley or other smaller divisions. They gave petty names too not relating to to their Pedigree, the Chief of each Clan being possesst of very great Estates of which many of them were deprived in the Reign of King James by a plantation and yet they never dispersed as other Septs of Ireland did but continue still in this Countrey and I suppose are the most Entire and Numerous of all the Irish Septs this day.

Now the County Stands as it hath done along time divided into Six Baronies, the smaller divisions being not like other parts of Ireland, where they are called in some places placelands in others quarters [blank] are here called Cartrons an uncertain way of measure. Some of these Cartrons Containing 100 acres others not Twenty so that they distinguish them by the great or small Cartron. The countrey is very populous and aboundeth with Corn and Cattle, the Corn being wholly consumed in the Countrey so that they neither Import or Export anything of the product of the Countrey but wooll and Cattle, it aboundeth with all sorts of Games and fowle great store of pheasant, Partridge, Growse &c. There are no great Loughs or rivers within the body of this County save one which is called Loughgawney which signifies the Calf Lough in which is an island containing sixty acres. There are two small Loughs within two miles of that and very near one another no River or Brook coming into them nor any issue from them but what is Subteranean the one of these having the Pike Fish in great plenty and no other fish in it but Trout which it hath in great plenty tho, but small ones. Near this Lough is the antientest Corporation in the County called by the name of St Johnstown antiently called Belanelee, signifying calves. It is governed by a Soveraigne and twelve Burgesses.

Within five miles of the said Johnstown Longford the Shiretown where the assizes & sessions are held. It is a Large Countrey Village having but few good houses in it, there runneth a small river thro it which affordeth little Fishes and is of Litle use save some few Mills it drives. There is an Old Abbey of the Dominican Order in it which was formerly governed by a prior and a Stone bridge lately built it was made a Corporation in the year [blank], governed by a Soveraign, two Bayliffs and 12 Burgesses. This is the Estate of the Right honble Francis Angier Earl of Longford, where the said Earl hath exceedingly Improved by rebuilding an antient house of great resort that was there and adding returns to it beautified it rarely within, adorned the place with Groves Inclosures Orchards and most delightful Gardens affording great variety of Trees and Flowers with most pleasant Fishponds and Canalls in which are Tench in great plenty, and Carp with store of Trout, Roach &c and hath built Stables and all other Office houses.

Near the confines of this County on the East is a very large Abbey called Monaster Lerha which signify half time. It was Governed by a Monk. Theres the Ruins of another Monastery called Abby Derge or the Red Abbey it was a nunnery. This County is in the diocese of Ardagh which Town of Ardagh is in the Middle of the County a place quite ruined there being only a few Thatched Houses. There is the Ruins of the Cathedral but clearly Demolished.

Here are two mountains in the County one about the middle and the other near the bounds of it Northward and a high hill with a small village under it called Granard from which the Lord Viscount Granard hath his Creation.

Nobility

Richard Earl of Ranelagh	Sir Tho Newcomen Bart.
Francis Earl of Longford	Sir Connell Ferall Knt.
Henry Lord Visco^t, Kingsland	Sir John Edgeworth Knt.
George Lord Visco^t, Lanesborough	Sir John Parker Knt.
Arthur Lord Visco^t, Granard	

All the lands belonging to the fferalls was seized and sequestred in this late War and Since the King's Restoration only 4 have been Restored vizt. Sr Connell ffarrell and such other lands as was antiently theirs, were given to soldiers and adventurers, there are many worthy Gent. that live in this County who had old Estates, and now have with much Industry Improved them. I shall mention some of them Sir John Edgeworth Knt. coming into his Father's Estate hath Improved it by building a fair house planted, Orchards and Gardens very Sumptuous and Impalled a fair Park for Deer and hath purchased land near him on which he hath planted a very good Countrey Town which hath a Market and two Fairs and is called Edgeworth Town antiently Masterinn, George Cunningham Esqr. hath built a fair house at Killinlosorogh which signifies a flaming wood.

John Kerr Dean of Ardagh hath built a fair house at Druing. Sir Thomas Newcomen Bart, hath built a stately house at Mosstown, antiently called Eenagh which signifies moss.

Sir Connell Ferrall Knight hath wrought much improvement at [blank] which Englished is a house or small stone by Inclosures Orchds Gardens &c, and hath made a Wooden Bridge over the River Einey at a place called Srooher from the Rapidness of the River in that place. All such soldiers as had Lotts in this County have all Improved on their proportions so that the County is much better than ever it was. It hath very much Red bog in the West part of it which occasioned the making of Sevll long Taghers or Causies to unite the lands and in these Red boggs there are Spacious parcells of good and profitable Lands and Woods.

b. From Arthur Young's *Tour of Ireland*, 1776

Arthur Young, an English writer whose main interest was agricultural improvement, visited Ireland on two occasions, in 1776 and 1777-8. He even settled briefly in Mitchelstown, Co. Cork, as agent for the Irish estates of Lord Kingsborough, but he stayed only a year and returned to England in 1778. Two years later the first part of his descriptive Tour was published. Young's method of gathering material was haphazard. He visited the houses of the gentry and recorded what he saw and heard of their estates. If there was no great house to receive him then the area got little mention. Longford was such a case. The scarcity of resident gentry meant that Young was satisfied to record what he saw while simply passing through the country. While he noted the good lands around Granard, the rest remained a 'cheerless' county, its economy enlivened only by the linen trade.

August 20th, took my leave of Farnham, and passed by Cavan to Granard; got in that neighbourhood, into a fine tract of dry, sound, gravelly land, which lets, on an average, at £1 1s, through the barony: use it very much for fattening some bullocks; cows chiefly, and a few sheep. The farms are in general large, many about 200 acres. It is all a limestone gravel. In the town of Granard, is one close of 50 acres, called Granard Kiln, immediately under a mound of earth, an antient Danish entrenchment, which regularly supports 50 fat cows, 100 sheep, 6 horses, and is reckoned the best spot in the county, worth 35s. an acre. The country, all the way from Cavan to near Carrickglass, within 2 miles of Longford, is exceedingly bare of trees.

Reached Ballynogh, the seat of W. G. Newcomen, Esq; who has many trees, and well planted hedge-rows, about him; he favoured me with the following particulars: about that neighbourhood, lands let at 13s. 6d. from 7s. to 20s. The rent of the whole country of Longford may be reckoned at 12s. an acre, on an average, of all that is cultivated, and one-sixth part bog and mountain, which yields no rent. The soil is, in general, a tolerable vegetable mould on the surface, for three or four inches deep; under that, two-inch thick of blue clay: which retains water under that yellow clay for two or three feet, and then every where lime-stone gravel. This is generally the soil of the whole county, except the barony of Granard, and a part of the county, called the Callaw, which is a light lime-stone rocky ground, producing fine wheat, and good sheep.

Leitrim lets at 4s. on an average. In Leitrim there are many mountain improvements, by setting fire to the heath in summer, liming it the following spring, marling upon that, and then plant potatoes, get great crops, and make fine land of it. The size of farms rise commonly to 5 or 600 acres, but the general size is about 100 acres, with many small ones; *Rundale*, or the hiring of farms in partnership, is very common, three or four families will take 100 acres. A great part of the country is let to tenants who do not occupy, but re-let at advanced rents to the poor people. The course of crops is: 1. Potatoes. 2. Potatoes. 3. Bere. 4. Barley, or Oats. 5. Oats. 6. Lay out for weeds, four or five years.

 1. Potatoes. 2. Bere. 3. Oats. 4. Oats. 5. Lay it out.
 1. Potatoes. 2. Flax. 3. Bere. 4. Oats. 5. Oats.

Of potatoes, they sow four barrels to an acre, each 64 stone, and get 40 in return; the price 5s. to 14s. average 8s. Of bere they sow 20 stone, and get 10 barrels. Of barley ditto, get 12. Oats they sow 2 barrels, at 14 stone, and get 15. The waste mountains are improving very fast, by families hiring spots of heath, building their cabbins on them, and improving them under a rent of 5s. to 8s. an acre. They bring it all in by potatoes, but use no lime, though they could have it cheap, for lime-stone is on the spot, and plenty of turf to burn it with; this is the case with Cornclanew, near Carrick Glass. While marle is found under the bogs, but scarce any of it used. The system of cattle most common, is to buy yearlings, at 40s., and keep them till three or four years old, and sell them lean at £5 to £5 10s. buying in some every year, and selling out the same number. Fatting cows is also very common, bought in in May, at £3 to £5 and sold out in October, at 30s. to 40s. profit. It is not reckoned bad land, if three acres fatten two. No cows for dairies, they are kept only by little people. Ploughing all with horses, a pair a-breast, but no drawing by the tail; this practice they utterly deny here. Land sells rack-rent at 18$^1/_2$ years purchase. Let for ever and well secured, 20 years purchase. The price has fallen within four years; rents have also fallen three shillings in the pound in six years, and are at present falling, from the low prices of grain. Tythes taken generally by the proctors, who are very civil to gentlemen, but exceedingly cruel to the poor. The country evidently encreases very much in population: the people are in better circumstances than they were 20 years ago, better cloathed, better fed, and more industrious; yet at present it is found, and I have had the same remark made to me, at many other places, that they only work to eat, and when provisions are plenty, will totally idle away so much of their time, that there is scarce any such thing as getting work done. The religion is principally Roman; no emigrations. There is a better yeomanry than is common in Ireland. Many farmers, of from 100 to 250 acres. Rent of a cabbin and garden, 30s. A cow's grass £1 10s. All the cottars have some land: all keep cows, and many pigs and geese. I remarked for some time late, that the geese are plucked, and upon enquiry, that every goose yielded three farthings or a halfpenny in feathers per annum. They make a dreadful ragged figure. The poor live upon potatoes and milk, it is their regular diet, very little oat bread being used, and no flesh-meat at all, except on an Easter Sunday, or Christmas-day. Their potatoes last them through the year; all winter long only potatoes and salt. Firing costs them 30s. a year for labour in the bogs. Building a mud cabbin, £4. Ditto of stone and lime, 37 feet by 15, £17. Another, 40 feet by 14, £11. These are the measures of two, which Mr. Newcomen has built at that expense. The linen manufacture spreads through Longford. It has encreased considerably, from a remarkable circumstance which happened three years ago, which was a gentleman unknown, giving £500 to be distributed to poor weavers, in loans of £5 each, to be repaid, at 25s. a quarter, to enable them to carry on their business with more ease. This had great effect. There are three bleach greens in the county; the weaving increases; spinning is universal throughout all the cabbins, and likewise through all the county of Leitrim, but there is not so much weaving as in Longford.

August 21st, to Strokestown, the seat of Thomas Mahon, Esq; Passed through Longford, a chearless country, over an amazing quantity of bog, and all improveable; a great one in particular, on the banks of the Shannon, two miles over, and I found it reached many miles beyond Lanesbro'.

c. From Samuel Lewis's *Topographical Dictionary* of *Ireland*, 1837

Samuel Lewis's Topographical Dictionary of Ireland, *published in 1837, was a remarkable compilation of information about Ireland in the decade before the Famine. Lewis, a London publisher, had already published topographical dictionaries of England and Wales in 1831 and 1833, and intended his Irish dictionary to complete the project. He encountered considerable difficulties in assembling material since much less had been written about Ireland than about other areas. His information was drawn from printed parliamentary papers and from reports of local gentlemen who were shown proofs of the entries for their own areas. The result was a comprehensive two-volume work of 1400 pages containing descriptions of the counties, towns and parishes of Ireland. Information was included on levels of population, landlords, churches, education and archaeological features. Despite Lewis's efforts, the* Dictionary *was greeted with a storm of protest on publication, and many people tried to cancel their subscriptions. However, comparison of contemporary sources with Lewis's entries shows that the inaccuracies were fewer than suggested although some of the historical information was dubious. His picture of Longford accords with other accounts.*

The county sent ten members to the Irish parliament, two for the county at large, and two for each of the boroughs of Longford, Granard, Lanesborough, and St Johnstown; but since the Union its sole representatives have been the two for the county, who are elected at Longford. The registered constituency consists of 201 £50, 105 £20, and 854 £10 freeholders; 67 £20 and 149 £10 leaseholders; and 5 £50 and 7 £20 rent-chargers, making a total of 1,388 voters. The county is included in the Home Circuit; the assizes and general quarter sessions are held at Longford, where the county gaol and court-house are situated: quarter sessions are also held at Ballymahon. The local government is vested in a lieutenant, 10 deputy-lieutenants, and 46 other magistrates, together with the usual county officers, including one coroner. There are 27 constabulary police stations, having in the whole a force of 1 sub-inspector, 3 chief officers, 25 sub-constables, 117 men, and 5 horses. The district lunatic asylum for this county and the King's, Queen's and Westmeath is at Maryborough; the county infirmary is at Longford, and there are dispensaries at Ballymahon, Edgeworthstown, Granard, and Keenagh, supported equally by Grand Jury presentments and private subscription. The amount of Grand Jury presentments for the year 1835 was £12, 606. 9s. 2d., of which £329. 11s. 7d. was for the roads, bridges, &c., of the county at large; £3,833. 6s. 10d. for the roads bridges, &c., of the baronies; £2,209.6s.2¹/₂d. for public buildings, charities, officers' salaries, and incidents; £2,678. 18s. 10d. for the police; and £3,556. 10s. 8¹/₂d. for repayment of advances made by Government. In military arrangements it is in the Western district, and there are barracks at Longford for infantry and cavalry, and at Granard for infantry, both together being capable of accommodating 15 officers, 391 men, and 202 horses.

The general outline of the county presents little to attract the eye or excite the imagination. It is for the most part flat and in many places overspread with large tracts of bog. Towards the north, where it borders on the county of Leitrim, it rises into bleak and sterile mountains. In its other extremity the country improves very much, particularly on the banks of the Inny, where the land is much more fertile and is well cultivated ...

The soil of this county, like the surface, is exceedingly various, changing from a light thin mould to a deep loamy clay, without any apparent variation in the geological arrangement: much of the north is in a state of nature, and the practicability of draining, reclaiming, and cultivating to any profitable purpose is exceedingly doubtful. Toward the south the prevailing character is a rich vegetable mould resting on blue clay, very retentive of moisture and based on a substratum of yellow marl, two or three feet thick, ultimately resting either on an excellent marl or limestone gravel. In this part of the country every kind of grain and green crop may be cultivated to the greatest advantage. The barony of Granard is mostly good land producing a short, close and sweet herbage; the elevated district between Edgeworthstown and Longford has a good soil, which yields abundant crops of grain, but westward of the latter place, except in the immediate neighbourhood of Newtown-Forbes, the land is much encumbered with surface water, the injurious effects of which could be easily obviated by a judicious system of draining. The level parts of the county are mostly in pasture, producing great varieties of acidulous plants occasioned by the overflowing of the rivers, or by the accumulation of surface water: these meadows, if properly drained and secured, would rank among some of the best in Ireland. Bogs are very numerous in many parts of the county, and everywhere capable of drainage and reclamation; but in consequence of the water being suffered to remain in them, numerous gullies or swallows are formed, which though always full never run over, although numerous small streams flow into them, whence it is evident that their waters must find a subterraneous passage to the Shannon, the Inny, or some other river, thus silently but forcibly pointing to the means by which the land may be made available to the service of man. The chief crops are oats and potatoes, but the sowing of wheat and barley is becoming more general; and flax, rape, clover, turnips and vetches are sometimes sown. Rape thrives peculiarly well on boggy soil, and the produce is everywhere very great. The practice of laying down land with grass or clover seeds is gaining ground every year. All the surplus grain is purchased in Longford and other markets, and sent down the Royal Canal to Dublin or Drogheda. Agricultural implements are of an inferior description, except with the gentry and wealthier farmers; one-horse carts of excellent construction are universal.

Great improvements have been made in the breed of cattle; the short-horned stock appears to be a decided favourite. A cross between the Durham and the long-horned native breed grows to a good size, and fattens well. Although this is not a sheep-feeding country, the breed of that useful and profitable animal has not been neglected; the New Leicester is decidedly a favourite with all the large landholders, but a cross between it and the small short-woolled sheep of the country suits the light and upland soils better. The horses are chiefly of a slight active breed, well adapted for light harness, but not equal as saddle-horses to those of Roscommon, Galway, and Sligo. Pigs are universally kept, and of every possible variety of breed; they are fattened for the merchants and curers of Longford, who ship great quantities of pork and bacon for Dublin, London, and Liverpool. Dairies upon an extensive scale are not very general, but great quantities of butter are made and chiefly sold in Longford and Ballymahon for the English markets. The meadows in the lower districts produce hay in great abundance, but it is much mixed with rushes and other aquatic plants, and it is everywhere cut too late in the season, the mowing seldom beginning till September, and is badly managed. Woods are very rare, although the land is everywhere well adapted to the growth of timber, and in many places throws up shoots spontaneously, particularly of oak, hazel, alder, and birch, which only require the protecting hand of man to attain their full growth; but cattle are everywhere suffered to browse upon them, and hence nothing but brushwood and stunted bushes remain. There is some good old timber at Castle Forbes, which, together with the plantations around Newtown-Forbes, shews to great advantage; there are also some good plantations at Edgeworthstown, others near Granard, on the shores of the lakes, on the road between Longford and Edgeworthstown, and in a few other places. The fences are generally good, being for the most part ditches faced with sods or stones, and having quickset hedges planted on the breast. Draining and irrigation appear to be quite unknown here, although no district in the province requires them more. The scented myrtle is found in all the bogs, which everywhere present an ample field for the pursuits of the botanist, as the plants are numerous and many rare species are found, particularly in the barony of Longford. Orchards and gardens are sometimes seen near the small farm-houses, and add greatly to their comfortable appearance and domestic economy...

Coarse linen cloth, and linen yarn, are manufactured to some extent and sent to markets in other counties: the first Earl of Granard took great pains to introduce this branch of manufacture among his tenantry at Newtown-Forbes. Flannels, friezes, and linsey-woolseys, chiefly for domestic consumption, are manufactured in several places. The rivers that water the interior of the county are the Camlin and the Kenagh. The source of the former is amid the numerous springs around Granard; its course is uncommonly winding, in consequence of the flatness of the valley through which it flows after quitting the hill of Granard, insomuch that the country is flooded to a great extent in winter: it runs westward and joins the Shannon at Tarmonbarry. The latter rises in the south and flows northward to the Shannon. The Fallen and Ownamount are insignificant streams. The Inny, which forms part of the southern boundary of the county, flows through a beautiful and rich country in a winding course by Ballymahon to Lough Ree: it contains salmon, trout, pike, perch, roach, tench, bream and eels: the last are highly esteemed. It is said that since the introduction of perch, all other kinds of fish except eels have grown scarce both in Lough Ree and in the Inny. Few rivers present so many facilities for water carriage: its course is very slow. The total fall from Finea to the Shannon is 90 feet, and the main obstructions to its navigation are a ridge of rocks between Newcastle and Ballymahon, and two shallows between the later town and the Shannon. The Royal Canal enters the county from Westmeath, by an aqueduct over the Inny near Tenellick, passing westward by Ballymahon, Keenagh, and Mosstown, to Killashee, whence a branch leads northward to the town of Longford, while the main line from the junction continues westward until it joins the Shannon at Richmond harbour a mile below Tarmonbarry. This line of communication through the heart of the country is of the greatest advantage to the commercial interests; boats of 20 tons convey bulky articles, and fly boats, travelling at the rate of 7 miles an hour, ply constantly between Longford and Dublin. The roads are numerous and well laid out, and the material of which they are made is abundant and of very good quality; but in general they are very wet throughout every part, a defect arising entirely from want of due attention to keep the drains and water courses open.

The remains of antiquity are very few. A large rath, usually called the Moat of Granard, stands at one end of the main street of that town; another, called Lisardowlin, situated near the road from Longford to Edgeworthstown, is by the people of this country generally believed to be the centre of Ireland. Monastic institutions were numerous, and for the most part held in great veneration and well endowed. Abbeyshrule belonged to the Canons Regular; Ardagh, to the Franciscans; Lerha or Laragh, to the Cistercians; the wealthy abbey of Longford was founded by the O'Farrels; there were also abbeys or priories at Moydow, Clone, Clonebrone, Derg, Druimchei, and Killinmore, besides those on the islands of Innismorey, Innisbofin, Inniscloran, and All Saints Island in Lough

Ree. Ruins of all the above still remain; but of the priories at Ballynasaggard, Kilglass, and St Johnstown, no vestiges of the original buildings remain, and their actual site is a matter of doubt. At Lanesborough are the ruins of a collegiate church or preceptory, originally founded by the Knights Templars. The remains of ancient castles are not so numerous here as in most of the other level counties. Granard castle is built on a hill rising to a considerable height above the town, and commanding an extensive view over all the level country. Besides Castle Forbes, the Forbes family had another fortified mansion at Longford, which was burned by the O'Nials in 1605. At Tenellick is the ruin of a strong castle, and near Ballymahon are the remains of two others. There are still remains of Rathcline castle, the chief residence of the O'Cuins; and not far from it are the ruins of a very ancient church. At Ballymahon was a strong castle erected to defend the ford of the Inny, the only traces of which are the cellars, under a house built on its ruins. Barnacor castle and Lot's castle, on the Inny, on the opposite banks, were both erected to protect the important pass or ford of that river, and at Castlecor are some remains of its ancient fortress. Fossil remains of various kinds have been discovered in the limestone caverns and fissures; many of them are those of animals unknown in these regions, and several others of species now extinct in Ireland. The bones and horns of the elk have been discovered in the marl at the foot of the Escars, and beneath several of the bogs, also in a small lake near Ballinalee the antlers and bones of the red deer are often found quite sound, having been preserved by the antiseptic properties of the bog water.

There are but few resident noblemen or gentry of large estates ... There are few parts of Ireland in which persons of limited income can live cheaper or better than here. In the towns are plentiful and cheap markets for beef, mutton, fowl, and fresh water fish, wild fowl in abundance, and the water fowl free from the fishy flavour of those from the sea coast. Cod and haddock from Galway, and oysters from the same shores, may be obtained at moderate prices. The diet and mode of living of the small farmers and others is very indifferent: they scarcely ever taste flesh meat, and not often anything but potatoes; yet they are strong, healthy, and active, and their general appearance is prepossessing. The women wear scarlet cloaks, with hoods which they seldom use, as they cover their heads with handkerchiefs: the rest of their dress consists indifferently of cotton chequer and linsey-woolsey. Those of the lowest order travel barefoot, carrying their shoes and stockings in their hands, till they draw near their place of destination; their fuel is invariably turf, which can be procured in great abundance and of very superior quality. Coal is sometimes brought by the canal for the use of the wealthier classes, but even these generally burn turf. The prevalent diseases are inflammatory and putrid fever in summer and autumn, and ague which latter is generally contracted in Meath, whither the labourers go to the harvest, and where they suffer much from the scarcity of fuel, which they had enjoyed in plenty at home. The lower orders are shrewd, intelligent, and industrious, fond of manly exercises and amusements, such as foot-ball, hurling, and wrestling, but on Sunday evenings the chief and invariable amusement is dancing. They are of a very proud and independent spirit, which manifests itself most conspicuously in their great repugnance to hire as servants, an occupation considered by them to be highly disreputable; hence they remain at home living in penury in a cabin and on a small patch of ground. They are exceedingly litigious, ever ready to have recourse to the law upon the most trivial subjects; they are also extremely superstitious: the first day of the year and of the month or week is considered the most proper times to commence an undertaking. No one removes to a new habitation on a Friday. A large candle is lighted on Christmas night; and suffered to burn out: should it be extinguished by accident, or otherwise, before it be completely burned away, it is considered as a certain prognostic of the death of the head of the family. The first of May and Midsummer-day are observed with great regularity, as are all the other festivals usual throughout the country: that of Hallow Eve concludes with a supper of boiled wheat buttered and sweetened, called Granbree. In the summer months, many individuals set out on pilgrimages either to holy wells in the vicinity or to Lough Derg, in Donegal, to which latter place persons in affluent circumstances have been known to walk barefoot as a penance. The places at which violent or sudden deaths have occurred, particularly if near a road, are marked by heaps of stones, to which every passenger deems it a duty incumbent on him to add one. The Irish language is scarcely ever heard, except in the mountainous districts among the old people; adults and children everywhere speak English. Of the ancient families of this county, scarce any traces now remain: titles of the most romantic kind were assumed and borne by the heads of several clans, all of which have long since fallen into disuse.

d. From the *Irish Catholic Directory*, 1842

The Irish Catholic Directory, *published annually since 1836, is an important source for the history of the Catholic Church in every area of Ireland. In its early years it was entitled the* Catholic Directory, Almanac, and Registry, *or Battersby's Registry. It was compiled and published by William J. Battersby of 10 Essex Bridge, Dublin, and revised 'by a Catholic priest approved of for that purpose'. It consisted of an almanac, setting out religious ceremonies and feast-days, and a register of the clergy of Ireland, with extensive supplementary material on topics ranging from architecture to temperance. In some years the Register included detailed information on ecclesiastical developments in various dioceses. In the case of Longford in 1842 it illustrated the growing confidence of the Catholic Church in the wake of the success of the Emancipation movement, and sketched the atmosphere of the country at the height of the repeal movement in which Battersby himself was involved. That new confidence was reflected in the building of St Mel's Cathedral, planned as one of the grandest cathedrals in Ireland and reflecting the gradual movement of the Church towards the 'devotional revolution' of the late nineteenth century.*

STATE OF RELIGION IN ARDAGH

It is unnecessary for us to offer even one observation on the state of Religion in Ardagh. The following which has already appeared in the Catholic Journals of the Empire, forming the most interesting and graphic picture of zeal and labour in the cause of Religion on Catholic Record, will place the glorious undertaking of St Mel's Cathedral, of which we give a view, in a position to challenge the warmest and most effectual co-operation of every catholic in the British Empire.

'The untiring labours of the Irish priesthood in the cause of religion, have been often the theme of universal eulogy; their zeal – their disinterestedness – their boundless ardour as well in the faithful discharge of their sacred duties, as in erecting, through the piety of a poor and persecuted people, temples worthy of the living God, are generously acknowledged, and, not withstanding the meddling efforts – the drivelling imbecilities of England's yet untaught and heartless aristocracy, shall continue to secure to them the lasting admiration and profoundest sympathies of the Catholic world. In no portion of Ireland have these edifying characteristics of her priesthood been more effectually displayed than in the unprecedented labours of the learned and venerable bishop of Ardagh, during the late visitation, and in the enthusiastic co-operation of his respected priesthood, in erecting in the centre of Ireland a Cathedral Church, which, in its style, the extent of its dimensions, the costliness of its materials, and beauty of its workmanship, bids fair to rival, if not surpass, the proudest specimens of ancient Catholic taste and glory. This distinguished prelate is ever found in the foremost ranks of pure and uncompromising patriotism; but whilst he directs the vast resources of his well-earned influence to the raising of his fallen and prostrate country from her degraded position, he is never unmindful of the more sacred duty of a Christian prelate, to elevate and advance the moral and religious condition of those committed to his pastoral care.

'Doctor Higgins has just now, and within the short space of four months, completed the visitation of his extensive diocese, containing forty-three parishes, and comprising portions of seven counties and three provinces. His visitation was productive of the most happy and beneficial results. During the whole of his progress through his diocese, so intense was the joy of the people to meet their good and venerated bishop, that on the day of visitation in each parish all servile work was suspended. Like the multitude on the mountain, thousands were everywhere seen, forgetful of the cares of this world, and attending with breathless silence to the pastor of their souls in the clear exposition of those things which appertain to the kingdom of Heaven. Even the precincts of the largest chapels were densely crowded, and in several places nearly to suffocation. His lordship addressed the people three times on each occasion, and never failed to produce the most powerful and thrilling effects on the minds of his hearers. Casting aside the persuasive and hollow words of human wisdom, he used only the simple and sublime language of the Gospel. It was obvious to the coldest of his hearers that his lips expressed the language of an ardent heart. This it was which gave his words such peculiar energy and force, and infused into the breasts of all a portion of that unbounded zeal which glowed in his own. The seed of the Gospel sown with a skilful and plenteous hand, and watered by the dews of heaven, has already produced rich and abundant fruit.

'The extent of his lordship's labours in the vineyard, during the present season, and the success with which they have been crowned, may be estimated by the fact that he has conferred the sacrament of confirmation on more than thirty thousand persons. In Ardagh parish, for instance, 1,272, in Mohill 1,267, in Granard 1,839, in Longford 2,150, &c. &c. The friends of religion will rejoice to learn that in these immense numbers were some hundreds of converts to the one Holy and Catholic church. In every parish it was his lordship's pleasing duty to express his approbation of the improved state of religion and morality, and to congratulate the people particularly on their steady adherence to the pledge of temperance, which he had lately administered to them.

'Next to his lordship's zeal for the spiritual temple of the Lord, the object nearest to his heart, is the advancement of the splendid cathedral of St. Mel. His appeals at every chapel, to the bounty and generosity of the people, for the completion of this glorious work, were powerful and impressive, and in every instance warmly and enthusiastically responded to. Though it was well known that his lordship would receive no subscriptions on the day of visitation, such was the ardour of the people, that several humble frieze-coated farmers urgently prayed him to receive at their hands, in many instances, the sum of £5. Inflamed by the apostolical labours of their bishop and the zealous co-operation of his clergy, they seemed to chide the shortness of time, and to long for the moment when they could record their generous anxiety for the glory of the House of the Lord.

'His lordship's visitation having closed on Sunday, the 24th of October, the following Wednesday was named for a general meeting of the clergy of Ardagh, to be held in Longford, to adopt some uniform mode of receiving in each parish the voluntary contributions of the faithful towards the erection of their cathedral church. Notwith-standing the inconvenient distance of many parishes, from the place of meeting, nearly one hundred priests assembled in Longford, at an early hour, on the appointed day. The meeting was held in the old chapel, the venerated bishop of the diocese in the chair. The resolutions were at once adopted, with that Christian harmony and perfect identity of feeling which have ever characterised the clergy of Ardagh. This unanimity amongst the assembled priests, as well as the chaste and apostolic style of the accompanying pastoral, drew forth the unbounded admiration and dignified panegyric of the Bishop of Olympus, who was present, and who emphatically observed that he felt amply repaid for the fatigues of a long journey in witnessing such edifying union and primitive zeal in the very centre of the land of his fore-fathers.

'Every glimmering of doubt of the speedy completion of St. Mel's is now dissipated given to the winds. The combined energies of a religious priesthood and people, guided by the wisdom of a prelate whom they respect and love, must surmount difficulties from which the cold and calculating worlding would shrink away in despair.

'The business of the meeting being over, his lordship with his clergy sat down to a sumptuous dinner in the rooms of the Catholic School-house. Dr Higgins was supported on the right by the Right Rev. Dr M'Donnell, Bishop of Olympus, and on his left by the distinguished and patriotic Bishop of Meath, the Right Rev. Dr Cantwell.

'The venerated Chairman proposed several toasts, which he prefaced in his usual happy and nervous style. On the healths of Drs M'Donnell and Cantwell being given, their lordships returned thanks in eloquent terms, and expressed their feelings of astonishment and delight at the rapid progress and surpassing beauties of the rising cathedral. Dr Cantwell, to whom the priests and people of Ardagh owe deep and lasting obligations, with peculiar warmth, assured the meeting that his late donation was but an instalment of his generous intentions towards St. Mel's cathedral. This announcement was received with overpowering demonstrations of gratitude. The other toasts of the evening were ably and eloquently responded to by the Very Rev. Doctors Slevin, O'Beirne, and M'Keon, who, on the part of their respective deaneries, evinced a generous rivalry in forwarding the holy cause, which had called them together. The entire proceedings were characterised by that joyous festivity, and religious harmony, which most naturally spring from the pleasing consciousness, of having fearlessly, and faithfully co-operated in doing the work of God.

'Notwithstanding his previous labours, Dr Higgins, unwilling that even the humblest labourer, employed at the cathedral, should not participate in the delightful festivities connected with the diocesan meeting, presided on the following day at a magnificent dinner, which he had previously ordered at Flood's Hotel, for all the mechanics and workmen engaged in the building. The vice-chair was taken by the excellent and patriotic curate of Longford, the Rev. Richard Davys, and to the right of the chair was Mr Mullen, the clerk of the works, whose steady and unremitting attention have earned for him the unqualified approbation of every admirer of St. Mel's cathedral. Though his lordship's humility would not shrink from contact with the poorest and most lowly of his flock, still his humble guests deeply felt and highly appreciated the honour his presence conferred upon them. During the evening there were occasional sparklings of native talent, with a refinement of manner, among these hardy mechanics, that is not always found in what the world calls the higher classes of society. The good-natured familiarity and eloquence of the Right Rev. host diffused the utmost happiness amongst them. If the conviction, of making a body of humble and deserving men happy, even for a day, be a luxury which the good alone can feel, then, indeed, under all the interesting circumstances attending this evening's entertainment, must the Right Rev. host have retired, enjoying the deepest sensation of pure delight.

'What a consoling picture does not the foregoing statement present to the mind of every Catholic interested for the purity of faith and the propagation of religion! We see in Ardagh a people flocking in crowds - in countless numbers, to receive the sacraments of the church. We see a priesthood, with no other claims than those, which lives of the most disinterested virtue confer upon them, yet possessing that unbounded influence, which state intrigue may in vain hope to suppress, but which, too long held sacred in Irish hearts, shall ever remain the unchanged and fruitful source of the blessings inseparable from the independence of the Irish church.'

At a general meeting of the clergy of the diocese of Ardagh, held in the chapel of Longford, on Wednesday, 27th October, 1841, Right Rev. Dr Higgins in the chair, (Right Rev. Dr M'Donnell, Bishop of Olympus, present,) the following resolutions were unanimously adopted:-

Resolved, 1st - That the zeal, and untiring efforts of Right Rev. Dr Higgins, for the erection of the splendid and magnificent cathedral of St Mel, which already challenges the admiration of all who have seen it, claim our warmest gratitude and thanks.

Resolved, 2d - That we hereby collectively and individually pledge ourselves to use our most strenuous efforts in co-operating with his lordship, and that we shall exert our influence with our respective flocks, to secure the contributions even of the most humble person, towards St Mel's Cathedral.

Resolved, 3d - That we consider the following to be the most effective means of raising contributions in our respective parishes - namely, that the clergyman of each parish, accompanied by some neighbouring clergymen, shall, on visiting each house in his parish, take down in a legible hand the names of the contributors, together with the amount of contribution; that this list of names, with the sums contributed, shall be presented on the altar to the Right Rev. Dr Higgins, who will read it aloud to the congregation, in presence of the clergymen by whom he will be accompanied, previously to his having the names of the contributors, &c. inserted in the diocesan registry.

Resolved, 4th - That the clergymen of each parish take with them as many copies of the pastoral address as there are houses in their parishes, and that they send a copy of it to every house, to be there religiously preserved.

Resolved, 5th - That we cannot separate without tendering our warmest acknowledgments to the bishops and clergy of Ireland, who have already generously co-operated in raising subscriptions in their respective dioceses towards the erection of St Mel's cathedral.

+ WILLIAM HIGGINS, Chairman.
MICHAEL O'BEIRNE, Secretary.

WILLIAM, BY THE GRACE OF GOD, AND THE FAVOUR OF THE HOLY SEE, BISHOP OF ARDAGH AND CLONMACNOISE, &C.

To the Faithful of these Dioceses, Health and Benediction.

'DEARLY BELOVED - Ever since it pleased Divine Providence to entrust us with the spiritual care of the faithful, in this extensive diocese, we have not ceased to be conscious that the due performance of so sacred and arduous a duty far exceeded our humble abilities; and that, unless aided from above, we could of ourselves do nothing.[a] We were well aware that although we might plant, it was only God himself that could give the increase,[b] and that without his assistance we could not so much as pronounce his holy name.[c]

'Deeply impressed with these awful truths, as well as with a sense of our insufficiency, we would have never undertaken the responsibility of becoming your chief pastor, and of thus rendering a fearful account of your stewardship[d] to him who might one day require your souls at our hands[e] had we not the encouraging assurance of his own unerring word, that he sometimes chooses the weak things of this world to confound the strong;[f] that human wisdom is but folly in his sight;[g] and that, though feeble and ineffectual in our own endeavours, we are rendered capable of all things[h] by the powerful influence of his grace.

'And we give thanks, dearly beloved, to the author of all good gifts,[i] whose helping hand, notwithstanding our weakness, has enabled us to propagate, in some degree, the glory of his name, and spread the blessings of religion among his people. In choosing us for so holy a purpose, he was not unmindful of our necessities; but mercifully cast our lot in a portion of his vineyard, where even an unskilful labourer could not fail to produce abundant fruit. We were not required to combat the errors of false philosophy, or to brave the sword of persecution; our task was merely to announce the word of God, with the simplicity of truth, and explain the laws of his church to a faithful and pious people.

'In the annual discharge of these sacred functions, dearly beloved, we always felt edified by your pious demeanour, and consoled by your progress in religion; but never had we such reason to rejoice as during our visitation of the present year. We have now brought that important duty to a close, having preached the truths of salvation in every parish of the diocese, and conferred the sacrament of confirmation on more than *thirty thousand* of the faithful. We have, moreover, received numerous converts into the bosom of the Catholic church, and witnessed the sincere repentance of almost every public or obstinate sinner. We have also perceived with unmingled delight, that the great bulk of the population had last year enrolled themselves at our hands, under the banner of sobriety, and scrupulously observed their promises to adhere to that virtue. We mention these things, as well to express our gratitude towards a merciful and bountiful God, as to place an edifying example before the community at large.

'But the main object of this brief address, dearly beloved, is to offer you our heartfelt thanks, as also those of our clergy, for the religious and generous ardour with which you have, both one and all, pledged yourselves to co-operate with us, to the utmost of your means in erecting in the centre of our diocese, to the glory of God a temple worthy of his holy name, and suited to the majesty of his religion. You are aware that that sacred and noble edifice, is already in a state of great forwardness; that in every diocese all over Ireland where contributions were sought for, they were freely and generously given; that even the poorest widows and orphans, *totally unconnected with our diocese*, have made unheard-of sacrifices to enable them to contribute; that the Ardagh priests have all given, according to their means; and it was only under these encouraging examples that we appealed to the people of our own diocese themselves. Let us here remark, that our cathedral will belong to *no one particular parish or district*; but being *diocesan*, claims the co-operation of *all*. Having explained this subject, in detail, during our late visitation, we shall now merely observe that the names of those who contribute, with the amount of their donations, will be enrolled in the diocesan register, enclosed in an iron safe, in the sanctuary of the church; that once every year, it will be placed on the chief altar, and that the bishop and his clergy, for ever, will then offer up, in the cathedral, with the adorable sacrifice of the mass, their fervent prayers, for the temporal and eternal advantage of all contributors.

'Your respective clergy dearly beloved, will make you acquainted with the time and manner of giving in your subscriptions, and we shall ourselves, in the course of the ensuing winter, once more visit every parish in the diocese on the same sacred subject; and in the presence of all the neighbouring priests, announce the names of the contributors, together with the sums they may subscribe, and give them our humble blessing, as also that of our clergy.

'In the meantime we earnestly entreat you, in the name of that holy religion, in whose sacred cause we are all equally interested, that you will treasure up something, either *daily, weekly, or otherwise*, in order that on the day we appear in your parish, no one, either rich or poor, may be found unprepared to fulfil his pledge of giving to God according to his means.

'In conclusion, let us implore you, dearly beloved, in the language of the Holy Scripture, to "do according to the ability of your hands; for the Lord maketh recompense, and will give to you seven times as much".ʲ

'And the peace of God, which surpasseth all understanding, keep your hearts and minds in Christ Jesus.ᵏ

'Ballymahon, Oct. 21, 1841.

'*The Ardagh Cathedral*, which is already in a state of great forwardness, will be of the purest Grecian architecture, and entirely built of the very finest cut stone, joined throughout with sheets of lead. Its front will exhibit six magnificent Ionic columns, enclosing a spacious portico. The Tower (nearly 200 feet high) will be partly composed of alternative tiers of Corinthian pillars. The interior will be divided into three aisles, and will contain seven marble altars; and the roof will be supported by 26 lofty Ionic columns of polished variegated marble. Its site is the town of Longford, the very centre of the diocese, and of Ireland. It will be dedicated in honour of St Mel, first bishop of this ancient see, and nephew of St Patrick, by whom, at the very commencement of his apostleship, he was consecrated in the same parish where the cathedral now stands. For the last 300 years a Catholic church of this splendour would not have been tolerated in Ireland, nor indeed had the Catholics, up to the present, adequate means, nor were they in sufficient numbers in Ardagh, to accomplish so glorious an undertaking. When finished, it will be the chastest, most extensive, and most elegant church of modern times, in any part of the United Kingdom.'

a. John xv, 5. b. 1st Cor. iii, 7. c. 1st Cor. xii, 3. d. Luke xvi, 2. e. Ezech. iii, 20. f. 1st Cor. i, 27. g. 1st Cor. iii, 19. h. Philipp. iv, 13. i. James i, 17. j. Eccl. xxxv, 18. k. Philipp. iv, 7.

INDEX